Catching History on the Wing

GET POLITICAL

www.plutobooks.com

Revolution, Democracy, Socialism
Selected Writings
V.I. Lenin
Edited by
Paul Le Blanc
9780745327600

Black Skin, White Masks
Frantz Fanon
Forewords by
Homi K.
Bhabha and
Ziauddin Sardar
9780745328485

Jewish History, Jewish Religion
The Weight of Three Thousand Years
Israel Shahak
Forewords by
Pappe / Mezvinsky/
Said / Vidal
9780745328409

The Communist Manifesto
Karl Marx and
Friedrich Engels
Introduction by
David Harvey
9780745328461

Theatre of the Oppressed
Augusto Boal
9780745328386

Catching History on the Wing
Race, Culture and Globalisation
A. Sivanandan
Foreword by
Colin Prescod
9780745328348

catching history on the wing

Race, Culture and Globalisation

A. SIVANANDAN

Foreword by Colin Prescod

PLUTO PRESS
www.plutobooks.com

The chapters in this book were first published in *Race & Class* and are reproduced by kind permission of the Institute of Race Relations.

This collection first published 2008 by Pluto Press
345 Archway Road, London N6 5AA

www.plutobooks.com

British Library Cataloguing in Publication Data
A catalogue record for this book is available from the British Library

ISBN   978 0 7453 2835 5   Hardback
ISBN   978 0 7453 2834 8   Paperback

Library of Congress Cataloging in Publication Data applied for

This book is printed on paper suitable for recycling and made from fully managed and sustained forest sources. Logging, pulping and manufacturing processes are expected to conform to the environmental standards of the country of origin. The paper may contain up to 70% post consumer waste.

10   9   8   7   6   5   4   3   2   1

Designed and produced for Pluto Press by
Chase Publishing Services Ltd, Sidmouth, EX10 9QG, England
Typeset from disk by Stanford DTP Services, Northampton
Printed and bound in the European Union by
CPI Antony Rowe, Chippenham and Eastbourne

CONTENTS

Acknowledgements   vi
Foreword by Colin Prescod   vii
Introduction: Unity of struggle   xiii

I THE PERSONAL AND THE POLITICAL   1

1. The liberation of the black intellectual   3
2. The hokum of New Times   19
3. La trahison des clercs   55

II STATE RACISM AND RESISTANCE   63

4. Race, class and the state: the political economy of
    immigration   65
5. From resistance to rebellion: Asian and
    Afro-Caribbean struggles in Britain   90
6. RAT and the degradation of black struggle   140
7. Race, terror and civil society   167

III GLOBALISATION AND DISPLACEMENT   177

8. Imperialism and disorganic development in the
    silicon age   179
9. New circuits of imperialism   193
10. A black perspective on the Gulf war   215
11. Poverty is the new black   222

Notes   229
Bibliography of writings by A. Sivanandan   244
Index   255

ACKNOWLEDGEMENTS

'Unity of struggle' was first published as 'The global context' in *Race & Class* (Vol. 48, no. 4, 2007); 'The liberation of the black intellectual' as 'Alien gods' in *Colour, Culture and Consciousness* (London, Allen and Unwin, 1974); 'The hokum of New Times' as 'All that melts into air is solid: the hokum of New Times' in *Race & Class* (Vol. 31, no. 3, 1990); 'La trahison des clercs' in *Race & Class* (Vol. 37, no. 3, 1996); 'Race, class and the state' in *Race & Class* (Vol. 17, no. 4, 1976); 'From resistance to rebellion' in *Race & Class* (Vol. 23, nos 2/3, 1981/2); 'RAT and the degradation of black struggle' in *Race & Class* (Vol. 26, no. 4, 1985); 'Race, terror and civil society' in *Race & Class* (Vol. 47, no. 3, 2006); 'Imperialism and disorganic development in the silicon age' in *Race & Class* (Vol. 21, no. 2, 1979); 'New circuits of imperialism' in *Race & Class* (Vol. 30, no. 4, 1989); 'A black perspective on the Gulf war' in *Race & Class* (Vol. 32, no. 4, 1991); 'Poverty is the new black' in *Race & Class* (Vol. 43, no. 2, 2001); 'The bibliography of writings' is an updated version of that prepared by Valerie Allport for 'A world to win', *Race & Class* (Vol. 41, nos 1/2, 1991).

FOREWORD

Colin Prescod

There is a generation of Black British community activists who emerged politically in the heady days of the late 1970s and early 1980s, for whom Sivanandan is possibly the most original influence in their lives. They were social workers, teachers, undergraduates and their lecturers, youth leaders, organisers of defence campaigns and members of emerging Black youth and feminist organisations at the grassroots, up and down the country – new generations of youth with Caribbean, Asian and African backgrounds. If they were close to the street, if they were trying to make sense of what was happening as, after 1979, Thatcherism began to bite, they were reading Sivanandan. Photocopies of his articles from *Race & Class* and well-worn copies of his IRR pamphlets were circulated amongst those who read. For those who wouldn't, or couldn't, read, hearing and seeing him speak was their inspiration. And he is a marvellous speaker, a rare combination of analyst, polemicist and orator – and a caller to arms. In fact, he writes in an idiom that rides on the rhythms of his conversational speech. The style is related to a rule of thumb for avoiding the turgid. In his own writing, just as with his editing of the writing of others, he cuts out the mortis that so often accompanies the self-conscious rigor (his joke!) of high academe. And this has marked him out from the other, more academically oriented, influential figures on the radical British scene since the 1960s.

Something of the calm authority with which he told our story, of how he insisted on grasping the meaning behind the immediate pain and irritation of experiencing racism, steadied us – steeled us. It was he who announced, in the telling and retelling of our particular British story, that we had moved from 'resistance to rebellion'. And it was he who cautioned against the siren seductions of consumerism, poignantly describing what ailed and goaded the souls of inner-city, working-class, Black folk and, at the same time, identifying their demands outside the frame of begging bowl, welfare cheque appeals as 'a different hunger'. For those who recall the first half of the 1980s as a watershed in Black British politics, Sivanandan was father, elder to them all.

Here was a Marxist who was not intimidated by taunts of revisionism, because he was a Marxist only, as if this is only an only, in the sense of using Marx's tools to analyse and unlock the conundrums of capitalism on a world scale. But what a craftsman he has been in the use of those tools. His anti-racism and his fierce opposition to the obscenities of injustice have always been inextricably bound up with a profound anti-imperialism – since imperialism, through its colonial and neocolonial successes, has been the major inventor and reinforcer of institutionalised racism on a global scale. And central to the analysis that he presents to new generations of British Black community has been the insistence that, although they might be pinned with the minority labels attached to their presences in the White centres of global capitalism, they are, in fact, part and parcel of the world's great majority – peasant and working-class, non-White masses. For as long as they remember, even as they first-foot in the First World, that they still have one foot in the Third World, they retain their authority to make radical demands of 'the system'.

Of course, there were and have been other significant figures presenting their analyses of the post-war Black British experience, but none have made their interventionist intention so transparent. The radical sociologists-cum-cultural analysts simply describe and follow after what emerges from the mass. Sivanandan has always given the impression of getting behind movements and campaigns in order to help push them forward. It was Sivanandan, unseen, who gave his willing ear and wise counsel to the courageous young founders of the Southall Monitoring Group and the Newham Monitoring Project on his doorstep in London, just as, half a generation later, he was still responding to the direct questions brought by the new organisers of community defence campaigns against discrimination and attacks on the fascist-infested estates of Tower Hamlets. With his unfailing ability to move seamlessly between theory and practice, and to travel from the particular experience of grievance or abuse to the general political context and back again to the particular organisational task, he would invent on-the-spot tool kits for these activists. It was he who made them understand that they would achieve the best political results only to the extent that they turned incidents into cases, made cases into campaigns, pushed campaigns until they became social issues and joined social issues with political movements. Sivanandan is one who has constantly underlined the distinctiveness and inventiveness of the 'Black' forged in late twentieth-century Britain. More than mere skin colour or ethnic flavour, and more than merely a victim reaction to racism read as a fact of life, it is the colour of those who have had no option but to stand against racism. Its target is not just racial discrimination but also the system of class within which racism is articulated. Its earliest constituency was working-class Black community but it has and does extend to all the new constituencies of those discriminated against who suffer and would resist injustice.

It was this grounding with the brothers and sisters that gave Sivanandan the authority to speak forthrightly to whole communities when, in the mid-1980s, they began to divide themselves into ghetto-ethnicities, often as a means of obtaining state hand-outs. He urged resisters to look every gift horse in the mouth and to bite the hand that fed where necessary. They had to be the beggars who would be the choosers. Then as now, he flipped everything, turned things over. He castigated self-styled and media-appointed community leaders, exposing their self-interest in using ethnic labels not only to access resources but also as a means of making the laziest appeals to what were uprooted, destabilised communities in transition, carrying humiliated colonial heritages and loaded with what the sociologists called crises of identity.

In the babel of our time, Sivanandan's has been the voice in the wilderness, warning of the weakening of political community that would accompany the shift to ethnicising our protest and struggle. And he has said this loudly into communities as well as into conferences of the welfare establishment – for the influential

King's Fund health brokers, as for CCETSW, the setters of professional community work agendas. His has been a distinctive, unequivocal voice, where others who really knew better have lacked the courage and integrity to make the same public stand.

That voice has continued to sound loud and clear over the past two decades; but it has taken on new timbres, new keys, as Sivanandan has witnessed and analysed the epochal changes brought on by globalisation. He was one of the first, not only to see, but also to demonstrate how the technological revolution has refashioned the whole world order, throwing up a new imperialism that has led to the further immiseration of the peoples of the global South and mass migration across the world. He has charted how the racism – against the poor, the Black, the dispossessed, the would-be migrant – that globalisation has latterly given birth to among the affluent of the global North, is culturally and economically, as well as colour, coded. 'Poverty is the new Black' says it all, really. His coinage of the term xeno-racism acutely exposes the self-serving belief that Europe's formidable hostility to the impoverished migrant workers on which so much of its basic prosperity depends is not just some nice people's social phobia about foreigners, but a system of belief and practice aimed at locking down, and locking in, the needy and the desperate. And the war on terror has spawned a new anti-Muslim racism, where minarets mark out the enemy within; a racism, as enacted by governments, that has proved an enemy to freedom of thought, freedom of movement, freedom of conscience, transparency of judicial process and rights to civil liberty.

Throughout it all, Sivanandan is ever there giving the Left, the activist intellectuals as well as the Black brothers and sisters, eyes to see with and ways to hone new weapons of struggle.

But the real reason for reprinting this selection of Sivanandan's seminal essays now is not just to recover history and the struggle from below, for new generations, though that in itself is a valid and necessary exercise. It is simply that incorporated within his articles – his methodology, if you like, though it's much more lively than that social scientist's term implies – is an approach to thinking through an issue, from a basic proposition and the specific evidence, which is still needed to make sense of the world today. In his 'thinking in order to do, not thinking in order to think', no orthodoxies get in the way of his whole-hearted commitment to clarity and truth. 'Race, class and the state', for example, which addressed race policy in the early 1970s through the prism of the Black experience, laid down a blueprint for examining the dialectic between the state and capital mediated through race. In it, through the way in which he marshalled his arguments, Sivanandan demonstrated how to evaluate the British state's apparently contradictory impulses, exposing, behind the smoke and mirrors, a coherent, repressive and exploitative policy. It is a practice from which we can learn today. 'RAT and the degradation of Black struggle', though aimed at ending a dangerous, superficial anti-racist training fad of the 1980s, contains essential truths about identity formation; the distinction that has to be made between individual and institutional racism, and the need for a fight for justice itself to be based on just principles. Both this essay and 'The hokum of New Times' show how to walk the tightrope of criticising friends and allies, when the situation demands, without selling them short to the enemy.

Sivanandan relishes language. His words soar and roar, his call to arms can be theatrical – he grabs you by the coat collar: 'Listen to the voice, the anxieties of the state'. And you do. His descriptions can be humorous: 'it was a sort of bazaar socialism, bizarre socialism', but the wit always contains an acute truth, such as that of Europe's 'common, market racism'. The rhythm and sweep of his language is often tantamount to poetry.

His slogans and pithy epigrams – 'we are here, because you were there', 'the people we are writing for are the people we are fighting for', 'we wear our passports on our faces', 'poverty is the new Black' – encapsulate real insights that will live with you months after you have closed this book. 'Disorganic development' sums up in two words the profound deformations foisted on the South by the old colonialism and the new imperialism – it is a way of understanding the world that continues to be valid.

Sivanandan is exciting and iconoclastic precisely because he refuses to be pigeon-holed. He cannot be reduced to a 'Black writer', an 'orthodox Marxist', a 'utopian'. He is all these and at once. And he is not just a polemical political essayist either. He has turned to fiction, using his sensibilities and commitment, to etch in the three-generational family saga *When Memory Dies*, the award-winning story of his country, Sri Lanka, and in *Where the Dance Is* to tell tales of lives and loves from Camden Town to Colombo.

But the backdrop to his output over four decades has been his work first as librarian, then as founding editor of *Race & Class* and finally as director of the Institute of Race Relations. Under his auspices the IRR has come to be more and more an institute against racism, but without ever changing its name. This direction was signalled in a now famous moment of transformation in the early 1970s, when the staff and progressive elements from its management took over the Institute's library, drove out the money-spinning neocolonialist founders from their own temple to race and, surviving on a shoe string, began to change its purpose and use.

Writing, for Sivanandan, is just another way of fighting. And most of his output has been in the form of pamphleteering, interventions into struggles, be they against state policies, the fascists, prejudiced trade-union leaderships, local authority bureaucrats, the Black middle class, the dogmatic Left, the postmodern intelligentsia, the war on terror, or the war on Iraq. The attempt – soaringly successful – to 'catch history on the wing' has driven his life and his writing; it is what makes it so compelling, it is what makes it resonate with truth.

INTRODUCTION: UNITY OF STRUGGLE*

Now is the time to catch history on the wing. But for those of us on the Left, the now is always now. And, however much we may disagree about ideology, belief or political line, what binds us still is a common, visceral hatred of injustice, the force that drives the green fuse of revolution.

We do not have to be at the barricades to be revolutionaries, we do not have to be grassrootists to be radical. To apprehend the social consequences of what we ourselves are doing and to set out to change it is in itself a revolutionary act.

And now globalisation, with its free-market system and imperial ideology has thrown up the objective circumstances which, in showing the relationship between our struggles, demand that we connect them. The way that globalisation has altered the role of the state, for instance, from welfare state to market state and so altered so many aspects of our lives. Or globalisation and the displacement of whole populations leading to forced migration and the consequences of that; globalisation and its racisms and their fall-outs; globalisation and the creation of unending poverty in the midst of growing prosperity, globalisation and imperialism – and war.

Hence, the struggles against globalisation and its ills are not separate struggles. The globalisation that throws up our several ills is also the globalisation that connects our resistances. In fighting our specific causes, we need also to be aware of the common cause they spring from and address ourselves to both at once – and so forge the alliances we need to win the battle. For globalisation is a complete system and unravelling one strand of it at a time does not unravel the whole. Single issue struggles may usher in piecemeal reform, but not radical change.

---

* Based on a talk to the IRR's conference, 'Racism, liberty and the war on terror', September 2006.

Take a look at the issue of immigration, for instance, and the different groups tackling the different problems thrown up by immigration laws and asylum policies – from incarceration and detention and deportation to deprivation, destitution and death – organisations such as JCWI, NCADC, BID, Black Women's Rape Action project, Schools Against Deportation, Medical Justice Network, Campaign to Close Campsfield, the Yarlswood Campaign, Statewatch, ILPA, CAMPACC, Stop Political Terror, Inquest, regional refugee networks and asylum-seeker led campaigns. They all address issues which originate in or derive from the policies of the government and strictures of the state. And the state in the global era is no longer, primarily, a nation state working on behalf of its people but a servitor of the global economy run by multinational corporations and the market. We have moved, in other words, from the welfare state of late industrial capitalism to the market state of global capitalism. If the nation state was the vehicle of industrial capitalism, the market state is the vehicle of global capitalism. It is the market, for instance, that sets the agenda for government policies on immigration and decides who are needed for the economy and who are not. And on that reckoning, asylum seekers are considered so much disposable waste and treated as such. Whereas the real waste is the waste of their talents and education.

But what has landed refugees and asylum seekers on these shores is the displacement of whole populations caused by the marauding incursions of global corporations into Third World countries in search of new markets, cheap labour, raw material, natural resources. *Oil.* To be successful, however, such incursions need the backing of friendly regimes in these countries. And what induces these regimes to be friendly is, first, the soft-soaping aid and development packages offered to them by the World Bank and the IMF, and the expertise and advice that come with their programmes, such as Structural Adjustment Programmes (SAPs) – which require the withdrawal of state subsidies for education and social services in favour of debt repayment (sops for SAPs). All of which ties the dependent countries into further dependency. If that doesn't work, there is always regime change – through assassination or economic sanctions, effected this time by the government of the United States and its satraps as agents of the multinationals. Or, failing that, through bombing the hell out of the offending regime and its people in pursuance, ostensibly, of a mission of mercy to save them for free elections and democracy. If, however, they, the people, fail to vote-in a friendly regime, they'll be bombed out of existence again, to make sure they understand that their liberators are our terrorists, and get it right the next time round.

That, in sum, is the trajectory of American-British imperialism today. Claiming to be democracies, however, and needing therefore to obtain the sanction of their electorates for their actions (often after the event), the American and British governments spin out false information based on faulty or twisted intelligence within a fundamentalist philosophy of good and evil, resurrecting a culture of primitive racism (we good, them evil) surrounded by a politics of spurious fear promoted on the back of the real fears of 9/11 and 7/7 and braced by anti-terrorist legislation. All of which leads, on the one hand, to the degradation of British values that the government so hypocritically upholds, and signifies, on the other, the Islamic war cloud hanging over your heads and the Muslim terrorist in your midst, squeezed in the tube train next to you.

Already immigration legislation had selected out asylum seekers for indefinite detention without trial, and summary deportation. Now anti-terrorist legislation is extending the same treatment to those who have already obtained the right to remain – and even to settled Asian communities. And the convergence of the two – the war on asylum and the 'war on terror' – one, the unarmed invasion, the other, the armed enemy within, has produced the idea of a nation under siege, and, on the ground, a racism that cannot tell a settler from an immigrant, an immigrant from an asylum seeker, an asylum seeker from a Muslim, a Muslim from a terrorist. All of us non-whites, at first sight, are terrorists or illegals. We wear our passports on our faces – or, lacking them, we are faceless, destitute, taken from our children, voided of the last shreds of human dignity.

But more insidious still is the damage done to the whole fabric of society and to the fundaments of democracy – constraining freedom of speech and assembly, undermining the rule of law and the independence of the judiciary, threatening the separation of powers and the conventions of an unwritten constitution, and Magna Carta. And then there is the increasing concentration of power in central government accompanied by the weakening and dissipation of local government – which is the closest thing there is to direct democracy, giving people a say in their own lives and engaging them in the political process. Finally, there is a whole range of laws (3,000 new criminal offences since the government came into power – i.e., one a day) which penalise anything from minor anti-social behaviour to demonstrating within a kilometre of parliament, thereby treating largely social problems to criminal solutions and ignoring the distinction between crime itself and the social causes of crime – which you'll remember was the avowed position of a government that once was Labour.

It is that adamantine resolve to deny the connection between cause and effect that has also prevented the government from seeing that, in the invasions of Afghanistan and Iraq and the systematic dismemberment of Palestine, it is they and their American bosses who have declared jihad on Muslims the world over and given sustenance to terrorism. And having refused to acknowledge it, they have no choice but to stir up more and more fear, in order to pass more and more draconian legislation that further erodes our liberties.

And in the interstices of an increasingly authoritarian state sprouts the culture of nativism, white ethnicism, in search of a flat, colourless, etiolated homogeneity, built on the shifting sands of assimilation and based on shifty British values. Inevitably, multiculturalism, which to me means simply unity in diversity, and which this country uniquely achieved in the '60s and '70s in the course of anti-racist struggles, has been ditched in favour of assimilation, meaning absorption of the lesser into the greater. But to make the term palatable, the government and the media have taken to substituting the word integration and/or cohesion for assimilation. The precise meaning of integration in practice, however, was set out as far back as 1966 by Roy Jenkins, an enlightened Labour Home Secretary who defined it 'not as a flattening process of assimilation but equal opportunity, accompanied by cultural diversity in an atmosphere of mutual tolerance'.

As for British values of tolerance, fair play, individual freedom – where, one might ask, do they count in the practice of government and its ministers? Why, besides, have the principles of the Enlightenment – liberty, equality, fraternity – not been extended in their fullness to the non-white peoples of the world? Surely, what we should be addressing in the era of rule by global corporations is not British values but universal values – embodied in human rights. Yet, it is this government which is making every effort to withdraw from the Human Rights Act, to which, in a moment of old Labour conscience, it acceded.

In the final analysis, though, all this talk of British values, social cohesion and individual responsibility is meaningless, given the government's commitment to the free market system, the *sine qua non* of globalisation. The market speaks to profit, not to values, to social control not to social cohesion, to personal greed not to individual responsibility. Its life-blood is privatisation not public ownership; its heart beats to the tune of giant corporations. It pauperises the Third World and feeds them scraps from the imperial table; it pauperises a third of its own people and feeds them scraps of social reform. It weighs up personal relationships in a balance-sheet of profit and loss – till we no longer listen to each other or hear the pain of the world. The market corrupts, and the free market corrupts freely.

That is what I mean when I say that globalisation is a complete system, and unravelling one strand of it does not unravel the whole. But the ills it throws up are so clearly connected – and overlap – that our struggles against them demand to be connected too. The fight against racism is connected to the flight against immigration laws, asylum and anti-terrorism, anti-terrorism to racism (anti-Muslim racism in particular), asylum and immigration, and so on. And they are all related in one way or another to the erosion of civil liberties, imperial foreign policy and the rise of the authoritarian state.

Let's leave the big picture for a moment, look at the enormity of the little everyday things that are happening to us. An old man, a life-long member of the Labour Party is muscled out of the party conference just because he heckled the Foreign Secretary. (An individual error, maybe, but where does the authority come from?) A 47-year-old is asboed and sent to prison for sixty days because he sang too loud in his Housing Association flat. Two Asians are taken off a flight because passengers found they were wearing too much clothing and speaking Arabic. (It happened to be Urdu.)

On another level, when did you ever hear of a neighbouring country kidnapping and imprisoning your elected MPs just because it didn't like the colour of their politics? The sheer arrogance of it is mindboggling, and yet Britain's ethical foreign policy closes its eyes to it because Israel is the cornerstone of American-British imperialism in the Middle East. Not only is Britain moving towards an authoritarian regime; it is promoting authoritarian regimes elsewhere.

Wherever you look, there is something rotten gnawing at the vitals of a free society. But it is hidden behind a façade of fake prosperity, lies made feasible by fear, and empty talk of democracy and values. But values come out of rights. And the rights that the struggles of the industrial working class won for us, and the values they bred, are under attack. It is up to us campaigners, dissidents, insurgents, as custodians of those rights and values, to connect with each others' struggles and take up the fight.

But how do we make the connections in practice and how do we turn that into a movement? Of course, there's no strategy that is valid for all of time. But my experience in the black, anti-racist struggles of the '60s and '70s – when we made black the colour of our politics and not the colour of our skins – when we fought on the factory floor and in the community, as a people and a class, and as a people for a class – tells me that only in being involved and supporting each other's struggles can we forge an organic relationship between us, not just ad hoc coalitions.

We cannot let ourselves be bogged down in our particularities and miss the wood for the trees. We need to have an international perspective, even as we take on national or local issues. We need to move, in our thinking, from the particular to the general and the general to the particular, both at once. And it is then that we can successfully turn individual cases into social issues, social issues into civic causes, and civic causes into a national movement.

PART I

THE PERSONAL AND THE POLITICAL

What does being black mean in terms of identity, struggle and intellectual engagement? Three essays examine these trajectories at three crucial points in time: 1974 marking the end of colonialism and the impact of Black Power, 1989 during Thatcherism and the decomposition of working-class struggle and 'the Left', 1995 as globalisation takes hold economically and post-modernism intellectually.

Each essay is about the challenge of not just following popular intellectual fads and taking the political line of least resistance but of staying true to the experience of the most oppressed in society. The 'black intellectual' of the early 1970s is asked to decolonise his mind, to decide whether he is 'a mercenary on hire to his people or a soldier in the people's army'. 'The hokum of New Times' takes on a pseudo-Marxist Left that bows to Thatcherism by accepting the end of class struggle and the reality of state power, and substituting in their place a personal, individualised, fleeting free-for-all. The values and traditions which came down from working-class movements are still alive in the communities of resistance of a new underclass. And there, the personal is not political: the political is personal. Under global capitalism where the culture of racism is the culture of violence, bred in the nexus of poverty and powerlessness, the need for commitment from intellectuals and academics is paramount. For it is they who are in the engine rooms of the Information Society. Instead of rising to the occasion, 'La trahison des clercs' reveals how far they have retreated into culturalism and post-modernism.

1

THE LIBERATION OF THE BLACK INTELLECTUAL*

Wherever colonisation is a fact, the indigenous culture begins to rot. And among the ruins something begins to be born which is not a culture but a kind of sub-culture, a sub-culture which is condemned to exist on the margin allowed by an European culture. This then becomes the province of a few men, the elite, who find themselves placed in the most artificial conditions, deprived of any revivifying contact with the masses of the people.

Aimé Césaire[1]

On the margin of European culture, and alienated from his own, the 'coloured' intellectual is an artefact of colonial history, marginal man par excellence. He is a creature of two worlds, and of none. Thrown up by a specific history, he remains stranded on its shores even as it recedes. And what he comes into is not so much a twilight world, as a world of false shadows and false light.

At the height of colonial rule, he is the servitor of those in power, offering up his people in return for crumbs of privilege; at its end, he turns servant of the people, negotiating their independence even as he attains to power. Outwardly, he favours that part of him which is turned towards his native land. He puts on the garb of nationalism, vows a return to tradition. He helps design a national flag, compose a People's Anthem. He puts up with the beat of the tom-tom and the ritual of the circumcision ceremony. But privately, he lives in the manner of his masters, affecting their style and their values, assuming their privileges and status. And for a while he succeeds in holding these two worlds together, the outer and the inner, deriving the best of both. But the

---

* This essay was written in 1974.

forces of nationalism on the one hand and the virus of colonial privilege on the other, drive him once more into the margin of existence. In despair he turns himself to Europe. With something like belonging, he looks towards the Cathedral at Chartres and Windsor Castle, Giambologna and Donizetti and Shakespeare and Verlaine, snow-drops and roses. He must be done, once and for all, with the waywardness and uncouth manners of his people, released from their endemic ignorance, delivered from witchcraft and voodoo, from the heat and the chattering mynah-bird, from the incessant beat of the tom-tom. He must return to the country of his mind.

But even as the 'coloured' intellectual enters the mother country, he is entered into another world where his colour, and not his intellect or his status, begins to define his life – he is entered into another relationship with himself. The porter (unless he is black), the immigration officer (who is never anything but white), the customs official, the policeman of whom he seeks directions, the cabman who takes him to his lodgings, and the landlady who takes him in at a price – none of them leaves him in any doubt that he is not merely not welcome in their country, but should in fact be going back – to where he came from. That indeed is their only curiosity, their only interest: where he comes from, which particular jungle, Asian, African or Caribbean.

There was a time when he had been received warmly, but he was at Oxford then and his country was still a colony. Perhaps equality was something that the British honoured in the abstract. Or perhaps his 'equality' was something that was precisely defined and set within the enclave of Empire. He had a place somewhere in the imperial class structure. But within British society itself there seemed no place for him. Not even his upper-class affectations, his BBC accent, his well-pressed suit and college tie afford him a niche in the carefully defined inequalities of British life. He feels himself not just an outsider or different, but invested, as it were, with a separate inequality: outside and inferior at the same time.

At that point, his self-assurance which had sat on him 'like a silk hat on a Bradford millionaire'[2] takes a cruel blow. But he still has his intellect, his expertise, his qualifications to fall back on. He redeems his self-respect with another look at his Oxford diploma (to achieve which he had put his culture in pawn). But his applications for employment remain unanswered, his letters of introduction unattended. It only needs the employment officer's rejection of his qualifications, white though they be, to dispel at last his intellectual pretensions.

The certainty finally dawns on him that his colour is the only measure of his worth, the sole criterion of his being. Whatever his claims to white culture and white values, whatever his adherence to white norms, he is first and last a no-good nigger, a bleeding wog or just plain black bastard. His colour is the only reality allowed him; but a reality which, to survive, he must cope with. Once more he is caught between two worlds: accepting his colour and rejecting it, or accepting it only to reject it – aping still the white man (though now with conscious effort at survival), playing the white man's game (though now aware that he changes the rules so as to keep on winning), even forcing the white man to concede a victory or two (out of his hideous patronage, his grotesque paternalism). He accepts that it is their country and not his, rationalises their grievances against him, acknowledges the chip on his shoulder (which he knows is really a beam in their eye), and, ironically, by virtue of staying in his place, moves up a position or two – in the area, invariably, of race relations.[3] For it is here that his skilled ambivalence finds the greatest scope, his colour the greatest demand. Once more he comes into his own – as servitor of those in power, a buffer between them and his people, a shock-absorber of 'coloured discontent' – in fact, a 'coloured' intellectual.

But this is an untenable position. As the racial 'scene' gets worse, and racism comes to reside in the very institutions of white society, the contradictions inherent in the marginal situation of the 'coloured' intellectual begin to manifest themselves. As a 'coloured' he is outside white society, in his intellectual functions he is outside black. For if, as Sartre has pointed out, 'that which defines an intellectual... is the profound contradiction between the universality which bourgeois society is obliged to allow his scholarship, and the restricted ideological and political domain in which he is forced to apply it',[4] there is for the 'coloured' intellectual no role in an 'ideological and political domain', shot through with racism, which is not fundamentally antipathetic to his colour and all that it implies. But for that very reason, his contradiction, in contrast to that of his white counterpart, is perceived not just intellectually or abstractly, but in his very existence. It is for him, a living, palpitating reality, demanding resolution.

Equally, the universality allowed his scholarship is, in the divided world of a racist society, different to that of the white intellectual. It is a less universal universality, as it were, and subsumed to the universality of white scholarship. But it is precisely because it is a universality that is particular to colour that it is already keened to the sense of oppression. So that when Sartre tells us that the intellectual, in grasping his contradictions, puts himself on the side of the oppressed ('because, in principle, universality is on that side'),[5] it is clear that the 'coloured' intellectual, at the moment of grasping his contradictions, *becomes* the oppressed – is reconciled to himself and his people, or rather, to himself in his people.

To put it differently. Although the intellectual qua intellectual can, in 'grasping his contradiction', take the *position* of the oppressed, he cannot, by virtue of his class (invariably petty-bourgeois) achieve an instinctual understanding of oppression. The 'coloured' man, on the other hand, has, by virtue of his colour, an *instinct* of oppression, unaffected by his class, though muted by it. So that the 'coloured' intellectual, in resolving his contradiction as an intellectual, resolves also his existential contradiction. In coming to consciousness of the oppressed, he 'takes conscience of himself',[6] in taking conscience of himself, he comes to consciousness of the oppressed. The fact of his intellect which had alienated him from his people now puts him on their side, the fact of his colour which had connected him with his people, restores him finally to their ranks. And at that moment of reconciliation between instinct and position, between the existential and the intellectual, between the subjective and objective realities of his oppression, he is delivered from his marginality and stands revealed as neither 'coloured' nor 'intellectual' – but BLACK.[7]

He accepts now the full burden of his colour. With Césaire, he cries:

I accept... I accept... entirely, without reservation...
my race which no ablution of hyssop mingled with lilies can ever purify
my race gnawed by blemishes
my race ripe grapes from drunken feet
my queen of spit and leprosies
my queen of whips and scrofulae
my queen of squamae and chlosmae
(O royalty whom I have loved in the far gardens of spring lit by chestnut candles!)
I accept. I accept.[8]

And accepting, he seeks to define. But black, he discovers, finds definition not in its own right but as the opposite of white.[9] Hence in order to define himself, he must first define the white man. But to do so on the white man's terms would lead him back to self-denigration. And yet the only tools of intellection available to him are white tools – white language, white education, white systems of thought – the very things that alienate him from himself. Whatever tools are native to him lie beyond his consciousness somewhere, condemned to disuse and decay by white centuries. But to use white tools to uncover the white man so that he (the black) may at last find definition requires that the tools themselves are altered in their use. In the process, the whole of white civilisation comes into question, black culture is re-assessed, and the very fabric of bourgeois society threatened. Take language, for instance. A man's whole world, as Fanon points out, is 'expressed and implied by his language':[10] it is a way of thinking, of feeling, of being. It is identity. It is, in Valéry's grand phrase, 'the god gone astray in the flesh'.[11] But the language of the colonised man is another man's language. In fact it is his oppressor's and must, of its very nature, be inimical to him – to his people and his gods. Worse, it creates alien gods. Alien gods 'gone astray in the flesh' – white gods in black flesh – a canker in the rose. No, that is not quite right, for white gods, like roses, are beautiful things, it is the black that is cancerous. So one should say a 'rose in the canker'. But that is not quite right either – neither in its imagery nor in what it is intended to express. How does one say it then? How does one express the holiness of the heart's disaffection (*pace* Keats) and 'the truth of the imagination' in a language that is false to one? How does one communicate the burden of one's humanity in a language that dehumanises one in the very act of communication?

Two languages, then, one for the coloniser and another for the colonised – and yet within the same language? How to reconcile this ambivalence? A patois, perhaps: a spontaneous, organic rendering of the masters' language to the throb of native sensibilities – some last grasp at identity, at wholeness.

But dialect betrays class. The 'pidgin-nigger-talker' is an ignorant man. Only common people speak pidgin. Conversely, when the white man speaks it, it is only to show the native how common he really is. It is a way of 'classifying him, imprisoning him, primitivising him'.[12]

Or perhaps the native has a language of his own; even a literature. But compared to English (or French) his language is dead, his literature passé. They have no place in a modern, industrialised world. They are for yesterday's people. Progress is English, education is English, the good things in life (in the world the coloniser made) are English, the way to the top (and white civilisation leaves the native in no doubt that that is the purpose of life) is English. His teachers see to it that he speaks it in school, his parents that he speaks it at home – even though they are rejected by their children for their own ignorance of *the* tongue.

But if the coloniser's language creates an 'existential deviation'[13] in the native, white literature drives him further from himself. It disorientates him from his surroundings: the heat, the vegetation, the rhythm of the world around him. Already, in childhood, he writes school essays on 'the season of mists and mellow fruitfulness'. He learns of good and just government from Rhodes and Hastings and Morgan. In the works of the great historian, Thomas Carlyle, he finds that 'poor black Quashee... a swift supple fellow, a merry-hearted, grinning, dancing, singing, affectionate kind of creature' could indeed be made into a 'handsome glossy thing' with a 'pennyworth of oil', but 'the tacit prayer he makes (unconsciously he, poor blockhead) to you and to me and to all the world who are wiser than himself is "compel me"' – to work.[14] In the writings of the greatest playwright in the world, he discovers that he is Caliban and Othello and Aaron, in the testaments of the most civilised religion that he is for ever cursed to slavery. With William Blake, the great revolutionary poet and painter, mystic and savant, he is convinced that:

> My mother bore me in the southern wild,
> And I am black, but O! my soul is white;
> White as an angel is the English child,
> But I am black, as if bereav'd of light.[15]

Yet, this is the man who wrote 'The Tyger'. And the little black boy, who knows all about tigers, understands the great truth of Blake's poem, is lost in wonderment at the man's profound imagination. What then of the other Blake? Was it only animals he could imagine himself into? Did he who wrote 'The Tyger' write 'The Little Black Boy'?

It is not just the literature of the language, however, that ensnares the native into 'whititude', but its grammar, its syntax, its vocabulary. They are all part of the trap. Only by destroying the trap can he escape it. 'He has', as Genet puts it, 'only one recourse: to accept this language but to corrupt it so skilfully that the white men are caught in his trap.'[16] He must blacken the language, suffuse it with his own darkness, and liberate it from the presence of the oppressor.

In the process, he changes radically the use of words, word-order – sounds, rhythm, imagery – even grammar. For, he recognises with Laing that even 'syntax and vocabulary are political acts that define and circumscribe the manner in which facts are experienced, [and] indeed... create the facts that are studied'.[17] In effect he brings to the language the authority of his particular experience and alters thereby the experience of the language itself. He frees it of its racial oppressiveness (black *is* beautiful), invests it with 'the universality inherent in the human condition'.[18] And he writes:

As there are hyena-men and panther-men
so I shall be a Jew man
a Kaffir man
a Hindu-from-Calcutta man
a man-from-Harlem-who-hasn't-got-the-vote.[19]

The discovery of black identity had equated the 'coloured' intellectual with himself, the definition of it equates him with all men. But it is still a definition arrived at by negating a negative, by rejecting what is not. And however positive that rejection, it does not by itself make for a positive identity. For that reason, it tends to be self-conscious and overblown. It equates the black man to other men on an existential (and intellectual) level, rather than on a political one.

But to 'positivise' his identity, the black man must go back and rediscover himself – in Africa and Asia – not in a frenetic search for lost roots, but in an attempt to discover living tradition and values. He must find, that is, a historical sense, 'which is a sense of the timeless as well as the temporal, and of the timeless and temporal together'[20] and which 'involves a perception not only of the pastness of the past, but of its presence'.[21] Some of that past he still carries within him, no matter that it has been mislaid in the Caribbean for over four centuries. It is the presence of that past, the living presence, that he now seeks to discover. And in discovering where he came from he realises more fully where he is at, and where, in fact, he is going to.

He discovers, for instance, that in Africa and Asia, there still remains, despite centuries of white rule, an attitude towards learning which is simply a matter of curiosity, a quest for understanding – an understanding of not just the 'metalled ways' on which the world moves, but of oneself, one's people, others whose life-styles are alien to one's own – an understanding of both the inscape and fabric of life. Knowledge is not a goal in itself, but a path to wisdom; it bestows not privilege so much as duty, not power so much as responsibility. And it brings with it a desire to learn even as one teaches, to teach even as one learns. It is used not to compete with one's fellow beings for some unending standard of life, but to achieve for them, as for oneself, a higher quality of life.

'We excel', declares the African,

> neither in mysticism nor in science and technology, but in the field of human relations... By loving our parents, our brothers, our sisters and cousins, aunts, uncles, nephews and nieces, and by regarding them as members of our families, we cultivate the habit of loving lavishly, of exuding human warmth, of compassion, and of giving and helping... Once so conditioned, one behaves in this way not only to one's family, but also to the clan, the tribe, the nation, and to humanity as a whole.[22]

Chisiza is here speaking of the unconfined nature of love in African (and Asian) societies (not, as a thousand sociologists would have us believe, of 'the extended family system'), in marked contrast to western societies where the love between a man and a woman (and their children) is sufficient unto itself, seldom opening them out, albeit through each other, to a multitude of loves. The heart needs the practice of love as much as the mind its thought.

The practical expression of these values is no better illustrated than in the socialist policies of Nyerere's Tanzania. It is a socialism particular to African conditions, based on African tradition, requiring an African (Swahili) word to define it. *Ujamaa* literally means 'familyhood'. 'It brings to the mind of our people the idea of mutual involvement in the family as we know it.'[23] And this idea of the family is the sustaining principle of Tanzanian society. It stresses cooperative endeavour rather than individual advancement. It requires respect for the traditional knowledge and wisdom of one's elders, illiterate though they be, no less than for academic learning. But the business of the educated is not to fly away from the rest of society on the wings of their skills, but to turn those skills to the service of their people. And the higher their qualifications, the greater their duty to serve. 'Intellectual arrogance', the Mwalimu has declared, 'has no place in a society of equal citizens.'[24]

The intellectual, that is, has no special privilege in such a society. He is as much an organic part of the nation as anyone else. His scholarship makes him no more than other people and his functions serve no interest but theirs. There is no dichotomy here between status and function. Hence he is not presented with the conflict between the universal and the particular of which Sartre speaks. And in that sense he is not an intellectual but everyman.

The same values obtain in the societies of Asia, sustained not so much by the governments of the day as in the folklore and tradition of their peoples. The same sense of 'family-hood', of the need to be confirmed by one's fellow man, the notion of duty as opposed to privilege, the preoccupation with truth rather than fact and a concept of life directed to the achievement of unity in diversity, characterise the Indian ethos. One has only to look at Gandhi's revolution to see how in incorporating, in its theory and its practice, the traditions of his people, a 'half-naked fakir' was able to forge a weapon that took on the whole might of the British empire and beat it. Or one turns to the early literature and art of India and finds there that the poet is less important than his poem, the artist more anonymous than his art. As Benjamin Rowland remarks: 'Indian art is more the history of a society and its needs than the history of individual artists.'[25] The artist, like any other individual, intellectual or otherwise, belongs to the community, not the community to him. And what he conveys is not so much his personal experience of truth as the collective vision of a society of which he is part, expressed not in terms private to him and his peers, but in familiar language – or in symbols, the common language of truth.

In western society, on the other hand, art creates its own coterie. It is the province of the specially initiated, carrying with it a language and a life-style of its own, even creating its own society. It sets up cohorts of interpreters and counter-interpreters, middlemen, known to the trade as *critics*, who in disembowelling his art show themselves more powerful, more creative than the artist. It is they who tell the mass of the people how they should experience art. And the more rarified it is, more removed from the experience of the common people, the greater is the artist's claim to *art* and the critic's claim to authority. Did but the artist speak directly to the people and from them, the critic would become irrelevant, and the artist symbiotic with his society.

It is not merely in the field of art, however, that western society shows itself fragmented, inorganic and expert-oriented. But the fact that it does so in the noblest of man's activities is an indication of the alienation that such a society engenders in all areas of life. In contrast to the traditions of Afro-Asian countries, European civilisation appears to be destructive of human love and cynical of human life. And nowhere do these traits manifest themselves more clearly than in the attitude towards children and the treatment of the old. Children are not viewed as a challenge to one's growth, the measure of one's possibilities, but as a people apart, another generation, with other values, other standards, other aspirations. At best one keeps pace with them, puts on the habit of youth, feigns interest in their interests, but seldom if ever comprehends them. Lacking openness and generosity of spirit, the ability to live dangerously with each other, the relationship between child and adult is rarely an organic one. The adult occupies the world of the child far more than the child occupies the world of the adult. In the result, the fancy and innocence of children are crabbed and soured by adulthood even before they are ready to beget choice.

Is it any wonder then that this tradition of indifference should pass on back to the old from their children? But it is a tradition that is endemic to a society given to ceaseless competition and ruthless rivalry – where even education is impregnated with the violence of divisiveness, and violence itself stems not from passion (an aspect of the personal), but from cold and calculated reason (an aspect of the impersonal). When to get and to spend is more virtuous than to be and to become, even lovers cannot abandon themselves to each other, but must work out the debit and credit of emotion, a veritable balance-sheet of love. Distrust and selfishness and hypocrisy in personal relationships, and plain cruelty and self-aggrandisement in the art of government are the practice of such a society, however elevating its principles. Government itself is the art of keeping power from the people under the guise of the people's will. And the working people themselves are inveigled into acquiescence of the power structure by another set of middlemen: the union bosses.

In the face of all this, the black man in a white society – the black man, that is, who has 'taken conscience of himself', established at last a positive identity – comes to see the need for radical change in both the values and structure of that society. But even the revolutionary ideologies that envisage such a change are unable to take into their perspective the nature of his particular oppression and its implications for revolutionary strategy. White radicals continue to maintain that colour oppression is no more than an aspect of class oppression, that colour discrimination is only another aspect of working-class exploitation, that the capitalist system is the common enemy of the white worker and black alike. Hence they require that the colour line be subsumed to the class line and are satisfied that the strategies worked out for the white proletariat serve equally the interests of the black. The black struggle, therefore, should merge with and find direction from the larger struggle of the working class as a whole. Without white numbers, anyway, the black struggle on its own would be unavailing.

But what these radicals fail to realise is that the black man, by virtue of his particular oppression, is closer to his bourgeois brother (by colour) than to his white comrade. Indeed his white comrade is a party to his oppression. He too benefits from the exploitation of the black man, however indirectly, and tends to hold the black worker to areas of work which he himself does not wish to do, and from areas of work to which he himself aspires, irrespective of skill. In effect, the black workers constitute that section of the working class which is at the very bottom of society and is distinguished by its colour. Conversely, the attitude of racial superiority on the part of white workers relegates their black comrades to the bottom of society. In the event, they come to constitute a class apart, an underclass: the sub-proletariat. And the common denominator of capitalist oppression is not sufficient to bind them together in a common purpose.

A common understanding of racial oppression, on the other hand, ranges the black worker on the side of the black bourgeois

[handwritten marginalia: Sounds like Sanders 2016 – will he change? ★Black lives matter]

against their common enemy: the white man, worker and bourgeois alike.

In terms of analysis, what the white Marxists fail to grasp is that the slave and colonial exploitation of the black peoples of the world was so total and devastating – and so systematic in its devastation – as to make mock of working-class exploitation. Admittedly, the economic aspects of colonial exploitation may find analogy in white working-class history. But the cultural and psychological dimensions of black oppression are quite unparalleled. For, in their attempt to rationalise and justify to their other conscience 'the robbery, enslavement, and continued exploitation of their coloured victims all over the globe',[26] the conquistadors of Europe set up such a mighty edifice of racial and cultural superiority, replete with its own theology of goodness, that the natives were utterly disoriented and dehumanised. Torn from their past, reified in the present, caught for ever in the prison of their skins, accepting the white man's definition of themselves as 'quintessence of evil... representing not only the absence of values but the negation of values... the corrosive element disfiguring all that has to do with beauty or morality',[27] violated and sundered in every aspect of their being, it is a wonder that, like lemmings, they did not throw themselves in the sea. If the white workers' lot at the hands of capitalism was alienation, the blacks underwent complete deracination. And it is this factor which makes black oppression qualitatively different from the oppression of the white working class.

The inability of white Marxists to accept the full import of such an analysis on the part of black people may be alleged to the continuing paternalism of a culture of which they themselves are victims. (Marxism, after all, was formulated in a European context and must, on its own showing, be Eurocentric.) Or it may be that to understand fully the burden of blackness, they require the imagination and feeling systematically denied them by their culture. But more to the point is that, in their preoccupation with the economic factors of capitalist oppression, they have ignored the importance of its existential consequences, in effect its consequences to culture. The whole structure of white racism

Racism is built on economic exploitation / cemented w/ white culture

is built no doubt on economic exploitation, but it is cemented
with white culture. In other words, the racism inherent in white
society is *determined* economically, but *defined* culturally. And any
revolutionary ideology that is relevant to the times must envisage
not merely a change in the ownership of the means of production,
but a definition of that ownership: who shall own, whites only or
blacks as well? It must envisage, that is, a fundamental change in
the concepts of man and society contained in white culture – it
must envisage a revolutionary culture. For, as Gramsci has said,
revolutionary theory requires a revolutionary culture.

But to revolutionise a culture, one needs first to make a radical
assessment of it. That assessment, that revolutionary perspective,
by virtue of his historical situation, is provided by the black
man. For it is with the cultural manifestations of racism in his
daily life that he must contend. Racial prejudice and discrimination, he recognises, are not a matter of individual attitudes, but
the sickness of a whole society carried in its culture. And his
survival as a *black* man in white society requires that he constantly
questions and challenges every aspect of white life even as he meets
it. White speech, white schooling, white law, white work, white
religion, white love, even white lies – they are all measured on
the touchstone of his experience. He discovers, for instance, that
white schools make for white superiority, that white law equals
one law for the white and another for the black, that white work
relegates him to the worst jobs irrespective of skill, that even
white Jesus and white Marx who are supposed to save him are
really not in the same street, so to speak, as black Gandhi and
black Cabral. In his everyday life he fights the particulars of white
cultural superiority, in his conceptual life he fights the ideology of
white cultural hegemony. In the process he engenders not perhaps
a revolutionary culture, but certainly a revolutionary practice
within that culture.

For that practice to blossom into a revolutionary culture,
however, requires the participation of the masses, not just the
blacks. This does not mean, though, that any ad hoc coalition
of forces would do. Coalitions, in fact, are what will not do.
Integration, by any other name, has always spelt death – for the

blacks. To integrate with the white masses before they have entered into the practice of cultural change would be to emasculate the black cultural revolution. Any integration at this stage would be a merging of the weaker into the stronger, the lesser into the greater. The weakness of the blacks stems from the smallness of their numbers, the 'less-ness' from the bourgeois cultural consciousness of the white working class.

Before an organic fusion of forces can take place, two requirements need to be fulfilled. The blacks must through the consciousness of their colour, through the consciousness, that is, of that in which they perceive their oppression, arrive at a consciousness of class; and the white working class must in recovering its class instinct, its sense of oppression, both from technological alienation and a white-oriented culture, arrive at a consciousness of racial oppression.

For the black man, however, the consciousness of class is instinctive to his consciousness of colour.[28] Even as he begins to throw away the shackles of his particular slavery, he sees that there are others besides him who are enslaved too. He sees that racism is only one dimension of oppression in a whole system of exploitation and racial discrimination, the particular tool of a whole exploitative creed. He sees also that the culture of competition, individualism and elitism that fostered his intellect and gave it a habitation and a name is an accessory to the exploitation of the masses as a whole, and not merely of the blacks. He understands with Gramsci and George Jackson that 'all men are intellectuals'[29] or with Angela Davis that no one is. (If the term means anything it is only as a description of the work one does: the intellect is no more superior to the body than the soul to the intellect.) He realises with Fanon that 'the Negro problem does not resolve into the problem of Negroes living among white men, but rather of Negroes exploited, enslaved, despised by a colonialist, capitalist society that is only accidentally white'.[30] He acknowledges at last that inside every black man there is a working-class man waiting to get out.

In the words of Sartre, 'at a blow the subjective, existential, ethnic notion of blackness[31] passes, as Hegel would say, into the objective, positive, exact notion of the proletariat... "The white symbolises capital as the Negro labour... Beyond the black-skinned men of his race it is the struggle of the world proletariat that he sings"'.[32]

And he sings:

> I want to be of your race alone
> workers peasants of all lands
> ...white worker in Detroit black peon in Alabama
> uncountable nation in capitalist slavery
> destiny ranges us shoulder to shoulder
> repudiating the ancient malediction of blood taboos
> we roll among the ruins of our solitudes
> If the flood is a frontier
> we will strip the gully of its endless
> covering flow
> If the Sierra is a frontier
> we will smash the jaws of the volcanoes
> upholding the Cordilleras
> and the plain will be the parade ground of the dawn
> where we regroup our forces sundered
> by the deceits of our masters
> As the contradictions among the features
> creates the harmony of the face
> we proclaim the oneness of suffering
> and the revolt
> of all the peoples on all the face of the earth
> and we mix the mortar of the age of brotherhood
> out of the dust of idols.[33]

2

THE HOKUM OF NEW TIMES*

New Times is a fraud, a counterfeit, a humbug. It palms off Thatcherite values as socialist, shores up the Thatcherite market with the pretended politics of choice, fits out the Thatcherite individual with progressive consumerism, makes consumption itself the stuff of politics. New Times is a mirror image of Thatcherism passing for socialism. New Times is Thatcherism in drag.†

Inevitably – since New Times' gestation in *Marxism Today* was marked by the latter's preoccupation with finding an electoral riposte to Thatcherism, in oppositional politics, taking a cue from Tory successes at the polls to formulate a programme for an anti-Thatcherite coalition of forces.[1] What was it about Thatcherism that appealed to such vast cross-sections of people? How could it be turned to Labour's benefit? How should Labour itself change in terms of principles, policies, pacts, in order to wrest the electorate from Thatcher?

There was an appreciation in these questions of the massive changes that Thatcherism was bringing about in society while Labour was still sulking in a troglodyte past, but, as yet, there was no understanding of the basis on which the Tories were able to carry these changes through. The answers owed not a little, therefore, to the Tory vision of change and tended to appropriate those areas in which the Tories were operating successfully (markets, share-

This essay was written in January 1990.
* Dedicated to those friends with whom, out of a different loyalty, I must now openly disagree.
† I am interested here in the 'economic, social and political shape' of New Times as presented in the special issue of *Marxism Today* (October 1988) and elsewhere, not in the eclectic manifesto for New Times as presented to the Communist Party of Great Britain (CPGB).

ownership, council housing) to see how they could be re-cast in a Leftish mode or mould. There was no understanding, that is, that the 'ideological hegemony' that *Marxism Today* was so quick to construct for Thatcherism was based on the Tories' instinctive and profound understanding of the sea-change in capitalist society issuing from the technological revolution in production, and of the consequent need to give people direction, guidance, ballast, 'assure them of certain certainties'. Labour was adrift, rudder-less, its moorings in the working class unhinged by the dissipation of the class itself, and hanging on to the driftwood of trade unionism, while Thatcherism charted an assured and defiant course through troublesome seas. 'Authoritarian populism' only explained why Thatcherism had found a hold among the people, but not why people were prepared to put up with it.

There was no attempt on the part of *Marxism Today* to rethink society from the ground up in terms of marxist analysis – no attempt to rethink marxism itself on the basis of the new liberatory revolution in the production process. But, then, they had already arrived at a re-interpretation of marxism down a different route: through a disillusion with Soviet Communism and a leaning towards its revised mode in Eurocommunism. The first acknowledged the failure of 'actually existing socialism' to enlarge bourgeois democracy and enrich individual freedom, and the second subscribed to the view that the only way the working class was ever going to capture power in advanced capitalist societies was through bourgeois electoral politics and not through violent revolution. The split within the CPGB, with the 'old guard' taking the *Morning Star* (the party newspaper) and the new appropriating *Marxism Today* (the party journal), signalled the change in the journal's direction towards a politics of the possible. But as yet it did not know quite what it stood for or where it was going. What was its philosophy? How did it see the world? Throwing out revolution and class-war empirically was all very well, but where was the ideological under-pinning for it? What was the journal's constituency? To whom was it speaking if no longer to the working class? Where would it locate itself, find domicile?

In the beginning...

The philosophy came from the theoretical practitioners whose own disillusion with communism and marxist orthodoxy sent them back to re-examining the original texts in search of the true marxism, re-interpreting them for our times and setting up schools of thought, in the process, to interpret the re-interpretations and to announce, through sundry disciplines and theories (philosophy, linguistics, semiotics, psychoanalysis, post-structuralism, deconstruction...), the consummate and conclusive finding that reality itself was a matter of interpretation, construction, presentation – of words, ideas, images. 'Philosophers', they might have said with a nod to Marx, 'have interpreted the world; our task is to change the interpretation.' And in an information society where 'the word is... as "material" as the world'[2] and a consumer society where the mode of presentation is all, their claims found a ready home in a 'with-it' *Marxism Today*.

The ideology, along with the constituency, came from another strand of intellectual marxism which provided theoretical confirmation that economic determinism and class reductionism were non-marxist and things of the past. The economic base did not determine, even 'in the last instance', the ideological and political superstructure. They were all more or less 'autonomous instances', 'articulating' with each other, influencing and being influenced, in all sorts of 'conjunctures'. Politics, therefore, was a matter of positioning in and through and vis-à-vis these conjunctures – and culture was the mode in which such positioning was expressed. Hence there was a cultural politics (as distinct from a political culture) or, rather, all sorts of cultural politics which, having challenged all sorts of 'social blocs' in civil society, would at some auspicious moment of time come together in a network of alliances heralding the transition from capitalism (to what they are not sure). Accordingly, the agent of change in the contemporary world was not the working class – which, in any case, had ceased (if it ever was) to be a class for itself and was therefore incapable of revolution – but the new social forces such as women, blacks, gays (and, soon, greens) who were themselves informed and impelled by the politics of the person. Later, the 'new marxists' would try to usher in a dimension of class through the backdoor of 'the politics of difference' but, for the nonce, it was the new social forces, irrespective of their differing class personae, which were the carriers of the new socialism or, rather, the trackers of the transition.

These, at any rate, were the building blocks of new marxist arguments, refine them how they would. How they put them together, from time to time, as required by various 'conjunctures', would of course differ from the way that I have played around with them here. But that is the great strength of this sort of autonomy: it allows you to be ad hoc, opportune, open-ended, pluralist. The only thing you have got to be sure of is your identity – and there was a politics around that too, autonomous of course, that you needed to construct, but to that anon.

As for domicile, location, *Marxism Today* was to find these in the thinking of a Left intelligentsia eviscerated of class and the counsels of a Labour Party thrashing around for a showing at the polls. In France and Italy the Eurocommunists were parties in their own electoral rights, but in Britain *Marxism Today*, having broken with the 'stalinists', had no comparable base – nor, presumably, having broken so violently with the theory and practice of the vanguard party, could it countenance one. Labour, besides, was the established party of socialism. The point was to influence it, infiltrate it or, more accurately, 'hegemonise' it. (Old marxists infiltrate, new marxists 'hegemonise'.)

Thus, New Times was born in the throes of political pragmatism under the sign of cultural theory bereft of economic reasoning. And the last proved disabling of the whole project. For, in throwing out the tool of economic analysis along with the ideological baggage of economism, the new marxists were unable to bring to New Times the understanding that all the seismic changes in society and culture that they were so adroitly and bravely describing stemmed from (and in turn contributed to) the revolutionary changes at the economic level, at the level of the productive forces, brought about by the new technology. Here was an ongoing revolution, the size, scope, comprehensiveness of which had never been known in the history of humankind and it was passing the Left by – till Thatcherism inadvertently brought it to their notice. And even then what the Left understood was the scientific and technical magnitude of its achievements summed up in Sir Ieuan Maddock's phrase that electronics had replaced the brain as once steam had replaced muscle. But its sociological size – that Capital had been freed from Labour – had escaped the Left altogether. The Labour Party was too sunk in its own stupor of trade unionism to see that the working class was decomposing under the impact of the new forces of production and that old forms of Labour organisation were becoming frangible.

The old marxists were, similarly, too wedded to orthodoxy to see that the old relations of production were disintegrating and new ones being born in their place. They had for so long been fighting for the emancipation of Labour from Capital that they could not bear to think that it was Capital that was now being emancipated from Labour.[3] So ensconced had they been in their own beliefs and dogmas and sentiments that they were fearful of venturing out into a changing world and taking it by the scruff of its neck.

And the new marxists, who had daringly abandoned all such fears and inhibitions and acknowledged and celebrated the cultural and social changes that were going on, were unable, because of their premature apostasy, to connect them concretely with the emancipation of Capital from Labour or root that emancipation in the economic basis of production. Instead, they held up the changes to justify their apostasy.

Determinacies

So that when *Marxism Today* finally came to acknowledge the importance of economic change for an understanding of New Times (in the special issue of October 1988), the economic was still given only a walk-on part on to the 'post-Fordist' stage. 'Coming to terms with New Times', wrote Martin Jacques in the editorial, 'means first understanding what New Times are, what they mean... At the heart of New Times is the shift from the old mass-production Fordist economy to a new, more flexible, post-Fordist order based on computers, information technology and robotics.'[4] But there the concern with the economic ceases – for 'New Times are about much more than economic change. Our world is being remade.' Yes, but how? 'Mass production, the mass consumer, the big city, big-brother state, the sprawling housing estate, and the nation-state are in decline: flexibility, diversity, differentiation, mobility, communication, decentralisation and internationalisation are in the ascendant.' That's fine as a description of what's going on, but where's the analysis? 'In the process our own identities, our sense of self, our own subjectivities are being transformed. We are in transition to a new era.'

Of course 'we are in transition to a new era'. Of course things are changing radically. And of course these changes are not just at the economic level. But the changes in society, culture, politics cannot just be juxtaposed with the economic; the economic cannot just be 'read off' from them any more than they could be read off from the economic. They derive from the economic – still.

Or take Stuart Hall's listings in his 'Brave New World' article[5] – one on the economy and the other on the 'broader social and cultural changes'. The first itemises

> a shift to the new 'information technologies', more flexible decentralized forms of labour process and work organization; decline of the old manufacturing base and the growth of the 'sunrise' computer-based industries; the hiving-off or contracting out of functions and services; a greater emphasis on choice and product differentiation, on marketing, packaging and design, on the 'targeting' of consumers by lifestyle, taste and culture rather than by the Registrar General's categories of social class; a decline in the proportion of the skilled, male, manual working class, the rise of the service and white-collar classes and the 'feminization' of the workforce; an economy dominated by the multinationals, with their new international division of labour and their greater autonomy from nation-state control; the 'globalization' of the new financial markets, linked by the communications revolution; and new forms of the spatial organization of social processes.

Brilliant, clear, to the point, exhaustive: all the elements of the 'post-Fordist' economy are there.

The 'social and cultural' list, general here, but worked out in the course of the article, lists 'greater fragmentation and pluralism, the weakening of older collective solidarities and block identities and the emergence of new identities associated with greater work flexibility, the maximization of individual choices through personal consumption'.

There is, of course, no causal connection here between the two, the economic and the social-cultural. They are 'associated', they may even be seen to be walking hand in hand, but the one does not follow from the other, influence the other, make the other possible. What is it that makes for 'greater fragmentation and pluralism' (List 2) unless it is the fragmentation of the working class and hence the obfuscation of class in general? And how has that been brought about if not by 'a shift to the new "information technologies"; more flexible, decentralized forms of labour process and work organization; decline of the old manufacturing base and the growth of the "sunrise" computer-based industries; the hiving-off or contracting-out of functions and services' and a 'decline in the proportion of the skilled, male, manual working class, the rise of service and white-collar classes and the "feminization" of the workforce' (List 1) – changes, that is, in the mode and relations of production? (Let's keep the old terminology for now because the new is yet to be born with the new post-Fordist 'system'.)

How have 'the older collective solidarities and block identities weakened' (List 2) except through 'the decline of the old manufacturing base', the rise of 'more flexible, decentralized forms of labour process and work organization', and 'the hiving-off or contracting-out of functions and services' (List 1)? And how have these come about if not through 'the shift to the new technologies' which enables Capital not only to do away with mass production lines and the mass employment of workers on the same factory floor but to move the workplace itself around, from one cheap labour pool to another, as required by profit and the market. (Note how, in his refusal to be 'determinist', Hall leaves out of his reckoning the massed up workers of the Third World, on whose greater immiseration and exploitation the brave new western world of post-Fordism is being erected, and cannot be persuaded back to them even when the item on 'multinationals with their new international division of labour' resonates with their presence.)

Similarly, 'the emergence of new identities' (List 2) cannot just be 'associated with greater work flexibility' (List 1); it is largely made possible by greater work flexibility which in turn is made possible by the new technology. And 'the maximization of individual choices through personal consumption' (List 2) comes also from retailers' ability to lay 'a greater emphasis on choice and product differentiation, on marketing, packaging and design, on the targeting of consumers by lifestyle, taste and culture...' (List 1) based on computerised information and supply systems which allow them to gear supplies to taste, demand and time.

And what is this 'spatial organization of social processes' Hall is talking about which exists apart from the spatial organisation of economic processes?

All the significant social and cultural changes that we are passing through today are similarly predicated on economic change.[6] To try to understand New Times without understanding that fundamental relationship is like trying to comprehend nineteenth-century society and culture without understanding the industrial revolution that gave rise to it. We are living through similar times where everything is being shaped, influenced, conditioned by the revolution in the productive forces.* Economic determinacy might be said to have flagged with the economic decline and 'class failure' of industrial capitalism in its last decades and to have been discredited by the success of 'the cultural revolutions of the 60s, 1968 itself...' and the 'theoretical revolutions of the 60s and 70s – semiotics, structuralism, poststructuralism...' (which Stuart Hall assures us were, along with feminism and psychoanalysis, 'key episodes in the passage to "New Times"'). And all of this

---

* 'The entire industrial revolution enhanced productivity by a factor of about 100...' but 'the micro-electronic revolution has already enhanced productivity in information-based technology by a factor of more than a million – and the end isn't in sight yet.'[7]

may have confirmed the theoretics that the economic was one of several ('autonomous', 'articulating') 'instances'. But today, when Capital has come out of its crisis, refurbished, regenerated and radicalised by the revolution in the productive forces – and Capital is nothing if not an economic project – how can we overlook the crucial role of the economic without offering hostages to Capital? Even as individuals, how can we here, now, caught on the crest of that revolution, impacted by it on all sides, believe that the economic shapes nothing? Even the question of personal transformation, the 'reforging of ourselves as individuals', and our preoccupation with our identities stem from the upheavals occasioned by the economic revolution of our times. Yes, we are being re-made, but if we overlook the occasion for that re-making, we overlook those myriad others who are being un-made by the self-same revolution.

The economic determines 'in the last instance' still – but shorn of its class determinacy. For the very revolution that restores the base/superstructure relationship to something like its former importance is also that which does away with the working class in its pristine form, shape, size, homogeneity of experience, unity of will, clout, and emancipates Capital from Labour. And the more Labour tries to hold Capital in thrall by withholding its labour, the more Capital moves towards its emancipation through yet more information technology, yet more labour-less productive regimes, yet more recourse to the captive labour force in the periphery. The relations of production, that is, have changed with the changes in the level of the productive forces: information (in the sense of data fed to computers, robots, etc.) increasingly replaces labour as a factor of production; Capital no longer needs living labour as before, not in the same numbers, in the same place, at the same time; Labour can no longer organise on that basis, it has lost its economic clout and, with it, whatever political clout it had, whatever determinacy it could exercise in the political realm. What is crucial here is not that the productive forces have altered the balance of dependency between Capital and Labour, but that they have altered it so radically as to allow Capital to free itself of Labour and yet hold Labour captive.

And that is what moves the terrain of battle from the economic to the political, from the base to the superstructure and appears to throw 'the language of politics more over to the cultural side'[8] and render the subjective important. However, the battle itself is neither about culture nor about the subject, but – still – about the ownership and control of the means of production and the exploitation of workers. Only now, the centre of gravity of that exploitation has shifted from the centre to the periphery and, within the centre, to peripheral workers, home workers, ad hoc workers, casual, temporary, part-time workers – all the bits and pieces of the working class that the new productive forces have dispersed and dissipated of their strength. Exploitation has not gone out with class determinacy or inequality and poverty with the working class as we know it. The battle is the same as before – only, it needs to be taken on at the political/ideological level and not at the economic/political level.

Thatcher's real lessons

Mrs Thatcher saw the time and seized it. That was her genius. The productive forces were pregnant with a new economic and social order. Labour and labourism blocked its passage. It required Mrs Thatcher to take a knife to the unions before the new order could be born. And with that deft bit of political surgery, she determined what course the new economic order should take, whose interests it should serve. And she sold it to the people in a clear, simplistic ideology that spoke to their self-interest and their self-esteem in a time of deep uncertainty and pother – with the help of a press which was itself dying for change and knew it could get it only from her. The time brought forth the woman. And she cast the time in her image.

The new marxists, in addressing Thatcherism as an electoral and ideological phenomenon, failed to give sufficient importance to the economic and social order it was constructing. Themselves predisposed towards a politics of position, their aim was rather to align the Labour Party with the new class of skilled and semi-skilled workers who were replacing the old Fordist mass worker, the expanding clerical and office workforce of the service sector which was replacing industry as the locus of employment and the new social forces that were increasingly replacing class constituencies.[9] These were the people who could swing the electorate Labour's way. What were their demands and aspirations? How should Labour refashion itself to meet the claims of the new share-owning working class? How could Labour be made to relate to the new social constituencies, such as women, blacks, greens, etc., which had no 'clear-cut class identity'? 'The whole point of Thatcherism as a form of politics has been to construct a new social bloc...' Could Labour do the same? Could it abandon its traditional class perspective and accept that a social bloc has to be 'constructed out of groups which are very different in terms of their material interests and social positions'? And could these 'diverse identities' be welded together into a 'collective will'? Thatcherism in its second term 'did not make a single move which was not also carefully calculated in terms of this hegemonic strategy. It stepped up the pace of privatisation. But it took care, at every step, to harness new social constituencies to it, to "construct" an image of the new share-owning working class, and to expand the bloc, symbolically, around the image of choice.' Could Labour relate to the fact that 'increasingly, the electorate is thinking politically, not in terms of *policies*, but of *images* – not that policies don't matter but that they don't "capture people's imaginations unless constructed into an image with which they can identify"'. If Labour was going to become the majority party in any deep sense, it had to find a strategy for modernisation and an image of modernity; instead of rallying and mobilising the past, it had to find a 'convincing alternative scenario to Thatcherism for the future'.

There is an outline of a programme here for Labour to win over the constituencies on which 'Thatcherism's electoral hegemony continues to rest', but it is not one that speaks to the needs of that third of the nation that Thatcherism has dispossessed, which after all is socialism's first constituency. And (hence?) there is no reference to the ideological shift that Labour would have to make to accommodate these new constituencies, though ideology, we are told, is 'critical' to the construction of new social blocs. What, in any case, is this (new) ideology that could relate to the interests of the new constituencies and the underclasses – and are the new social forces a classless monolith? Or (alternatively?)* is there a 'hegemonic strategy' that needs to be builded around images that would 'expand the bloc symbolically' – for, 'elections are won or lost not on so-called real majorities but on (equally real) symbolic majorities'. These images, would they be the same sort of images around 'choice', around a new share-owning working class, etc. that Mrs Thatcher constructs? And how shall these speak to the dispossessed, how capture their political imagination? Or are there alternative images/policies that Labour can construct which can still keep it socialist at heart?

How, again, should Labour relate to the race, sex, gender-based social movements? On what terms? What is so profoundly socialist about these new social forces is that they raise issues about the quality of life (human worth, dignity, genuine equality, the enlargement of the self) by virtue of their experiences as women, blacks, gays, etc., which the working-class movement has not just lost sight of but turned its face against. But if these issues are fought in terms of the specific, particularistic oppressions of women qua women, blacks qua blacks and so on, without being opened out to and informed by other oppressions, they lose their claim to that universality which was their particular contribution to socialism in the first place. And they, further, fall into the error of a new sectarianism – as between blacks versus women, Asians versus Afro-Caribbeans, gays versus blacks and so on – which pulls rank, this time, not on the basis of belief but of suffering: not who is the true believer but who is the most oppressed. Which then sets out the basis on which demands are made for more equal opportunities for greater and more compound oppressions in terms of quotas and proportions and that type of numbers game. That is not to say that there should be no attempt to redress the balance of racial, sexual and gender discrimination, but that these solutions deal not with the politics of discrimination but

---

* The writings of the new marxists are so non-committal as to make definition difficult.

its arithmetic – giving more weightage to women here and blacks there and so rearranging the distribution of inequality as not to alter the structures of inequality themselves. In the process, these new social movements tend to replace one sort of sectarianism with another and one sort of sectional interest for another when their native thrust and genius was against sectarianism and for a plurality of interests.

Equally, what is inherently socialist about the issue-based new social forces such as the Green and Peace movements is the larger questions they raise about the quality of the environs we live in or whether we live at all. But to the extent that the Green Movement is concerned more, say, with the environmental pollution of the western world than with the ecological devastation of the Third World caused by western capitalism, its focus becomes blinkered and narrow and its programmes partial and susceptible to capitalist overtures. Or, to come at it from the opposite direction, it is precisely because the Green Movement overlooks the centrality of capitalism and imperialism in the despoliation of the planet that it overlooks also the narrowness of its campaigns (the US Greens attack 'addictive consumerism' while ignoring the inability of whole sections of the population to consume at all) and the limitation of its vision (the German Greens boast that their movement is 'neither to the right nor to the left but in front').[10] And for that self-same reason it fails, too, in its claim to connect the global and local, the collective and the individual – and therein fails its own trust and promise.

So, too, does a Peace Movement which does not, for instance, see that to preserve the world from a holocaustal nuclear war also involves preserving the Third World from a thousand internecine wars sponsored and financed by the arms industry of the West.

There are simple, basic connections to be made here within and between the various movements. They are connections which are organic to socialism, but they can only develop if the new social movements open themselves out to the larger social issues and to each other; move out in a centrifugal fashion without losing sight of the centripetal – move out, that is, from their particularities to the whole and back again to themselves, enriching both, in an unending traffic of ideas, struggles and commitments; weave the specific and the universal into a holistic pattern of socialism which, so far from failing the parts, continues to be informed by them.

But that is not how the new marxists visualise the new social forces. They do not ask what it is in the philosophy and practice of these movements that needs to be constantly reviewed and rectified if they are to make a continuing contribution to a modern progressive socialism. They do not seem to accept that there can be contradictions within and between the movements or that their practice often plays into the hands of capitalism and is therein negated. Instead, they tend to romanticise the movements – feminism especially, as though in a backlash of socialist guilt, romancing the feminine now where once they romanced the class – regarding them as the catalysts or, in their language, 'the leading edge' of change.* Perhaps they needed to, as a tactic, as a gun trained on the male, heterosexual citadels of socialism. But it is one that has backfired precisely because it has not looked to its own fallibility. It is not enough to ask what it is that the new social forces bring to the socialist movement without also asking what it is within these movements that could be corrupting of socialism.

But then, the axes on which the new social movements revolve are single-issue and identity-based politics which are of themselves self-defining and enclosed particularities tending to burrow into themselves for social truths and answers. Identity politics, in fact, seems to claim that the struggles of the self over its various personae – social, sexual, gendered – are by their very nature (for one does not struggle alone) social and political struggles: they impinge on how society regards women, blacks, gays, etc. and challenge the prevailing mores and ideology, in a sort of metaphysical dialectic between the personal and the political. The laboratory of social change, it would appear, is the self, but the self is also in the world and so the world changes with the changing of the self and the self with it.

---

*   In pursuing 'the leading edge of change', the new marxists ignore the basis of change.

At the still point of the turning world. Neither flesh nor fleshless; Neither from nor towards...[11]

Eliot was also a dialectical metaphysician.

The new politics

Politics is not just out there any more, says Rosalind Brunt – in study groups and meetings and vanguard parties – but here in the person, in 'the continuous making and remaking of ourselves, and ourselves in relation to others'.[12] It is in the way people experience the world through 'the many, and increasing, identities it offers: ... a colour, a gender, a class, a nationality; "belonging" to a family, having a child of your own; relating to colleagues, friends, comrades, lovers'. It can no longer be said that there is a politics outside ourselves – politics is in the person – or that to be political is to talk about '*the* system, *the* state, *the* working class, *the* Third World' – everything is political. 'What people do as political acts', remarks Beatrix Campbell in the same issue of *Marxism Today* (with a caveat that she is possibly being 'trivial here'), 'is they read, they buy, they refuse to buy, and they commit all sorts of acts which are about participation in the culture. It's only nut-cases in ever declining political organizations who think the only political act is to go to a meeting.'[13]

Power, for Brunt, is 'not simply a force coming from above and governed by one set of people, the ruling class'. Power is everywhere and 'it operates horizontally as much as vertically, internally as well as externally'. Even sex, goes on Rosalind Brunt paraphrasing Foucault, 'so far from... being a natural, biological given, central to our identity... is socially and culturally constructed and has a history brimming with power points...'. But 'where there is power there is also a "multiplicity of points of resistance"', particularly in the way that historical identities are constructed – in 'reverse discourse', for example, where a homosexual subject, say, can 'start to speak on his/her own behalf, and begin to shift to another, more "empowering" discourse that describes an identity that transcends the original vocabulary of pathology and illness. Hence the self-defining movements of "gay" and "lesbian" politics – a defiant and celebratory "coming out"…'[14]

That, according to the new-timers, is what is exhilarating about New Times: the shift to the subject, the personal, the individual. Everything is in our hands now. We are not determined by 'impersonal structures', 'objective contradictions' and 'processes that work "behind men's (sic) backs"'.[15] We are not conditioned by class, class is no more – the working class certainly, not as we knew it, anyway – and the dominance of production relations has gone with it. Everything has been thrown on to the cultural side. 'All interests, including class ones', says Stuart Hall, 'are [now] culturally and ideologically defined.'[16] That is where the struggle is. That is where we challenge the various power blocs in civil society. And 'far from there being no resistance to the system', Hall assures us, 'there has been a proliferation of new points of antagonism, new social movements of resistance organised around them, and consequently, a generalisation of "politics" to spheres which hitherto the Left assumed to be apolitical: a politics of the family, of health, of food, of sexuality, of the body'. Or, as Beatrix Campbell puts it, 'there's a plethora of collective comings and goings in what you might call "civil society" that are outside the political system'.[17] There is, that is, not just one power game any more but several, and not just one political line but a whole lot of political positions – and hence 'a politics which is always positional'.[18]

And personal. Because the personal is the political. And personal politics is also about the politics of consumption, desire, pleasure – because we have got choice now. New Times affords us choices, all sorts of choices, of how we dress, eat, live, make love, choices of style, design, architecture, the social spaces we occupy. The individual has been opened up to the 'transforming rhythms and forces of modern *material* life'. Commodified consumption? Maybe, but 'have we become so bewitched', asks Stuart Hall, 'by who, in the short run, reaps the profits from these transactions and missed the deep democratization of culture which is also part of their hidden agenda? Can a socialism of the 21st century revive, or even survive, which is wholly cut off from the landscapes of popular pleasures, however contradictory a terrain they are? Are we thinking dialectically enough?'[19]

Equally, are we thinking socialist enough? And what, in any case, is this dialectic about materialism which is not itself materialist? Should we become so bewitched by 'the deep democratisation of culture' that we miss out on those who reap the profits from 'these transactions'? How do you gauge democratisation – by its spread or the spread of effective choice – and how deep is it that it deprives a third of the population of such choice? And why 'in the short run'? Because profit is short and culture long? Or because subversion is a commercial proposition only in limited runs and the transactors know when to call the tune, change the demand, 'democratise' some other (reactionary) bits of culture. In an age of 'designer capitalism', as Robin Murray terms it, who 'shapes' our life-styles? Who still sells us the ideas that sell us the things that we buy? Who lays out for us 'the landscapes of popular pleasures'? Should we not be suspicious of those pleasures which, even in a post-Fordist era, tend to be turned out like hamburgers, mass-produced and mass-oriented? Should we not, instead, find pleasure in being creative in ourselves and in our relationships with others now that we have got the time to be creative in? Can a socialism of the twenty-first century survive which does not develop landscapes of creative leisure for people to be human in?

New Times also sets great store by the feminist concept of the personal is the political. But how that concept has been interpreted (because it lends itself to such interpretation) and used has led to disastrous consequences in Left local authority politics, especially as regards race, and in the fight against racism generally. By personalising power, 'the personal is the political' personalises the enemy: the enemy of the black is the white as the enemy of the woman is the man. And all whites are racist like all men are sexist. Thus racism is the combination of power plus prejudice. Remove the prejudice and you remove the cutting edge of power; change the person and you change the office.

Hence the fight against racism became reduced to a fight against prejudice, the fight against institutions and practices to a fight against individuals and attitudes. And those Left councils which carried out anti-racist policies on this basis found themselves not only ineffectual but open to the accusation that their approach to the collective good often ended up in individual injustice. The McGoldrick affair – where a white headteacher was suspended because her alleged (personal) racism was said to stand in the way of Brent Council's wholly valid policy to recruit more black teachers – was a case in point. Another was the lesson introduced into some Racism Awareness Training (RAT) classes whereby people were so sensitised to the pejorative use of the term 'black' that they baulked at asking for black coffee. Which then gave credence to stories such as the one broadcast by the *Daily Mail* that Haringey Council had banned teachers and children from singing 'Baa Baa Black Sheep' in its schools as it was racist.[20]

All of which went to create the image of the 'Loony Left' which, as Stuart Hall so rightly says, bolstered 'Thatcherism's hidden "moral agenda" around those powerful subliminal themes of race and sex' and helped her win the election.[21] But if, as Hall insists, the Left is to learn from its mistakes, it must also be said that it was precisely the 'policies' arising from the personal is the political 'line' (around 'those powerful subliminal themes of race and sex') that played into the hands of the Right and provided them the modicum of truth necessary to sustain the Loony Left image in the public mind.

The 'personal is the political' has also had the effect of shifting the gravitational pull of black struggle from the community to the individual at a time when black was already breaking up into ethnics. It gave the individual an out not to take part in issues that affected the community: immigration raids, deportations, deaths in custody, racial violence, the rise of fascism as well as everyday things that concerned housing and schooling and plain existing. There was now another venue for politics: oneself, and another politics: of one's sexuality, ethnicity, gender – a politics of identity as opposed to a politics of identification.

Carried to its logical conclusion, just to be black, for instance, was politics enough: because it was in one's blackness that one was aggressed, just to be black was to make a statement against such aggression. If, in addition, you 'came out' black, by wearing dreadlocks say, then you could be making several statements. 'The one which I think is important', declared a black intellectual in a radio programme recently, 'is the statement it makes to the white people that I have to deal with as a professional, as a scholar, as a historian and other things which I do, and it tells them that there are certain things they can't do to me because I have a power behind me that they can't comprehend.'[22] Equally, you could make a statement, by just being ethnic, against Englishness, for instance; by being gay, against heterosexism; by being a woman, against male domination. Only the white-straight-male, it would appear, had to go find his own politics of resistance somewhere out there in the world (as a consumer perhaps?). Everyone else could say: I am, therefore I resist.

Of course, the individuals who could leave the black community to its problems and mind their own were those who were not directly affected by them: the emerging black middle class of functionaries and intellectuals. The functionaries found commitment, if not profit, in ethnicity and culture, the intellectuals found struggle in discourse. That way they would not be leaving the struggles of the community behind but taking them to a higher level, interpreting them, deconstructing them, changing the focus of struggle on the sites of another practice, theoreticist this time.

The flight of the intellectual, however, is not confined to the black community – that is a particular type of flight: new, raw, immediately noticeable, because the blacks have achieved some sort of upward social and economic mobility only in the last two decades or so. It is part of a larger, smoother, more sophisticated flight of Left intellectuals from class – a flight that was already intimated in the philosophical excursions of theoretical marxism and the politics of Eurocommunism but found objective justification in 'post-Fordism' and the disintegration of the working class.

The new class

From then saying 'farewell to the working class' to electing themselves the new agents of change in 'new times' was but a short and logical step. For the shift from industrial to post-industrial society or, more accurately, from industrial to information society did not just remove the industrial working class from its pivotal position but threw up at the same time a new information 'class'. Since, however, information operated differently at two different levels: at the economic, as a factor of production (information in the sense of data fed to computers, robots, etc.), and at the political, as a factor of ideology, so to speak (information as fed to people), the combined economic and political clout of the old working class also got differentiated – with the economic going to the technical workers and the political to the 'information workers', the intelligentsia. And in a society 'overdetermined' by the political/ideological, the intelligentsia, who had hitherto no class as such, had come into their own. Except that the Right intelligentsia knew that the means of information were in the hands of the bourgeoisie and they were merely the producers of ideas and information and ideology that kept the bourgeoisie in situ, while the Left intelligentsia were convinced that the ideas and information and ideology they produced would overwhelm, if not overthrow, the bourgeoisie itself.

Every mode of production, as Marx has said, throws up its own classes. Capitalism is still the 'mode' in his sense, but the method of production has undergone such qualitative change as to shift the balance of influence between the economic, political, ideological instances and, with it, the balance of class forces. In today's post-industrial society that balance has shifted to the middle classes and its most vociferous wing, the intelligentsia, who as purveyors of information, ideas, images, life-styles find themselves in an unusual position of power to influence the way people think and behave – or, as the new marxists would put it, the way the 'subject' is 'constructed' and, since ideologies 'work on and through the subject', the way politics is constructed too. For the New Times intelligentsia this means dragging marxism with them to their own intellectual terrain, altering the battle-lines to suit their bent and equipment, engaging in wars of position that never lead to a war of overthrow or 'manoeuvre', challenging not the coercive power of the state but altering the ideological hegemonies in civil society, not through the instrument of the party as before but through the construction of alternative social blocs that would coalesce existing Left/centre parties. Central to the project, of course, are the new social forces.

But the mode is still capitalist, the struggle is still against its coercive power as embodied in the state. The working class might have disintegrated, but the bourgeoisie has, for that very reason, got stronger. There is still exploitation and oppression and hunger among the vast majority of the world's population. There is poverty and unemployment right here, in our midst, that arises from the unequal distribution of wealth.* That again is in the hands of the state, held there by the state.

There may well be all sorts of 'resistance to the system', as Stuart Hall suggests, in civil society today, all sorts of new social movements and 'a politics of the family, of health, of food, of sexuality, of the body'.[24] And they may even succeed in pushing out the boundaries of individual freedom. But the moment they threaten to change the system in any fundamental way or go beyond the personal politics of health, food, sexuality, etc., they come up against the power of the state. That power does not need to be used at every turn, just to intimate that it is there is sufficient to change the politics of the new social forces, personal politics, to a politics of accommodation.

Civil society is no pure terrain of consent where hegemonies can play at will; it is ringed around, if not with coercion, with intimations of coercion – and that is enough to buttress the system's hegemony. It is only in challenging state power that you expose the coercive face of the state to the people, sharpening their political sense and resistance, providing the temper and climate for

---

* In May 1988, 8.2 million people in Britain were dependent upon supplementary benefit. In the year 1988/89 tax cuts for individuals in the richest 1 per cent of tax payers were £22,680 per person, a sum greater than the total income of any single person in the bottom 95 per cent of the population.[23]

'the construction' of more effective 'social blocs'. Conversely, you cannot take on the dominant hegemonies in civil society without at some point – at the point of effectiveness, in fact – falling foul of the system.

It is inconceivable that we should go on talking about resistances in civil society and ignoring the power of the state when Mrs Thatcher has used exactly that to limit the terrain of civil society, keep government from the people, undermine local democracy, abrogate workers' rights, hand over water to businessmen, make education so narrow and blinkered as to make the next generation safe for the Tories. The Greater London Council (GLC) might have succeeded in constructing all sorts of social blocs and movements (the pride and joy of the new marxists) to challenge Tory hegemony, but all that Mrs Thatcher had to do was abolish it. The abolition, though, might have been stayed if the social blocs and forces that the GLC had generated and/or supported had a politics that could have opened out to each other and formed a solid phalanx of resistance to the encroachments of the Thatcherite state. Instead, their politics of position only helped them to take it lying down.

Nor is civil society an even terrain of consent, a plateau of consent, with no 'cliffs of sheer fall'. It drops sharply for the poor, the black, the unemployed. For them, the distinction between the mailed fist and the velvet glove is a stylistic abstraction, the defining limit between consent and force a middle-class fabrication. Black youth in the inner cities know only the blunt force of the state, those on income support (8 million on today's count)[25] have it translated for them in a thousand not so subtle ways. If we are to extend the freedoms in civil society through a politics of hegemony, those who stand at the intersection of consent and coercion should surely be our first constituency and guide – and a yardstick to measure our politics by. How do you extend a 'politics of food' to the hungry, 'a politics of the body' to the homeless, a 'politics of the family' for those without an income?* How do any of these politics connect up with the Third World?

---

* In 1985, 15.42 million people (10 per cent of the population) were living in poverty or on its margins, a rise of 33 per cent since 1979. Families with children

The touchstone of any issue-based or identity-based politics has to be the lowest common denominators in our society. A women's movement that does not derive its politics from the needs, freedoms, rights of the most disadvantaged among them is by that very token reformist and elitist. Conversely, a politics that is based on women qua women is inward-looking and narrow and nationalist and, above all, failing of its own experience. So too the blacks or gays or whoever. So too are the Green and Peace movements Eurocentric and elitist that do not derive their politics from the most ecologically devastated and war ravaged parts of the world. Class cannot just be a matter for identity, it has to be the focus of commitment.

But even if, as the new marxists have it, class is only one of a subject's many identities, it is still his or her class identity surely that makes a person socialist or otherwise. What makes for that identity may be an individual's direct experience of hardship, or it may stem from one's capacity to see in his or her own oppression or oppressions as a woman, a black, a black gay, etc., the oppression of others, or it may derive quite simply from 'the truth of one's imagination'. But unless it informs and underlines the subject's other identities, the politics of identity becomes a narrow, sterile, self-seeking exercise. You don't have to live in poverty and squalor to be a socialist, as Beatrix Campbell so derisorily implies,[26] but the capacity to identify yourself with those who do, helps. By the same token, the 'politics of pleasure', which the new marxists warn us we must not knock, could hardly be one of socialism's priorities – nor the pursuit of personal gain its morality. Class, even as metaphor, is still the measure of a socialist conscience.

But there's the rub. The new marxists do not see the self as something forged in and forging the struggle to change the world, but as fragmented identities inhabiting different social worlds, 'with a history, "produced", in process. These vicissitudes of the

---

experienced a steeper rise in poverty than other people on low income. 6.45 million people in families with children (26 per cent of all families with children) were living in poverty or on its margins, an increase of 55 per cent since 1979. In 1987 there were 107,000 households who were homeless; 64 per cent were households with dependent children; 14 per cent had a member who was pregnant. (*Poverty*, Summer 1988 and Winter 1988/9.)

subject have their own histories which are key episodes in the passage to new times' such as 'the cultural revolutions of the 1960s... feminism's slogan that "the personal is the political"... the theoretical revolutions of the 60s and 70s – semiotics, structuralism, post-structuralism – with their concern for language and interpretation'.[27] And it is this 'return of the subjective with a vengeance' that New Times proudly presents.

The 'return' of the subject to the centre of the political stage brings with it, of course, the politics of the subject: individualism, consumption, choice, the market, sexuality, style, pleasure, 'international humanism'.

The big waffle

Individualism, for New Times contributor Charlie Leadbeater, is what the Left now needs 'at the core of its vision of how society should be organised' – a 'socialist individualism', of course, a 'progressive individualism', an 'expansive individualism', a 'democratic individualism' even, in contrast to Mrs Thatcher's 'constrained, narrow, materialistic individualism'.[28] Labour and the Left had abrogated individual rights and choices through statism, and Thatcherism had seized upon them to construct its own vision of society. It was time now for the Left to re-appropriate the individual – an individual with responsibilities, however, not just rights. For 'if the Left stands for one thing, it should be this: people taking responsibility for all aspects of their lives'. No more nanny state, no more asking 'what can the state, the council, the professionals, do to solve this problem for people'. Should this sound like Thatcherism, Leadbeater hastens to assure us that, in addition to individual responsibility, there would also be collective provision. But how, if not through the state and local authority – and for whom, if not the needy? And are we then not returning to the 'theological collectives... of state and class'? Through 'intermediate collectives', answers Charlie Leadbeater, composed perhaps of 'individuals, private initiatives, even companies...' operating within a 'space' provided and regulated by the state.[29] But how is this different from Heseltine's compact for the inner cities?

The individual must also have choice, in consumption, life-style, sexuality and so on, because 'the dynamic area of most people's lives is where they can assert their difference from others'. There's 'new marxism' for you, and yet the old man whose name they take in vain said that it was 'only in community with others' that the individual has 'the means of cultivating his gifts in all directions, only in community... is personal freedom possible'.

But that apart, the question of choice in Leadbeater's scheme of things does not emerge from the position of the choiceless, those deprived of choice, deprived of purchasing power. It relates, in the first instance, to those who already have and stresses, therefore, the importance of the market in delivering choice. When Leadbeater does turn to the problems of the less well-off, it is to tag on feeble provisos to market solutions, such as regulating competition, or to offer up sundry collective actions which are themselves 'conceived and expressed individually'.

The stress on the individual leads Leadbeater to the market and Thatcherism, the anxiety not to be found out leads him to 'collectivism', and he ends up as a man divided against himself in 'individually-based collectivism' – i.e., as a social democrat. At one point he even goes beyond 'collective action' to mention 'redistribution', but it is not the redistribution of wealth. That, though, would have been to shift the centre of gravity of new marxist argument from consumption to distribution – which, after all, is where socialism begins. The fulfilment of choice in an unequal society is always at the expense of others and is, in that, a negation of choice, of freedom.

It is in Stuart Hall's writing, however, that consumption reaches higher, even more lyrical, levels and requires to be quoted at length if only for its poetry. If 'the preoccupation with consumption and style' appears trivial, he warns us, it is

> more so to men, who tend to have themselves 'reproduced' at arm's length from the grubby processes of shopping and buying and getting and therefore take it less seriously than women, for whom it was destiny, life's

'work'. But the fact is that greater and greater numbers of people (men and women) – with however little money – play the game of using things to signify who they are. Everybody, including people in poor societies whom we in the West frequently speak about as if they inhabit a world *outside* of culture, knows that today's 'goods' double up as social signs and produce meanings as well as energy. There is no evidence that, in a socialist economy, our propensity to 'code' things according to systems of meaning, which is an essential feature of our sociality, would *necessarily* cease – or, indeed, should.[30]

I don't understand the last sentence and even the previous one seems meaningless to me – or it is in 'code'. But what 'social signs' do 'today's goods' have for the poor in 'poor societies' except that they have not got them, the goods. And what 'meaning' or 'energy' do they produce except that those who have do not give and those who haven't must take? Who are these people who, in our own societies, 'with however little money play the game of using things to signify who they are' unless it is those who use cardboard boxes under Waterloo Bridge to signify that they are the homeless? They know who they are: they are the poor and they do not have 'things' to play games with. It is they – both men and women – who think, who know that 'the preoccupation with consumption and style' is trivial. And Hall's bringing in male sexism in matters of 'shopping and buying and getting' does not elevate consumption any higher. If, on the other hand, what Hall is trying to say is that poor people find meaning, express themselves, in 'consuming' the goods they can't afford precisely because they are poor, that again is special pleading to bring consumption closer to the heart of socialism.

Consumption is also where Robin Murray, alas, stubs his socialist toe. He first, like the other New Timers, excoriates the Left for being reluctant to take on the question of consumption. And like Stuart Hall, in another passage to New Times, Murray too develops a powerful argument for those movements in civil society which have taken on the market and the state over those issues of consumption where 'the social and the human have been threatened': such as 'the effects of food additives and low-level radiation, of the air we breathe and the surroundings we live in, the availability of childcare and community centres, or access to privatised city centres and transport geared to particular needs'.[31] But he cannot help singing a paean to the market: 'which local council pays as much attention to its users as does the market research industry on behalf of commodities? Which bus or railway service cuts queues and speeds the traveller with as much care as retailers show to their just-in-time stocks?' One would have thought that the motive of market researchers and retailers alike was profit, not use value.

With 'the return of the subjective' has also gone the notion of imperialism out of new marxist reckoning – the ravaging of the Third World, the exploitation of its peoples, the theft of its resources, ecological devastation. The Third World is no longer out there as an object of struggle; it is here, in the minds of people, as an anodyne to consumption, in the personal politics of the subject – an object of western humanism, the occasion for individual aid, a site for pop culture and pop politics. The 'famine movement', the new marxists call it,[32] 'people aid' to the Third World – making the plight of the Third World come through to people through mass gigs, mass runs, telethons – mass culture at the service of 'mass politics' – the politics of selfish consumption relieved by relief for the Third World – altering, if not the fate of the Third World, the views of government to alter the fate of the Third World – (governments tied up with multinational corporations, governments governed by multinational corporations) – altering people's politics, lifting people's horizons 'beyond even the boundaries of Europe, to Africa...' – a mass movement for the moment, initiated not by the Left but outside it – by caring people – by pop stars who put '"caring for others" on the map' of rock culture (because 'every fan knows how much it costs a star to give a free performance...') – millionaire pap merchants effecting a peaceful transition for the young from pap culture into pap politics.

'Who would have guessed in 1979, or even perhaps in 1983', ask Stuart Hall and Martin Jacques writing in 1986, 'that the plight of the Third World would generate one of the great popular movements of our time?' And not just that: 'with the rise of the Band Aid/ Live Aid/ Sport Aid phenomenon, the ideology of selfishness – and thus one of the main ideological underpinnings of Thatcherism – has been dealt a further, severe blow'. In fact, 'the famine movement's capacity to mobilise new forces', especially the youth, has 'helped to shift the political centre of gravity'.[33]

On the contrary, all that it shifted was the focus of responsibility for the impoverishment of the Third World from western governments to individuals and obscured the workings of multinational corporations and their agents, the IMF and the World Bank. Worse, it made people in the West feel that famine and hunger were endemic to the Third World, to Africa in particular (the dark side of the affluent psyche), and what they gave was as of their bounty, not as some small recompense for what was being taken from the poor of the Third World. And, in the language of the new marxists (more or less), a discourse on western imperialism was transmogrified into a discourse on western humanism.

What New Times represents, in sum, is a shift in focus from economic determinism to cultural determinism, from changing the world to changing the word, from class in and for itself to the individual in and for himself or herself. Use value has ceded to exchange value, need to choice, community to identity, anti-imperialism to international humanism. And the self that new timers make so much play about is become a small, selfish inward-looking self that finds pride in life-style, exuberance in consumption and commitment in pleasure – and then elevates them all into a politics of this and that, positioning itself this way and that way (with every position a politics and every politics a position) into a 'miscellany of movements and organisations' stretching from hobbies and pleasure to services.[34]

A sort of bazaar socialism, bizarre socialism, a hedonist socialism: an eat, drink and be merry socialism because tomorrow we can eat drink and be merry again... a socialism for disillusioned marxist intellectuals who had waited around too long for the revolution – a socialism that holds up everything that is ephemeral and evanescent and passing as vital and worthwhile, everything that melts into air as solid, and proclaims that every shard of the self is a social movement.

Of course, the self is fragmenting, breaking up. But when in Capital's memory was it never so? Capital fragments the self as it fragments society, divides the self as it divides labour, develops some aspects of the self at the expense of others, encourages specialisation, compartmentalises experience and hands it over to professionals for interpretation, conceptualisation, and keeps the self from becoming whole.

Up to now we had the homogenising influence of class to hold us together, but this, as the new marxists so rightly point out, was a flattening process, a reductive process, mechanical, and as destructive of the creative self as Capital.* That influence of class is gone from us and all its comforting, stultifying adhesions of procedures and organisation. There is nothing 'objective' to hold us together, our selves are let loose upon the world, and even the freedoms won in that great period of industrial working-class struggle are being threatened.

The emancipation of Capital from Labour has left a moral vacuum at the heart of post-industrial society, which is itself material. The 'universalist' bourgeois values which Bill Warren wrote about – 'equality, justice, generosity, independence of spirit and mind, the spirit of inquiry and adventure, opposition to cruelty' – and which sprang precisely from the creative tension between Capital and Labour are endangered by Capital's emancipation. The Factory Acts which took children out of work and women from the mines and gave them the light of day, the Education Acts that opened their minds out to other worlds and the world, the Public Health Acts which stopped the spread of disease and plagues – all came out of the tension, the hostility between Capital and Labour.

---

* 'Capitalism... destroys the human possibilities it creates... Those traits, impulses and talents that the market can use are rushed (often prematurely) into development and squeezed desperately till there is nothing left; everything else within us, everything nonmarketable, gets draconically repressed, or withers away for lack of use, or never has a chance to come to life at all.' (Berman, *All That Is Solid Melts Into Air*).[35]

Freedom of speech, of assembly, the right to withhold one's labour, universal suffrage, sprang not out of bourgeois benefice but from working-class struggle. All the gains of the period of industrial capitalism were the creative outcome of social contradictions – the heart of dialectical materialism. The welfare state was its apotheosis.

Those contradictions are not as eloquent any more. The 'service class' of the post-industrial society which has displaced the working class of industrial society does not contest Capital but is accommodating of it and secretes a culture of accommodation, a petit-bourgeois culture. Where once the tension between the bourgeoisie and the working class produced 'bourgeois' culture and 'bourgeois' freedoms, the lack of tension, of hostility, of 'class hatred' even, produces a petit-bourgeois culture and petit-bourgeois values.

But there are still the values and traditions that have come down to us from the working-class movement: loyalty, comradeship, generosity, a sense of community and a feel for internationalism, an understanding that unity has to be forged and re-forged again and again and, above all, a capacity for making other people's fights one's own – all the great and simple things that make us human.

Communities of resistance

Where those traditions have taken hold and come alive today are in the struggles of the people in those spaces that Thatcherism and new marxism alike have obscured from public view: in the inner cities, among the low paid and the poor, in the new underclass of homeworkers and sweat-shop workers, casual and part-time workers, ad hoc and temporary workers, thrown up by the putting-out system in retailing, the flexi-system in manufacturing, and the hire and fire system in the expanding service sector, and among refugees, migrants, asylum seekers: the invisible workers who have no rights, no claims, no roots, no domicile and are used and deported at will.

By their very nature and location, the underclass are the most difficult to organise in the old sense of organisation. They do not submit to the type of trade union regimen which operates for the straight 'official' workforce – but they come together, like villagers, through hearsay and common hurt, over a deportation case here or a death in custody there, to take on the immediate power of the immigration officer or the police and to go beyond it, if that's where it takes them, to oppose the power of the state itself as it presents itself on the street. They come together, too, over everyday cases of hardship to help each other's families out, setting up informal community centres to help them consolidate whatever gains they make. These are not great big things they do, but they are the sort of organic communities of resistance that, in a sense, were pre-figured in the black struggles of the '60s and '70s and the insurrections of '81 and '85.

Broadwater Farm was such a community. Relegated to a concrete ghetto and deprived of basic amenities and services, jobless for the most part and left open to crime, the inhabitants of the estate came together to create a life for themselves. They set up a nursery, provided meals and a meeting-place for pensioners, established a recreation centre for youth and built up, in the process, a political culture that resisted police intrusion and proceeded to take on the judiciary and the press over the mistrial (the press trial in fact) of Silcott, Braithwaite and Raghip.

In 1979 the whole of Southall – Asian, Afro-Caribbean, white, the young, the old, women and men, shop-keepers and householders – shut shop and went off to demonstrate against the incursion of the National Front into their town and were savagely beaten up by the police. Hundreds were injured when mounted police and riot police charged into the crowds – and Blair Peach, a white anti-racist campaigner and teacher, died at the hands of the Special Patrol Group. But that death did not die in the memories and campaigns of white groups and black organisations who took up the question of police accountability and brought it to the attention of a larger and larger public. From these campaigns came the setting up of local police-monitoring groups and council police committees. People were alerted now to the deaths, especially of young blacks, in police or prison custody, and from that has grown a distrust of inquest procedures and the demands for public inquiries in their stead. In April 1989, on the tenth anniversary of Blair Peach's death, activists from all over the UK and Europe gathered in Southall to commemorate his memory and pledge themselves to his legacy of struggle against racism and fascism.

It was also from the failure, well-nigh wilful, of the police to protect working-class Asian families from racial harassment and attack, following Mrs Thatcher's 'this country might be rather swamped by people with a different culture' pronouncement, that the call for the self-defence of the black community arose. And when a few months later Judge Argyle imposed savage sentences on the Virk brothers for defending themselves with spanners and jacks (they were repairing their car at the time) against the unprovoked attack of a racist gang, the Asian community, elders and youth alike, realised that it was as futile to look to the judiciary for justice as it was to the police for protection. From that 'self-defence is no offence' campaign sprang similar campaigns – in Newham, for instance, on behalf of Asian youth who had defended young children against racist attacks on their way from school (the case of the Newham 8). Which in turn raised the question of the pastoral role of teachers in protecting children against racial harassment.

The most celebrated of these campaigns arose from the defence of Manningham against impending fascist attack by twelve young Asians (allegedly) armed with molotov cocktails. They were charged with conspiracy, a charge so wholly disproportionate that it outraged ordinary people and brought to the defence campaign support from a whole cross-section of groups – women, gays, students – who had hitherto not made the 'racial attack' issue their own. Meetings across the country, regular newsletters and mass marches were to alert communities everywhere to the issues involved: problems in policing, attacks by fascists and racists in black areas, racism and political bias in the criminal justice system, a wish by the state to smash militant black organisations. It was the success of the community defence campaign as much as the legal representation in court (which was itself 'changed' by the community) which got the twelve acquitted.

These campaigns in turn were to strengthen the resolve of local authorities to outlaw racism, from council housing for instance. And in November 1984 Newham Council took the unprecedented step of evicting a white family, the McDonnells, for persistent harassment of their black neighbours.

Similarly, the issue of deportation and of the rights of children to join their parents, taken up by trade unions and legal and civil rights bodies, were initially raised by women's organisations – black and white. And from these issues the realisation arose that the question of deportation and children's rights had got to be seen and fought in the larger context of the quality of family life generally – and gave rise to the campaigns over child benefit, unsavoury surveillance by the state of marriages (to make sure they were not bogus), the racist and sexist nature of nationality laws and the 'internal', unseen, unknown, unaccountable control of black families – via the police, education, welfare and social services.

It is a community of women again, predominantly middle-aged women, which has helped keep alive in Britain the issues of Israeli terror in the Occupied Territories, protested against the treatment of women Palestinian prisoners, collected funds for the children detained during the *intifada*, confirmed their fellow women in Israel in their struggle against the occupation. Week in and week out for two years a Women in Black picket stands each Saturday in silent protest outside the Israeli airlines office in London – informing people, collecting signatures, arguing the issues with passersby. The irony is that these women are for the most part Jewish women and that the catalyst for their movement came from a realisation in Jewish feminist circles that their politics of identity was too narrow, historicist and self-indulgent – and betraying of a sisterhood that should embrace Palestinian women as well.

Recently, the campaign to prevent the deportation of Tamil asylum-seekers to the UK involved a fight between the judiciary and the Home Office over their legitimacy. But the whole issue of the would-be-refugees, tortured by the Sri Lankan government, brought up Britain's role in the training of the armed forces and intelligence networks of repressive regimes and the implications of tourism into such countries. And when two Tamil asylum-seekers working (for want of work permits) as night security guards in a Soho amusement arcade were burnt to death, the issue became one about the super-exploitation of a new rightless, peripatetic section of the working class and led to an exposé of the profits made by the leisure industry.

It was, again, the migrant workers and the Refugee Forum which fought for the rights of Kurds who had to flee Turkey in 1989. The feeding, housing, clothing of the Kurds, help with translation, appealing for the right to remain, were all undertaken by community groups themselves. Outrage over arbitrary detentions and deportations by the Home Office (which led to the self-immolation of two Kurdish asylum-seekers) brought out various migrant and black communities on to the streets in dem-onstrations and meetings.* Just as in the case of the Tamils, the Kurds too threw up crucial issues which the 'movement' had to embrace: the conditions of work in East London's sweat-shops (where the Kurds found employment), the use of chemical weapons (by Iraq) on the Kurds, Britain's collusion through NATO with Turkey's armed forces and, therefore, its harassment and torture of the Kurdish minority.

The joint struggles of refugee, migrant and black groups in Britain not only help to sustain the links between racism and imperialism and between racial oppression and class exploitation, but have also been at the forefront of the attempts to build a network of European groups against a new European racism[36] in the run-up to 1992. And only last month (November 1989) activists from black settler groups, migrants, refugees and asylum seekers based in Holland, Germany, France, Denmark and the UK came together in a conference in Hackney to launch a Communities of Resistance Campaign across Europe.

All these activities may constitute a 'miscellany of movements', 'a plethora of collective comings and goings' outside mainstream party politics, as the new marxists describe them. But there the

---

* These are not the party-hacks' meetings that Beatrix Campbell inveighs against but practical meetings to work out rotas for volunteers at community centres, panels of lawyers to take up cases, etc.

resemblance to anything they have in mind ceases. In the first place, these are collectivities, movements, that issue from the grassroots (if the term may still be used) of economic, social and political life, from the bare bone of existence, from people who have nothing to lose but their chains, nothing to choose but survival, and are therefore dynamic, open, organic. They are not inward-looking, navel-gazing exercises like identity politics or narrow self-defining particularities like single-issue politics. They do not, in other words, issue from the self but from the community, not from choice but from need and are organic in the sense of sharing a common life.

Secondly, these movements do not stop at the bounds of civil society or confine their activities to its boundaries. They know from experience that beyond civil society lies the state, behind civil society lurks the state, on every street corner the state, at the Job Centre and the town hall, in the schools and at the hospital, whether demanding your rights or asking for guidance or just trying to lead an ordinary family life – local state or central, it matters little, as Thatcherism goes on eroding local authority, except that that too is now their fight. The struggles stretch from civil society to state and back in a continuum, effecting material changes in the life and rights of ordinary people and extending, in the process, the bounds of civil society itself.

Thirdly, what these movements throw up, by their very nature, are not diverse cultural politics but a multi-faceted political culture which finds authority in practice, tests theory in outcome, and works towards a wider political movement commensurate with our times, but unrelenting still of its struggle against Capital. The point is to overthrow capitalism, not to join it in order to lead it astray into socialism.

Hence and fourthly, these movements have little sympathy with the notion of the personal is the political because this has tended in practice to personalise and fragment and close down struggles. The personal is the political is concerned with what is owed to one by society, whereas the political is personal is concerned with what is owed to society by one. The personal is the political is concerned with altering the goal posts, the political is personal is concerned with the field of play. The personal is the political may produce radical individualism, the political is personal produces a radical society. The personal is the political entraps you in the self-achieving, self-aggrandising life-style of the rich, the political is personal finds value in the communal life-style of the poor.

Finally, there is an unspoken morality about these movements which stem from a simple faith in human beings and a deep knowledge that, by himself or herself, the individual is nothing, that we need to confirm and be confirmed by each other, that only in the collective good our selves can put forth and grow.

This means that to come to consciousness of one's own individual oppression (which the new marxists so eloquently point to as a sign of new times) is to open one's sensibilities out to the oppression of others, the exploitation of others, the injustices and inequalities and un-freedoms meted out to others – and to act upon them, making an individual/local case into an issue, turning issues into causes and causes into movements and building in the process a new political culture, new communities of resistance that will take on power and Capital and class.

Moralistic? Morality is material when it is forged on the smithy of practice into a weapon of ideology. 'If you want to know the taste of a pear', a Chinese saying goes, 'you must change its reality by eating it.'

3

LA TRAHISON DES CLERCS*

Global capitalism has been let loose on the world. Racism and poverty are locked in deadly embrace. The industrial working class has decomposed under the impact of the technological revolution. The intellectuals have defected, and walled themselves up behind a new language of privilege. Those who are poor, and are powerless to do anything about their poverty, are also those who, by and large, are non-white, non-western, Third World. Poverty and powerlessness are imbricated in colour and race. Discrimination and exploitation feed into each other.

There's nothing new in that. But the relationship was clearer under industrial capitalism which made no bones about exploitation, about reifying work and turning workers into so many units of labour. And discrimination – racial, gendered – was an aid to such exploitation. And the only way workers could survive was by bonding together in the workplaces and in their communities and wresting from the bosses a living wage for themselves and some sort of life for their children. The Factory Acts, the Education Acts, the Public Health Acts all came out of that bitter fight, as did the so-called bourgeois freedoms of speech and of assembly, the free press, universal suffrage. They were not devolved from bourgeois benefice, they were wrought in the white heat of battle between capital and labour. And in that same battle were thrown up the values and mores of modern society: public honesty, political responsibility, solidarity, accountability.

But capital, by and large, has won the battle – for now anyway. The technological revolution has dis-aggregated the workforce, removed it from its congeries of thousands on the factory floors

* This essay was written in May 1995.

and shipyards and coal mines, and diffused it across the globe while, at the same time, 'aggregating' capital into multinationals and concentrating it across the globe. And the fall of communism has strengthened the hand of capital, given it free rein.

Capital is no longer rooted in one place, importing cheap labour. It can, instead, take up its plant and walk to where labour is cheap and captive and plentiful. And that invariably means the under-developed countries of the Third World. As within the Third World itself, capital can move from one reserve pool of labour to another at will, extracting the last ounce of profit from the daughters and sons of illiterate peasants drawn by western consumer culture into the quick-fix, feel-good, hi-tech money economies of the city.

We are back to primitive accumulation, plunder on a world scale. Only, this time, the pillage is accompanied by aid, sustained by expert advice and underpinned by programmes and policies that perpetuate dependency. The IMF, the World Bank, SAPs, GATT are just a few of the organisations, schemes, projects which, under the guise of developing the Third World, plunder it, under the guise of giving it aid, throw it into eternal debt and, under the guise of promoting democracy, set up governments accountable to them and not to their own people.

But then, western governments are themselves in thrall to multinational capital. The state no longer controls capital, capital controls the state. Monetarism and the market are one expression of it, the European Union is another. Trade no longer follows the flag, the flag follows trade. Western governments go where multinationals take them, to set up regimes that are friendly to capital. Democracy is the ploy that gives the West entry, aid is the gift that bids it stay. Trade agreements and patents and intellectual property rights then lock them into paralytic dependency.

And along with that dependency goes a certain paternalism – reluctant but habitual – which decrees that second-hand double deckers, third-rate experts and 'thraada' (a Sinhalese word meaning rubbishy, decadent) cultural exports such as paedophilia and baby-buying are good enough for Third World countries. Racism is tied into dependency. No longer credo or ideology, racism is an everyday fact of dependent life: a historical deposit of slavery and colonialism, which lies in the interstices of dependency and seals it. At best, it allows of charity, not of equality; of patronage, not justice; of compradorism, not freedom.

The term Third World may, after the fall of communism, no longer serve as a valid category in terms of its original paradigm, but, in terms of the exploitative relationship between the richest and poorest nations of the world, there is still a Third World – and it is still demarcated from the other two by race and power. And in the context of global capitalism, 'Third World' is a term that is more evocative of its status than ever before: the First World is naturally, organically, capitalist: the Second World opts to be capitalist: the Third World has capitalism thrust upon it. The only difference now is that the bourgeoisie of the Third World is not a national bourgeoisie opposed to international capital on behalf of its people, but an international bourgeoisie in cahoots with international capital in the exploitation of its people – and such a bourgeoisie is colourless.

Such an understanding of capitalism-sans-frontiers, and the worlds it throws up, not only sheds light on the displacement of whole populations within and between Third World countries and continents, but also on the forced migration of peoples to the West in search of asylum. And, invariably, these are political refugees fleeing the authoritarian governments that the West has set up and/or sustained in the interests of multinational capital. To decry them, then, as economic refugees is to overlook the basic fact that it is your economics that create our politics that make us refugees in your economies. Racism and imperialism work in tandem, and poverty is their handmaiden.

And it is that symbiosis between racism and poverty that, under those other imperatives of multinational capitalism, the free market and the enriching of the rich, has come to define the 'underclass' of the United States and, increasingly, of Britain and Western Europe. It is not so much a class that is under as out – out of the reckoning of mainstream society: de-schooled, never-employed, criminalised and locked up or sectioned off. If they are an underclass, they are an underclass within that deprived,

one – third society – asset-stripped

immiserated third of society that monetarism and the market have
created – a replica of the Third World within the first. And it is
that one-third society, asset-stripped of the social and economic
infrastructure that gave it some sense of worth and some hope
of mobility, that provides the breeding ground for fascism. It
is there, where the poorest sections of our communities, white
and black, scrabble for the leftovers of work, the rubble of slum
housing and the dwindling share of welfare, that racism is at its
most virulent, its most murderous.

And that is the racism that interests me – the racism that kills
– not so much the racism that discriminates. Not because racial
discrimination is not important, but because it is racist violence
that sets the agenda for state racism, official discrimination, in
particular. It provides the rationale for the government's numbers
game – no immigrant, no rivers of blood. And it follows, too, in
the wake of some of the government's asylum policies which have
led to the illegal transport of human cargo and to the throwing
overboard of stowaways by ships' captains unwilling or unable
to pay the massive fines imposed on them for carrying illegals
– policies that run right across Europe. The sheer violence of that
racism resonates right through society – on the playing fields of
the national game, in the headlines of the yellow press, in the
canteen culture of the police force – and parades as humour in the
performances of Bernard Manning, Jim Davidson and their ilk.

The culture of racism is a culture of violence, bred in the nexus
of 'colour' and poverty and powerlessness, both global and local,
at once – not just out there in the tropics, as Eliot might have
said, but 'squeezed in the tube-train next to you' – and requires
to be addressed at that level of complexity and immediacy, both
at once.

Implicating academics.

But at the very moment that we need analysis and strategy
and commitments, the intellectuals and the academics have either
retreated into culturalism and ethnicism, or, worse, fled into
discourse and deconstruction and representation – as though to
interpret the world is more important than to change it, as though
changing the interpretation is all we could do in a changing world.
The first is a retreat, the second a betrayal.

The retreat into culturalism and ethnicism is a retreat from
the struggle against racism – a struggle *for* culture, not *against
racism* – a struggle for a particular way of life and not for the
general quality of life, or even for a standard of living – because
that would be to 'privilege' (their word) the economic dimension
of racism over the cultural. And cultural politics is careful to set
its face against such economic determinism. That way, it does
not have to confront economic power (including the state), only
cultural power (including cultural centres of authority, as they
term it). And such power can be personal, vested in the individual,
and/or in the office of the individual. Hence the personal is the
political: the fight for my blackness or Asian-ness, as they would
call it, is also my fight against racism. Granted, but the converse
is not necessarily true: the political is not necessarily personal:
the fight against racism does not necessarily help my Asian-ness.
The one is about cultural politics as it affects some sections of
society, the other is about political culture as it affects the whole
of society.

> not true
> in my
> exp

I have collapsed here a number of cultural schools, but what
they all have in common is a penchant for culture and cultural
politics, and a contempt for class or economic determinism. But
then those who deride economic determinism are those whose lives
are not economically determined. For the poor and the deprived,
the first and fundamental determinant is economic. Culture for the
comfortable is expression and cultural politics, a pre-occupation
with their identities, their proclivities, their hang-ups. Culture for
the less well-off is more escape than expression, and politics is
the struggle to have some say over their own lives.

For the postmodernists, such arguments are too simplistic, such
a narrative too totalising, such a schema too foundationalist.
According to them, we live in an age, or, rather, a condition (note
the temporality of the word) in which everything is transitory,
fleeting, contingent; everything is fractured, fragmented, free-
floating. 'Everything that is solid melts into air.' Knowledge itself
has been shaken to its foundations, they say, and can no longer
be based on unchanging laws. There are no grand narratives
that explain the world in its totality, no universal truths. And no

ultimate answers, not even answers that can command any sort of consensus.

There are only processes and provisionality and ever-changing perspectives – through which subjects are 'constituted', identities are 'negotiated', problems 'represented'. Thus, there is no racism in schools, only 'a racialisation process', no ghettos but a 'racialisation of space', no 'binary oppositions' such as old racism/new racism but all sorts of racisms feeding off and into each other.

In an Information Society, besides, it is communication that matters, and what is real is that which is conveyed, communicated – and language, as communicant, is the first reality. The medium is the message, the word is the deed, the reality is in the interpretation. Experience of itself is nothing till it is 'linguisised', discoursed, represented – till it is played around with in word games and language games, abounding in tropes and metaphors and sleight-of-hand imagery, where one image transforms into another before your very eyes, and experience disappears before the anodyne of presentation and the will to act is sapped. You have the experience, but they have the meaning. Between the experience and the act falls the interpretation.

Let me give you an example. There's a school of thought that hangs out in the East End of London. I say a school of thought in the sense that there's a school there, a building, and it has produced a thought: to contain racism (as opposed to challenging it) through 'educational and cultural work among [white] adolescents who may be drawn into this type of activity [i.e., racial harassment of ethnic minorities] through a quest for homing devices associated with the territorial assertion of racialised identities'. For: 'the lethal aspect of racial harassment is not the material damage done, but the hidden wounds inflicted as it sets in motion the ancient regression from room to womb and turns the womb into a kind of tomb'. And this from an ethnicity unit in the East End where, out on the street, Quddus Ali is being beaten to within an inch of his life, where fascists are carrying out their educational and cultural work much more successfully, where a BNP candidate was voted on to the local council. Unabashed by all this, however, our intrepid scholars predict that once 'racism is declared a no-go area for these young people, they [would] look elsewhere for ways of constructing a white working-class ethnicity' – and, then, they (the scholars, that is) would hopefully be ready with their postmodern kit to 'offer a more general model for the recomposition of white working-class identities along non-racist lines'. Provided, of course, that these youngsters have not been 'subjected to censorious or self-righteous homilies from the moral, doctrinaire and symbolic school of anti-racism'. So, it is anti-racists who are turning reformed characters back into racist thugs. The solution, clearly, is to get anti-racists off the streets and house them safely in universities.

In another time, these intellectual playboys of the western world would be of little consequence: they would not affect the struggle on the ground. But in post-industrial society, where information is paramount and does aid or alter material fact, the intellectuals are in the engine room of power: they are the workers of mind and brain, if you like, that run the Information Society. And, it is they who are the best placed and best equipped to unmask governments, counter disinformation, invigilate the communication conglomerates – (not Britannia, but Murdoch, rules the waves) – and, in the process, rekindle the drive for a just and equal society that the unprecedented prosperity, unleashed by the technological revolution, promises. In place of which, they blame modernity for having failed to abolish 'poverty, ignorance, prejudice and the absence of enjoyment' (the list is Lyotard's) and so decide to abolish modernity instead. And to justify their betrayal, the postmodernists have created a whole new language of their own which allows them to appropriate struggle without engaging in it and, while appearing radical, further their own interests – a class in itself and for itself. (Poor Marx.)

Hence we have discourse sans analysis: information that never becomes knowledge – theory that never becomes practice. Deconstruction sans construction: you disassemble dominant value systems, but have none of your own to replace them – and that vacuum is a virtue. And the temporal sans the eternal. But it is animals that live in time, humankind lives in eternity, in continuity, in meta-narrative. That's why we have recall and memory, reflection and tradition, values and vision. The notion that everything is contingent, fleeting, evanescent is the philosophical lode-star of individualism, an alibi for selfishness, a rationale for greed. They are the cultural grid on which global capitalism is powered, and the postmodernist intellectuals have helped to keep it in place, lent it their skills, their ideas – usurers in the temple of knowledge. It is time we drove them from the temple.

PART II

STATE RACISM AND RESISTANCE

Within the space of a few years, from the early 1960s on, the terms of debate on 'race' in Britain had been set, a common language developed in which that debate was conducted and its fundamental assumptions established. Blacks were the problem; fewer blacks made for better race relations; immigration control was the answer; social control would follow. The intellectual backing for these assumptions was provided by the policy-oriented research of the Institute of Race Relations. The struggle to change the assumptions led to a struggle within the Institute itself and transformed both the Institute and the terms of debate.

'Race, class and the state' emerged from that struggle and the author's involvement in it – to provide the first coherent class analysis of the black experience in Britain, overturning in the process the old race relations orthodoxies of both Right and Left.

This pioneering analysis of the political economy of race and migration, throwing a light on the real intent behind government strategies, has set the standard for all future analysis of state racism.

The changing nature of racism, of the state and of black people's resistances and of the relationship between all three inform all the essays here. Black organisations and movements are examined critically and dialectically too. And when they depart from the struggles for justice, become partial, self-serving or even 'a part of the problem not the solution', Sivanandan is the first to say so.

'From resistance to rebellion' is a landmark history of black protest from 1940 to 1981 in the UK, which has become the starting point for black historiography. 'RAT and the degradation of black struggle' – written to expose the dangers in personalising anti-racist programmes – succeeded in changing the parameters of town-hall funded anti-racist work. It also enunciates the crucial, strategic distinction between personal racialism and institutional or state racism.

Racism does not stay still, but changes its shape, size, contours, purpose, function with changes in the system. After 9/11 and 7/7, the war on terror at home and abroad, multiculturalism itself came under attack as anti-Muslim racism became institutionalised. 'Race, terror and civil society' examines the interconnections between the new racism thrown up by globalisation and modern empire, the increasing threat to civil liberties and the alienation of young Muslims.

4

RACE, CLASS AND THE STATE: THE POLITICAL ECONOMY OF IMMIGRATION*

For Wesley Dick[1] – poet and prisoner
In some answer to his questions

Within ten years Britain will have solved its 'black problem' – but 'solved' in the sense of having diverted revolutionary aspiration into nationalist achievement, reduced militancy to rhetoric, put protest to profit and, above all, kept a black underclass from bringing to the struggles of the white workers political dimensions peculiar to its own historic battle against capital. All these have been achieved in some considerable measure in the past decade and a half – and the process has already thrown up the class of collaborators so essential to a solution of the next stage of the problem: the political control of a rebellious 'second generation'. And it is to this exercise that the White Paper of 1975 addresses itself.

The political economy of immigration

The laissez-faire era

But to understand the politics of the White Paper, to see what it tells us about state power in one particular aspect – black labour – but an aspect which, like a barium meal, reveals the whole organism of the state and relates black experience to white

* This essay was written in April 1976.

65

struggle – one must first reappraise the Immigration Acts. Britain, after the war, like most Western European countries, was faced with a chronic shortage of labour. This shortage was in some measure alleviated by the half a million or so refugees, displaced persons and prisoners of war who were admitted to Britain between 1946 and 1951. But even so, the Ministry of Labour found it necessary to systematise the recruitment of workers from other parts of Europe. Between 1945 and 1957 there was a net immigration of more than 350,000 European nationals into the United Kingdom.[2]

Unlike most other European countries, however, Britain was in a position to turn to an alternative and comparatively uncompetitive source of labour in its colonies and ex-colonies in Asia and the Caribbean. Colonialism had already under-developed these countries and thrown up a reserve army of labour which now waited in readiness to serve the needs of the metropolitan economy. To put it more graphically, colonialism perverts the economy of the colonies to its own ends, drains their wealth into the coffers of the metropolitan country and leaves them at independence with a large labour force and no capital with which to make that labour productive. And it is to these vast and cheap resources of labour that Britain turned in the 1950s.

At first the supply of labour from these countries was governed by the demand for it in the metropolis. Except for a few thousand workers who were recruited directly into London Transport and the British Hotels and Restaurants Association from Barbados (from 1956), no effort was made to relate employment to vacancies. Instead it was left to the free market forces to determine the size of immigration. And this on the whole, as the excellent study by Ceri Peach shows, worked very well.[3] Thus periods of economic expansion led to a rise in immigration, periods of recession to a decline – and this sensitiveness of supply to demand characterised the whole 'stop-go' period of the 1950s.

But if the free market economy decided the numbers of immigrants, economic growth and the colonial legacy determined the nature of the work they were put to. It was inevitable that in a period of full employment the indigenous worker would move upwards into better paid jobs, skilled apprenticeships, training programmes, etc., leaving the dirty, hard, low-paid work to immigrant labour. Although, that is, the shortage of labour was general, the more dynamic and attractive sectors of industry were able to draw the best qualified labour from both the non-growth industries as well as the immigrant labour force. The non-growth sector (including the public services), on the other hand, had only new entrants to the labour market to turn to. (In practice, though, prejudice decreed that qualified immigrants were more available to the latter than to the former.) Thus the jobs which 'coloured immigrants' found themselves in were the largely unskilled and low status ones for which white labour was unavailable or which white workers were unwilling to fill – in the textile and clothing industries, engineering and foundry works, transport and communication, or as waiters, porters, kitchen hands.

And since the opportunities for such work obtained chiefly in the already overcrowded conurbations, immigrants came to occupy some of the worst housing in the country. The situation was further exacerbated by the exorbitant rents charged by slum landlords. Attempts on the part of the newcomers to break the landlords' hold by buying their own homes were often frustrated either by the difficulties of obtaining loans from regular sources or by the prohibitive rates of interest charged by the irregular ones – or even by the refusal of owners to sell to 'wogs' and 'nig-nogs'. When immigrants eventually managed to buy their own property and were able to house their fellows, they were accused of overcrowding – sometimes sleeping five and ten to a room. (That there was excellent precedent for this in the dormitories of Eton and Harrow went unnoticed and unremarked.) In the course of time the 'immigrants' became ghetto-ised and locked into the decaying areas of the inner city. And a ghetto, in the words of Ceri Peach, 'is the geographical expression of complete social rejection'.[4]

Everyone made money on the immigrant worker – from the big-time capitalist to the slum landlord – from exploiting his labour, his colour, his customs, his culture. He himself had cost the country nothing. He had been paid for by the country of his origin

– reared and raised, as capitalist under-development had willed it, for the labour markets of Europe. If anything, he represented a saving for Britain of all the expense involved in feeding and clothing and housing him till he had come of working age. For, as André Gorz has pointed out, 'the import of "ready-made" workers amounts to a saving, for the country of immigration, of between £8000 and £16000 per migrant worker, if the social cost of a man is estimated for Western European countries as between five and ten years of work'.[5] And the fact that in the early years of migration, the 'coloured' worker came to Britain as a single man – as a unit of labour – unaccompanied by his family meant an additional saving to the country in terms of social capital: schools, housing, hospitals, transport and other infra-structural facilities. A fraction of the saving made from the import of these ready-made workers – let alone their active contribution in labour and taxes – could have served to increase social stock and improve social conditions if the government had so willed. But capital and the state were concerned with the maximisation of profit, not with the alleviation of social need.

By the late 1950s, however, the contradiction between the social and economic needs of Britain, *thrown up* – not caused – by immigration, became more defined. The shortage of workers, as Ceri Peach shows, made immigrants economically acceptable; the shortage of housing made them socially undesirable. 'The colour prejudice of landlords and landladies coupled with the shortage of houses made the crowding, and in some cases the overcrowding, of much of the accommodation available to the migrants inevitable and this, in turn increased their image of undesirability.' From being refused accommodation on the grounds that they were coloured, they were now refused houses on the grounds that they would overcrowd. 'It is surely an ideal system,' concludes Peach, 'in which prediction produces its own justification.'[6]

Ideal, that is, for capital – for it gets labour without the overheads (so to speak), profit without pain, gain without cost. Having already deprived one section of the working class (the indigenous) of its basic needs, it now deprives it further in order to exploit another section (the blacks) even more – but, at the same time, prevents them both from coming to a common consciousness of class by intruding that other consciousness of race. It prevents, in other words, the horizontal conflict of classes through the vertical integration of race – and, in the process, exploits both race and class at once.

To put it differently, the profit from immigrant labour had not benefited the whole of society but only certain sections of it (including some sections of the white working class) whereas the infrastructural 'cost' of immigrant labour had been borne by those in greatest need. That is not to say that immigrants (qua immigrants) had caused social problems – Britain, after all, was a country of net emigration – but that the *forced* concentration of immigrants in the deprived and decaying areas of the big cities highlighted (and reinforced) existing social deprivation; racism defined them as its cause. To put it crudely, the economic profit from immigration had gone to capital, the social cost had gone to labour, but the resulting conflict between the two had been mediated by a common 'ideology' of racism.

Prelude to control

That same 'ideology' detonated the race riots of 1958 – and revealed to the state that considerations of social need had now to be weighed against considerations of economic gain. Racism, though economically useful, was becoming socially counterproductive. And the state, which had hitherto acted in the economic interests of the ruling class, was now compelled to modify that role and assume its other function of appearing to act in the interests of society as a whole – in the 'national interest'. The first step was to slow down immigration, thin out the black presence, the second to manage racism, keep it within profitable proportions – relief for the depressed areas, urban aid, would follow. The economy in any case had, for the time being, absorbed all the unskilled labour it could (though it still required skilled and professional workers). Additional units of labour applied to existing (outworn, outmoded) plant would not yield the returns that would make such addition justifiable. On the other hand, automation and new technology – capital intensive production – would help Britain to compete with the rest of Europe in markets made more competitive by the loss of its colonies. That same 'loss', however, would make it possible for Britain to renege on its Commonwealth ties and look to the Common Market for the labour it required – when the time was ripe. The stage was set for immigration control.

To end immigration altogether would have been one answer. But given the periodic labour shortages characteristic of the capitalist countries of Western Europe, given the structural needs of late capitalism for the import of foreign workers, it was no answer at all. Migrant labour, precisely because it was migrant – seasonal and contractual, filling in the labour gaps in times of expansion and being fired in times of recession – served to absorb the shocks of alternating booms and depressions. And by virtue of the fact that it was foreign, migrant labour yielded extra profit to the employer.[7] Most of Western Europe had worked out a migratory mechanism combining both these functions. Labour, on short-term permits, on contract, ensured the buffer function; and the fact that it was foreign, recruited from the under-developed southern extremities of Europe, ensured that it would not – by virtue of nationality laws freely agreed to – have the same rights as the indigenous worker and could therefore be discriminated against. And to discriminate is to exploit, to derive a surplus value larger than that afforded by the exploitation of the native worker.[8] Together they, contract labour and nationality laws, fulfilled a third function – a political one: they prevented the integration of migrant labour into the indigenous proletariat and thereby mediated class conflict.

Britain, still outside the European community but periodically knocking at its door and gifted with a vast reserve of labour in the colonies and Commonwealth, was loath to let go of either and tried to hang on to both. Initially it recruited migrant workers from Europe on a permit basis. Between 1946 and 1951, 100,000 European workers had entered Britain. But the availability of labour in the colonies and ex-colonies and its sensitivity to demand made labour on contract unnecessary.[9] And as for a discriminatory mechanism, in place of nationality laws there was the fact of race. Black labour was inherently 'discriminatable'. It was alien per se – and automatically excluded from integration into a racist white working class.

It had suited Britain, therefore, to import the workers it needed from its colonies and ex-colonies: it was the quickest way of getting the cheapest labour at minimum (infrastructural) cost – and without the fuss and bother of barriers. It worked, in effect, like any internal migratory movement: a movement of population from the periphery to the centre as and when the need arose. And in that sense it was unrestrained, laissez-faire. But to characterise the laissez-faire period of immigration as an essay in British absent-mindedness – the sort of aristocratic whimsy that gathers and loses empires on the spin of a wheel – or as a conscious 'open-door' policy designed to benefit the poor orphaned children of empire as befitted a once and only mother country – an aspect of British high-mindedness – is a load of bull-shit.[10] So ingrained were these views among radical analysts that when, over the 'Kenyan Asian' affair (in 1968), Labour went even more Tory than Tory, the 'experts' instead of abandoning their analysis, mourned instead the death of Labour idealism or, more concretely, the passing of 'the liberal hour' – and of Roy Jenkins, its finest flower.

The fact of the matter was that laissez-faire immigration and laissez-faire discrimination had thrown up social problems which, after the riots of 1958 and the growing militancy of a black underclass were taking on political proportions that the government – irrespective of party – could not ignore. It had to put an end to 'coloured immigration' and yet have recourse to a reserve pool of labour when required. The crux of the problem, therefore, was not migration, but settlement – and not discrimination but *racial* discrimination. For the purposes of exploitation, it was labour and not colour that had to be discriminated against – and that could be done on the basis of citizenship, of nationality, rather than of race. And since nationality laws by definition distinguished between citizen and alien, foreign or migrant labour would be automatically subject to discrimination. To change British nationality laws so as to put Commonwealth citizens on a par with aliens was the most obvious solution – and it had the added advantage of debarring settlement as a matter of right. But, on the other had, it would spell the end of a historical relationship which ensured the continuing dependency of the colonial periphery on the centre. (No one, bar the tear-stained liberals, believed the sentimental bull about mother-country obligations.) The aim, therefore, was to move gradually towards the European model of contract labour (and a European configuration with the poor south as its periphery) without forgoing the 'Commonwealth' relationship. Eventually the Commonwealth relationship would have to be subordinated to the European relationship – and then the nationality laws would need to be tidied up – but for the time being a solution had to be found that did not require such a change.

This meant, in concrete terms, that immigrants from the Commonwealth countries, though remaining British subjects under British nationality law, would be debarred from entering (and settling in) Britain except as and when required by the British economy. Thus the formal links with the Commonwealth would be maintained but the right of individual citizens to automatic entry would be denied. In terms of British nationality law, this would mean that a British citizen was not completely a British citizen when he was a black British citizen – somewhat on the lines of the American constitution which once decreed that a 'Negro' was three-fifths of a person. Nevertheless it would be a solution to black settler immigration: if it did not end settlement altogether it would at least reduce the numbers.

From status to contract

Accordingly the Commonwealth Immigrants Act of 1962 restricted the admission of Commonwealth immigrants for settlement to those who had been issued with employment vouchers. The vouchers themselves were chiefly available to those who had jobs to come to (A vouchers) and to those with skills and qualifications 'likely to be useful in this country' (B vouchers). A third category, C vouchers, for unskilled workers gradually disappeared and became a dead letter by September 1964.[11] And, as though to compensate for the discrimination now institutionalised in the Immigration Act, a Commonwealth Immigrants Advisory Council (CIAC) was set up to advise the Home Secretary on immigrant welfare and integration.

When the Labour government came to renew the Commonwealth Immigrants Act in the White Paper of August 1965, it made further restrictions on 'coloured' immigration – reducing the number of vouchers in the A and B categories to a ceiling of 8,500 per year and doing away with the unskilled category C altogether. It also reduced the categories of skill and qualifications required of B voucher applicants to doctors, dentists, nurses, teachers and graduates in science and technology. The policy was now firmly established that immigration from the black Commonwealth should be geared to the requirements of the British economy.[12] And since the manpower needs of this period were infrastructural – the schools (including medical schools), hospitals, houses, etc., that the state had decided not to invest in during an earlier period – it was to the skilled and the professional that employment vouchers were increasingly issued. Over 75 per cent of the vouchers issued in the first half of 1966 alone were to such personnel, whereas for the whole of 1965 the figure was 55 per cent. Or take another statistic: of the 3,976 B vouchers[13] (A vouchers accounted for 306) issued to India in 1966, 1,511 went to doctors, 922 to technology graduates, 667 to teachers and 469 to science graduates (and 407 to others).[14] Any lingering pretence that the employment of Commonwealth immigrants aided the Commonwealth was dispelled by a system which creamed off the most skilled and professional personnel from these countries while keeping out their unskilled.

It was also a system which took discrimination out of the market-place and gave it the sanction of the state. It made racism respectable and clinical by institutionalising it. But in so doing it also increased the social and political consequences of racism. And to counter these the state set out to develop a more coherent policy of integration. Thus, the White Paper replaced the CIAC with the National Committee for Commonwealth Immigrants (NCCI). In fact, the announcement of other legislation to deal with 'racial discrimination in public places and with the evil of incitement to racial hatred' preceded the White Paper. But an examination of the politics of integration (as opposed to the sociology of integration) belongs to the second half of this paper. Here it is intended to pursue the investigation into immigration policies to see how they effected the transition of Commonwealth (and therefore British) citizens from the status of citizens to labourers on contract.

The Commonwealth Immigrants Act of 1968 is not essential to that investigation – except in that the circumstances which necessitated its enactment highlighted yet more the contradiction between British nationality laws and the Immigrants Acts and once again pointed to the passage of the Commonwealth citizen from status to contract.

In 1967, following on the Africanisation policies of the Kenyatta government, British Asians in Kenya, who had not opted for Kenyan citizenship at independence (1963) and had stayed loyal to the 'mother country', were granted only temporary residence. They were in effect asked to go home to Britain. Already in 1965 and 1966 six thousand Asians, possessing British citizenship, who were not subject to immigration control, had entered the UK. But after the Kenyan legislation of 1967, the numbers increased and the British (Labour) government, with an eye to all those other British Asians and British Chinese whom Britain had used and abandoned on the darker shores of the once empire, decided that they were not as British as their passports warranted. They were only as British as Commonwealth citizens. And since they were liable to the voucher system, the British Asians in Kenya would also be liable to the same procedure for admission – but would be allocated special vouchers as distinct from work vouchers.

Given the devaluation of British citizenship in 1962, the distinction between Commonwealth citizens and Kenyan British Asians was only a legal nuance – except that, unlike the former, the Kenyan Asians had nowhere but Britain to go to: they were potentially stateless. And this aspect plus the fact that they were more middle-class and British than the normal run of immigrants particularly outraged British liberal opinion. But the blacks, post-

1962, had seen the Act merely as the correction of an anomaly in the policy of reducing all black British citizens to the lowest common denominator of contract labour.

As usual, new anti-discriminatory legislation and integrationist policies went hand in hand with the new Immigrants Act – but these again will be dealt with in the next section.

The 1962 and 1965 Immigrants Acts had ensured the supply of skilled and professional workers from the black Commonwealth; for the seasonal unskilled jobs Britain turned to 'foreign workers'. The Kenyan Asian episode had temporarily swelled the number of settlers beyond immediate employment needs (the voucher system, in this case, was a device to phase-in the Kenyan 'exodus'). And the 1968 Act had in effect brought 'coloured' UK passport-holders within the provisions of the Immigration Acts. Black settler migration was firmly under control, but it was still settler and not migrant. Once in, the black 'immigrant' could remain in the UK indefinitely – and after five years he had the right to British citizenship. He was still not a fully-fledged '*Gastarbeiter*'.

That situation was remedied by the Immigration Act of 1971 which put him, finally, on the same footing as the foreign worker: he could only come in on a permit to do a specific job in a specific place for an initial period of not longer than twelve months. He could not change his job without the permission of the government – which meant that he was dependent on his employer for recommendation: he had to be a good little wage-slave. He may, like any other alien, apply for UK citizenship at the end of four years, provided that he has been 'of good behaviour'. On the other hand, he could, if the Home Secretary so wished, be deported on the ground that it was 'conducive to the public good as being in the interest of national security or of the relations between the UK and any other country or for other reasons of a political nature'.

The immigrant was finally a migrant, the citizen an alien. There is no such thing as a 'Commonwealth immigrant' anymore. There are those who came from the Commonwealth before the 1971 Act came into force (January 1973) but these are not immigrants; they are settlers, black settlers. There are others who have come after the Act; they are neither settlers nor immigrants, they are simply migrant workers, black migrant workers. And the migratory mechanism – the combination of contract labour and discriminatory nationality laws – which ensures that the *Gastarbeiters* of Europe are no more than second-class production factors yielding surplus surplus value as well as acting as a buffer, a shock absorber, between boom and depression now applied to migrant workers from the 'Commonwealth' except that time and distance and fares and race made them less accessible to the British labour market than their European counterpart. Then there are the workers, since Britain's entry into Europe in 1975, from the European *community* with free access to work in Britain. And there are aliens and colonials and patrials and non-patrials and white Commonwealth... All of which makes a mess of nationality laws and discrimination less tidy – and for those reasons must claim the government's attention in the near future. But all of which also leaves the divisions and sub-divisions within the non-indigenous sector of the working class – apart from the divisions between them, a sub-proletariat, and the native workers – looking something like this:

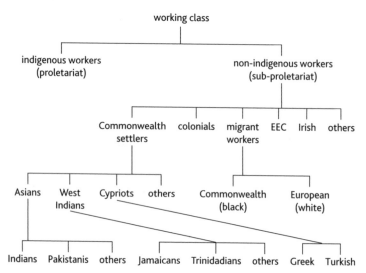

Britain now had two main reserve pools of labour: in the under-developed south of Europe and in the under-developed Third World – one for unskilled and/or seasonal labour, the other for skilled and professional – one, to put it crudely, to do the dirty work, the other to provide the infrastructural facilities (transport, hospitals, welfare) needed to keep the workers working – but neither exclusively so.[15] In a sense, Britain was now a neo-colonial power with two peripheries. And if migrant labour helped to perpetuate both these dependencies, the older was also anchored in that other history of colonialism.

The Politics of Integration

From institutional racism...

Thus the state had achieved for capital the best combination of factors for the exploitation of labour while appearing, at the same time, to have barricaded the nation against the intrusion of an 'alien wedge'. It had atomised the working class and created hierarchies within it based on race and nationality to make conflicting sectional interests assume greater significance than the interest of the class as a whole. It had combined with the trade union aristocracy to reduce the political struggle of the labour movement to its bare economic essentials – degraded the struggle to overthrow the system to the struggle to be well off within it – and in the process had weaned the trade unions from the concerns of the labour movement to the concerns of government. And when the black proletariat threatened to bring a political dimension, from out of their own historic struggle against capital, to the struggles of the working class, state policy had helped trade unions to institutionalise divisive racist practices within the labour movement itself.

But racism is not its own justification.[16] It is necessary only for the purpose of exploitation: you discriminate in order to exploit or, which is the same thing, you exploit by discriminat-ing. So that any other system of discrimination, say on the basis of nationality, would – if available – do equally well. During the laissez-faire period of immigration, racism helped capital to make extra profit off black workers (extra in comparison to indigenous workers) – and the state, in the immediate economic interests of the ruling class, was content to leave well enough alone. But in the 1960s the state, in the long term and overall interests of capital (as against its temporary and/or sectional interests), entered into the task of converting immigrant settler labour to migrant contract labour. One of the benefits of such labour, as has been shown, is that it is automatically subject to discrimination on the basis of nationality laws and inter-state agreements. The British government, however, had – for reasons outlined earlier – no wish to change the nationality laws in order to stop 'coloured immigration' – some of the Caribbean countries were still colonies anyway.[17] Hence it resorted to a system of control which, in being specifically (though not overtly) directed against the 'coloured' Commonwealth, was essentially racist.

The basic intention of the government, one might say, was to anchor in legislation an institutionalised system of discrimination against foreign labour, but because the labour happened to be black, it ended up by institutionalising racism instead. Instead of institutionalising discrimination against labour it institutionalised discrimination against a whole people, irrespective of class. In trying to banish racism to the gates, it had confirmed it within the city walls.

The whole thing was particularly 'untoward' because once immigration control had helped to minimise the number of blacks settling in Britain, the 'black problem' itself would have become more manageable. And the lessons of America had not been lost on Britain. Hence in order to counter-act the consequences of the Immigration Acts and to stop black militancy from infecting the body politic, the government embarked on a programme of 'integration'.

The Commonwealth Immigrants Advisory Council of 1962, however, was no more than a gesture towards integration: its function was to advise the Home Secretary on matters of immigrant welfare. But with the White Paper of 1965 integration began to assume the proportions of a philosophy. In fact the government had, in introducing further controls on immigration, pointed out that the purpose of reducing the numbers coming in was to improve matters for those already within – to improve race relations. 'Without integration,' opined a future minister, 'limitation is inexcusable; without limitation, integration is impossible.'[18] Accordingly the government replaced the CIAC with the National Committee for Commonwealth Immigrants (NCCI), with lots of money and staff and local liaison committees – and, to vest the effort with sanctity, set the Archbishop of Canterbury at its head. It was an independent body, however, free of government control, but linked to it through a minister in the Home Office with 'special responsibility for immigrants'. The Committee's brief was 'to provide and coordinate on a national basis efforts directed towards the integration of Commonwealth immigrants into the community'.

The government also introduced the first piece of anti-discriminatory legislation in the form of the Race Relations Act of 1965, but this was a half-hearted affair which merely forbade discrimination in 'places of public resort' and, by default, encouraged discrimination in everything else: housing, employment, etc. The incorporation, in the Act, of a clause to 'penalise incitement to racial hatred' turned out to be more useful in imprisoning blacks (and right-wing extremists) than in arresting the exalted nativism of the Rt. Hon. Enoch Powell, Ronald Bell Q.C. and others of their ilk and silk. The discrimination provisions of the Race Relations Act were to be implemented by the Race Relations Board and its local conciliation committees.

But the concern of integration during this period related more to the Asians than to the West Indians. The latter, it was felt, had 'largely been brought up to regard themselves as British', whereas 'Pakistanis and Indians... showed almost no interest in being integrated'.[19] The Asians, with their different cultures and customs and language and dress, their extended families and sense of community, and their peculiar preference to stay with their own kind, were a society apart. But they were also a people who were industrious and responsible, anxious to educate themselves, prepared to work hard and move up the social and economic ladder, honest, diligent, 'politic, cautious and meticulous' – all virtues which shored up bourgeois society. Besides they too had their creeds and their castes and their classes. They may not be assimilable, but they were certainly made for integration – a parallel society to be accommodated in a pluralist set-up. All that was required was an acceptance of the principles of cultural pluralism on the part of the 'host' population. And it was not as though Britain had not had a tradition of accommodating other cultures and other peoples – only, this time, they happened to be a little more different and a lot more visible. Hence the precision with which the Home Secretary, Roy Jenkins, defined integration in May 1966: 'not as a flattening process of assimilation but as equal opportunity accompanied by cultural diversity, in an atmosphere of mutual tolerance'.[20]

The West Indians, on the other hand – it had been assumed – were a part of British culture, an aspect of it, a sub-culture. They spoke the same language, wore the same clothes, followed the same religions. They were not a society apart – only their colour was different. They could be assimilated into the mainstream of British society.[21] All that was necessary to make them acceptable to the 'host' society was to banish colour prejudice, outlaw racial discrimination.

The NCCI and Race Relations Board, however, did not succeed in even getting that programme off the ground. The Board was virtually a non-starter, so feeble and narrow were the provisions of the 1965 Act. The National Committee discovered discrimination everywhere it went but was frustrated into educating people out of their attitudes. 'Education in school and out of school, education of adults as well as children, education of newcomers as well as the indigenous population, education through conferences, through committee work, through social activities, through the Press...' dragged on its first annual report in the tones of a forlorn manifesto. Hence in 1966 both bodies jointly commissioned the PEP (Political and Economic Planning) to investigate the extent of racial discrimination. Its report, published a year later, produced evidence to show what everybody knew: that racial discrimination varied in extent from 'the massive to the substantial'.

... to domestic neo-colonialism

The purpose of the Board as far as the state was concerned was to carry that lesson to employers and local officials. And it was a lesson to be taught not in anger or in punishment but in sorrow and conciliation. The very structure and personnel of the Board and its conciliation committees, marked by the presence of local firms and interests (and token blacks) and the absence of black workers from the factory floor, bear witness to the point and purpose of the Act.

And yet there have been protestations that the Board has failed. Failed for the masses of the blacks, yes. But it succeeded in what the state meant it to do: to justify the ways of the state to local and sectional interests – and to create, in the process, a class of coloured collaborators who would in time justify the ways of the state to the blacks. One has only to look at the successful cases handled by the Board to see how much of it relates to the alleviation of marginal and often middle-class discrimination. In the year April 1969 to March 1970, for instance, the highest percentage of success recorded related to discrimination in clubs: 50 per cent, the lowest to dismissals in employment: 4 per cent. Or take a look at the Board's journal, *Equals*, not just for the 'black' columnists who rage on the page they are paid for, but to see how the blacks are making it in the system. Sewa Singh Sodi can now play darts for his local against a club that once operated a colour bar. Mr Trevor McDonald is 'the first black staff reporter to present news on British national TV', Mr Yunus Chowdry is the first black man to reach the National Executive of his union, the National Union of Dyers, Bleachers and Textile Workers, a veritable trade union aristocrat with his own little fiefdom. There is also a first black mayor somewhere in Wales, a first black woman deputy mayor in Camden, and of course there is the black black Lord, Lord Pitt – not the first, but close. And all within the last couple of years.

The 1968 Act also re-formed the existing organisation, the NCCI, to create the Community Relations Commission – in order to complement the work of the Race Relations Board.

The Commission's task as defined by the Act was to 'promote harmonious community relations', to coordinate national action to this end through its local community relations councils, to disseminate information about matters affecting minority groups and to advise the Home Secretary.

In theory, the Commission attempted to combat racial discrimination, the Board to penalise it. In practice, they were both educational and advisory and tended to overlap each other. In effect, they were to one degree or another both instruments of mediation – between sections of the ruling class, between the sectional interests and the blacks and, on the national level, between whites and blacks.

In its seven years of existence, the Commission has succeeded in saturating the key areas of society with information, advice and literature explaining West Indian and Asian peoples to white groups and individuals in positions of influence and power – employers, police, political parties, churches, local authorities, voluntary groups, educationalists, trade unions, the media. It has held conferences and seminars, often jointly (but in an elder capacity by virtue of its specialised and/or statutory position) with bodies such as the National Union of Journalists, Inner London Education Authority, Library Association and Department of Education and Science – to inform the future holders of power: trainees in youth work, community work, teaching, policing, etc. Only in matters of employment and labour relations and the sophistry of statistics has it seemed to rely on the efforts of that 'independent' body, the Runnymede Trust.

In the structure of its local community relations councils, the Commission revealed the success of its local, grassroots effort. In the main appointed by the statutory body, the Commission, and paid by the local authority, but always governed by Councils which are an exact replica of the local power structure (businessmen, police, political parties, trade unions, headmasters, clergy), the office of the Community Relations Officer defines, exactly, 'integration' as the absorption and negation of black discontent: the accommodation within the local status quo of factors that threaten the status quo, the expansion of the status quo itself to accommodate such factors.

But most important of all, the Commission took up the black cause and killed it. With the help of its 'black' staff and its 'black' experts, with the help of an old colonial elite and through the creation of a new one, it financed, assisted and helped to set up black self-help groups, youth clubs, supplementary schools, cultural centres, homes and hostels. It defined and ordained black studies; it investigated black curricula; it gave a name and a habitation to black rhetoric. And finally, almost in a last blaze of glory, the Commission, funded for this purpose by the Gulbenkian Foundation, brought together at a residential conference in an opulent hotel in January 1975 a cross-section of black activists, gave up the platform to the most militant blacks and itself sat in the aisles, servicing the black people. Aptly, in view of the new dependent relationship that the black community was entering into, the Conference was named 'Black People: The Way Forward'. And out of that conference has emerged a new black committee one of whose functions will be to advise the Gulbenkian Foundation (shades of Ford) where to put its money – in itself an indication that the black programmes can now be safely left in private enterprise.

The Commission's task is over. The Race Relations Bill (February 1976) sees that its work is good and that its work is done. It has taught the white power structure to accept the blacks and it has taught the blacks to accept the white power structure. It has successfully taken politics out of the black struggle and returned it to rhetoric and nationalism on the one hand and to the state on the other. It has, together with the Board, created a black bourgeoisie, especially West Indians (the Asian bourgeoisie was already in the wings), to which the state can now hand over control of black dissidents in general and black youth in particular. Britain has moved from institutional racism to domestic neo-colonialism.

In terms of the larger picture, what has been achieved in half a decade is the incorporation of a whole generation of West Indian militants. The Asians had already settled into the cultural pluralist set-up ordained for them by the state as far back as a decade ago.

They had their own TV and radio programmes, their mosques and their temples, their shops and cinemas and social centres. More importantly, they had thrown up leaders and spokesmen who spoke to and worked with the state. They had remained parallel in terms of culture, they had merged in terms of class. Only in regard to the Asian working class was there any trouble. Their strikes at Courtauld's and Woolf's and Mansfield Hosiery and Imperial Typewriters had threatened the system as few strikes did – for they were subsidised and supported by the community, united across divisions of labour and possessed of a genius for organisation and obstinacy against all sorts of odds (including trade union ones).

The strategy of the state in relation to the Asians had been to turn cultural antagonism into cultural pluralism – in relation to the West Indians, to turn political antagonism into political pluralism. The process, in the case of the Asians, was first to free them from cultural oppression so as to help them 'modernise' their own class hierarchies and social structure – and then slot them into mainstream society. The West Indians, however, had to undergo a different process – for they were an aspect of British culture and society and yet outside it, even antithetical to it. Their similarities might have arisen from a master–slave history into which they had been locked in deathly embrace, but that same history had produced a culture and a politics that were mortally anti-white and anti-capital. The task, therefore, was to separate their antagonisms: to leave them anti-white but make them pro-capital. The task was to free them from the dishonour of racism so that they could honour the blandishments of capital. They had to be allowed to move upwards within the existing system so that they would not threaten to transform it into a different system.

But there was still 'the second generation'. All the other blacks had been found a place within the system, but the young blacks stood outside it. As though to confirm the dialectics of history they, the British born, carry the politics of their slave ancestry. And so it is to them that the state now turns its attention in the Race Relations Bill of February 1976 and the White Paper that heralded it.

The Politics of the White Paper

Listen to the voice, the anxieties of the state:

> the character of the coloured population resident in this country has changed dramatically over the decade. Ten years ago, less than a quarter of the coloured population had been born here: more than three out of every four coloured persons then were immigrants to this country... About two out of every five of the coloured people in this country now were born here and the time is not far off when the majority of the coloured population will be British born.

Some of these the state has already mobilised by affording them places in universities and colleges of higher education, others it has taken care of – in borstals, mental homes and prisons. But some, in a completely unprecedented new phenomenon, have picked up the gun – not of course in the organised manner of a revolutionary political party or even as a movement (for as one small fragment of a very small minority, black youth qua black youth cannot have a mass base) but as self-ordained soldiers of the people.[25] That is not to romanticise their futile ambition to lay siege to the state but to acknowledge, even while acknowledging the romanticism of the act, the deep dark concern out of which their commitment springs. It is to acknowledge their gesture as a new language of resistance – and to refute the definition which the state through years of indoctrination has persuaded the black underclass to accept as the language of gangsterism. It is to refute, in the particular, that other romanticism of anti-organisation blacks which holds that unemployed black youth or, rather, anti-employment black youth are 'gunning for a wage'.[26] It is, in other words, to refute the 'ideology' of these political romanticists that if every dissident section of society did its own thing, capitalism would lie down and die – it is to refute the politics of spontaneism which Gramsci equates with opportunism.

And it is to assert that 'the union of spontaneity and conscious leadership, or discipline *is* the real political action of subaltern classes, in so far as this is mass politics and not merely an adventure by groups claiming to represent the masses'.[27]

For, the anxiety of the state about rebellious black youth stems not from the rhetoric of professional black militants (whose dissidence it can accommodate and legitimise within the system) but from the fear of the mass politics that it may generate in the black underclass and in that other discriminated minority the migrant workers and perhaps in the working class as a whole – particularly in a time of massive unemployment and urban decay.

Almost a decade earlier the Home Secretary had warned the country against the future depredations of the second generation and argued for timely attempts at 'civilised living and social cohesion'. Now in the White Paper the same Home Secretary pointed out the 'politically grave consequences' of continued racism.

> If... job opportunities, educational facilities, housing and environmental conditions are all poor, the next generation will grow up less well-equipped to deal with the difficulties facing them. The wheel then comes full circle, as the second generation find themselves trapped in poor jobs and poor housing. If, at each stage of this process an element of racial discrimination enters in, then an entire group of people are launched on a vicious downward spiral of deprivation.

Thus the Bill's intention is not just to outlaw discrimination but to carry the fight against discrimination into every area of society – housing, education, employment, trade unions, local government, vocational training bodies, etc. And more significantly, it means to *enforce* the law. The law is no longer an instrument of education; it is an instrument of compulsion. More, it will redress the balance of discrimination in some areas by discriminating in favour of the disadvantaged blacks; for it acknowledges at last that although 'they may share each of the disadvantages with some other deprived group in society... few other groups in society display all their accumulated disadvantages'. 'It is no longer necessary to recite the immense danger, material as well as moral, which ensues when a minority loses faith in the capacity of social institutions to be impartial and fair.' And that is why the government believes that 'it is vital to our well-being as a society to tap these reservoirs of resilience, initiative and vigour in the racial minority groups and not allow them to lie unused or to be deflected into negative protest on account of arbitrary and unfair discriminatory practices'.

Hence the new Race Relations Commission which will replace both the Board and the Commission 'will have a major *strategic* role in *enforcing* the law in the *public interest*' (emphasis added).

However that interest is defined – as 'the public interest' or the national interest or, unashamedly, the ruling class interest – it is certainly the interest of capital. For capital requires racism, not for racism's sake but for the sake of capital. Racism changes in order that capital might survive.

5

FROM RESISTANCE TO REBELLION: ASIAN AND AFRO-CARIBBEAN STRUGGLES IN BRITAIN*

On 25 June 1940 Udham Singh was hanged. At a meeting of the Royal Asiatic Society and the East India Association at Caxton Hall, London, he had shot dead Sir Michael O'Dwyer, who (as the Lieutenant Governor of the Punjab) had presided over the massacre of unarmed peasants and workers at Jallianwala Bagh, Amritsar, in 1919. Udham was a skilled electrician, an active trade unionist and a delegate to the local trades council, and, in 1938, had initiated the setting up of the first Indian Workers' Association, in Coventry.

In October 1945 at Chorlton Town Hall in Manchester the fifth Pan-African Congress, breaking with its earlier reformism, pledged itself to fight for the 'absolute and complete independence' of the colonies and an end to imperialism, if need be through Gandhian methods of passive resistance. Among the delegates then resident in Britain were Kwame Nkrumah, Jomo Kenyatta, George Padmore, Wallace-Johnson, C.L.R. James and Ras Makonnen. W.E.B. DuBois, who had founded the Pan-African Congress in America in 1919, presided.

In September 1975 three young West Indians held up a Knightsbridge restaurant for the money that would help set up proper schools for the black community, finance black political groups and assist the liberation struggles in Africa.

Of such strands have black struggles in Britain been woven. But their pattern was set on the loom of British racism.

* This essay was written in October 1981.

In the early period of post-war reconstruction, when Britain, like all European powers, was desperate for labour, racialism operated on a free market basis – adjusting itself to the ordinary laws of supply and demand. So that in the sphere of employment, where too many jobs were seeking too few workers – as the state itself had acknowledged in the Nationality Act of 1948 – racialism did not debar black people from work per se. It operated instead to deskill them, to keep their wages down and to segregate them in the dirty, ill-paid jobs that white workers did not want – not on the basis of an avowed racialism but in the habit of an acceptable exploitation. In the sphere of housing, where too many people were seeking too few houses, racialism operated more directly to keep blacks out of the housing market and to herd them into bed-sitters in decaying inner-city areas. And here the racialism was more overt and sanctioned by society. 'For the selection of tenants', wrote Ruth Glass scathingly,

> is regarded as being subject solely to the personal discretion of the landlord. It is understood that it is his privilege to bar Negroes, Sikhs, Jews, foreigners in general, cockneys, socialists, dogs or any other species which he wants to keep away. The recruitment of workers, however, in both state and private enterprises is a question of public policy – determined explicitly or implicitly by agreements between trade unions, employers' associations and government. As a landlord, Mr Smith can practise discrimination openly; as an employer, he must at least disguise it. In the sphere of housing, tolerance is a matter of private initiative; in the sphere of employment, it is in some respects 'nationalised'.[1]

That same racialism operated under the twee name of colour bar in the pubs and clubs and bars and dance-halls to keep black people out. In schooling there were too few black children to cause a problem: the immigrants, predominantly male and single, had not come to settle. The message that was generally percolating through to the children of the mother country was that it was their labour that was wanted, not their presence. Racialism, it would appear, could reconcile that contradiction on its own – without state interference, laissez-faire, drawing on the traditions of Britain's slave and colonial centuries.

The black response was halting at first. Both Afro-Caribbeans and Asians, each in their own way, found it difficult to come to terms with such primitive prejudice and to deal with such fine hypocrisy. The West Indians, who, by and large, came from a working-class background – they were mostly skilled craftsmen at this time – found it particularly difficult to accept their debarment from pubs and clubs and dance-halls (or to put up with the plangent racialism of the churches and/or their congregations). Fights broke out – and inevitably the police took the side of the whites. Gradually the West Indians began to set up their own clubs and churches and welfare associations – or met in barbers' shops and cafes and on street corners, as they were wont to do back home. The Indians and Pakistanis, on the other hand, were mostly rural folk and found their social life more readily in their temples and mosques and cultural associations. Besides, it was through these and the help of elders that the non-English speaking Asian workers could find jobs and accommodation, get their official forms filled in, locate their kinsmen or find their way around town.

In the area of work, too, resistance to racialism took the form of ad hoc responses to specific situations grounded in tradition. Often those responses were individualistic and uncoordinated, especially as between the communities – since Asians were generally employed in factories, foundries and textile mills, while recruitment of Afro-Caribbeans was concentrated in the service industries (transport, health and hotels). And even among these, there were 'ethnic jobs', like in the Bradford textile industry, and, often, 'ethnic shifts'.

A racial division of labour (continued more from Britain's colonial past than inaugurated in post-war Britain) kept the Asian and Afro-Caribbean workers apart and provided little ground for common struggle. Besides, the black workforce at this time, though concentrated in certain labour processes and areas of work, was not in absolute terms a large one – with West Indians outnumbering Indians and Pakistanis. Hence, the resistance to racial abuse and discrimination on the shop floor was more spontaneous than organised – but both individual and collective. Some workers left their jobs and went and found other work. Others just downed tools and walked away. On one occasion a Jamaican driver, incensed by the racialism around him, just left his bus in the High Street and walked off. (It was a tradition that reached back to his slave ancestry and would reach forward to his children.) But there were also efforts at collective action on the factory floor. Often these took the form of petitions and appeals regarding working conditions, facilities, even wages – but, unsupported by their white fellows, they had little effect. On occasions, there were attempts to form associations, if not unions, on the shop floor. In 1951, for instance, skilled West Indians in an ordnance factory in Merseyside (Liverpool) met secretly in the lavatories and wash rooms to form a West Indian Association which would take up cases of discrimination. But the employers soon found out and they were driven to hold their meetings in a neighbouring barber's shop – from which point the association became more community oriented. Similarly, in 1953 Indian workers in Coventry formed an association and named it, in the memory of Udham Singh, the Indian Workers' Association. But these early organisations generally ended up as social and welfare associations. The Merseyside West Indian Association, for instance, went through a period of vigorous political activity – taking up cases of discrimination and the cause of colonial freedom – but even as it grew in numbers and out of its barber's shop premises and into the white-run Stanley House, it faded into inter-racial social activity and oblivion.[2]

Discrimination in housing met with a community response from the outset: it was not, after all, a problem that was susceptible to individual solutions. Denied decent housing (or sometimes any housing at all), both Asians and Afro-Caribbeans took to pooling their savings till they were sizeable enough to purchase property. The Asians operated through an extended family system or 'mortgage clubs' and bought short-lease properties which they would rent to their kinsfolk and countrymen. Similarly, the West Indians operated a 'pardner' (Jamaican) or 'sou-sou' (Trinidadian) system, whereby a group of people (invariably from the same parish or island) would pool their savings and lend out a lump sum to each individual in turn. Thus their savings circulated among their own communities and did not go into banks or building societies to be lent out to white folk. It was a sort of primitive banking system engendered by tradition and enforced by racial discrimination. Of course, the prices the immigrants had to pay for the houses and the interest rates charged by the sources that were prepared to lend to them forced them into overcrowding and multi-occupation, invoking not only further racial stereotyping but, in later years, the rigours of the Public Health Act.

Thus it was around housing principally, but through traditional cultural and welfare associations and groups, that black self-organisation and self-reliance grew, unifying the respective communities. It was a strength that was to stand them in good stead in the struggles to come.

There was another area, too, where such organisation was significant – and offered up a different unity: the area of anti-colonial struggle. There had always been overseas students' associations – African, Asian, Caribbean – but in the period before the First World War these were mostly in the nature of friendship councils, social clubs or debating unions. But after that war and with the 'race riots' of 1919 (in Liverpool, London, Cardiff, Hull and other port areas where West African and *lascar* seamen had earlier settled) still fresh in their mind, West African students formed the West African Students' Union in 1925, with the explicit aim of opposing race prejudice and colonialism. It was followed in 1931 by the predominantly West Indian, League of Coloured Peoples. This was headed by an ardent Christian, Dr Harold Moody, and devoted to 'the welfare of coloured peoples in all parts of the world' and to 'the improvement of relations between the races'. But its journal, *The Keys*, investigated and exposed cases of racial discrimination and in 1935, when 'colonial seamen and their families', especially in Cardiff, were being subjected to great economic hardship because of their colour, indicted 'the Trade Union, the Police and the Shipowners' of 'cooperating smoothly in barring coloured Colonial Seamen from signing on ships in Cardiff'.[3]

The connections – between colonialism and racialism, between black students and black workers – were becoming clearer, the campaigns more coordinated. And to this was added militancy when in 1937 a group of black writers and activists – including C.L.R. James, Wallace-Johnson, George Padmore, Jomo Kenyatta and Ras Makonnen – got together to form the International African Service Bureau. In 1944 the Bureau merged into the Pan-African Federation to become the British section of the Pan-African Congress Movement. From the outset, the Bureau (and then the Federation) was uncompromising in its demand for 'democratic rights, civil liberties and self-determination' for all subject peoples.

As the Second World War drew to a close and India's fight for *swaraj* stepped up, the movement for colonial freedom gathered momentum. Early in 1945 Asians, Africans and West Indians then living in Britain came together in a Subject Peoples' Conference. Already in February that year, the Pan-African Federation, taking advantage of the presence of colonial delegates at the World Trade Union Conference, had invited them to a meeting at which the idea of another Pan-African Congress was mooted. Accordingly, in October 1945 the Fifth Pan-African Congress met in Manchester and, inspired by the Indian struggle for independence, forswore all 'gradualist aspirations' and pledged itself to 'the liquidation of colonialism and imperialism'. Nkrumah, Kenyatta, Padmore, James – they were names that were to crop up again (and again) in the history of anti-racist and anti-imperialist struggle.

Three years later India was free and the colonies of Africa and the Caribbean in ferment. By now, there was hardly an Afro-Caribbean association in Britain which did not espouse the cause of colonial independence and of black struggle generally. Asian immigrants, however, were past independence (so to speak) and the various Indian Leagues and Workers' Associations which had earlier taken up the cause of *swaraj* had wound down. In their place rose Indian Workers' Associations (the name was a commemoration of the past) concerned with immigrant issues and problems in Britain, though still identifying with political parties back home, the Communist Party and Congress in particular. So that two broad strands begin to emerge in IWA politics: one stressing social and welfare work and the other trade union and political activity – though not exclusively so.

In sum, the anti-racialist and anti-colonial struggle of this period was beginning to break down island and ethnic affiliations and associations and to re-form them in terms of the immediate realities of social and racial relations, engendering in the process strong community bases for the shop floor battles to come. But different interests predicated different unities and a different racialism engendered different though similar organisational impulses. There was no one unity – or two or three – but a mosaic of unities. However, as the colonies began to be free and the immigrants to become settled and the state to sanction and institute racial discrimination, and thereby provide the breeding ground for fascism, the mosaic of unities and organisations would resolve itself into a more holistic, albeit shifting, pattern of black unity and black struggle.

By 1955 the first 'wave' of immigration had begun to taper off: a mild recession had set in and the demand for labour had begun to drop (though London Transport was still recruiting skilled labour from Barbados in 1956). Left to itself, immigration from the West Indies was merely following the demand for labour; immigration from the Indian subcontinent, especially after the restrictions placed on it by the Indian and Pakistani governments in 1955, was now more sluggish. But racialism was hotting up and there were calls for immigration control, not least in the House of Commons. There had always been the occasional 'call', more for political reasons than economic; now the economy provided the excuse for politics. Pressure was also building up on the right. The loss of India and the impending loss of the Caribbean and Africa had spelt the end of empire and the decline of Britain as a great power. All that was left of the colonial enterprise was the ideology of racial superiority; it was something to fall back on. Mosley's pre-war British Union of Fascists was now revived as the Union Movement and was matched for race hatred by a rash of other organisations: A.K. Chesterton's League of Empire Loyalists, Colin Jordan's White Defence League, John Bean's National

Labour Party, Andrew Fountaine's British National Party. And in the twilight area, between these and the right wing of the Tory Party, various societies for 'racial preservation' were beginning to sprout. Racial attacks became a regular part of immigrant life in Britain. More serious clashes occurred intermittently in London and several provincial cities. And in 1954, 'in a small street of terraced houses in Camden Town [London], racial warfare was waged for two days', culminating in a petrol bomb attack on the house of a West Indian.[4] Finally, in August 1958 large-scale riots broke out in Nottingham and were soon followed in Notting Hill (London), where teddy-boys, directed by the Mosleyites and the White Defence League, had for weeks gone on a jamboree of 'nigger-hunting' under the watchful eye of the police.

The blacks struck back, and even moderate organisations like the Committee of African Organisations, having failed to obtain 'adequate unbiased police protection', pledged to organise their own defence. The courts, in the person of a Jewish judge, Lord Justice Salmon, made amends by sending down nine teddy-boys and establishing the right of 'everyone, irrespective of the colour of their skin... to walk through our streets with their heads erect and free from fear'. He also noted that the teddy-boys' actions had 'filled the whole nation with horror, indignation and disgust'. It was to prove the last time when such a claim could be made on behalf of the nation. Less than a year later a West Indian carpenter, Kelso Cochrane, was stabbed to death on the streets of Notting Hill. The police failed to find the killer. It was to prove the first of many such failures.

The stage was set for immigration control. But the economy was beginning to recover and the Treasury was known to be anxious about the prospect of losing a beneficial supply of extra labour for an economy in a state of expansion – though the ongoing negotiations for entry into the EEC promised another supply. Besides, the West Indian colonies were about to gain independence and moves towards immigration control, it was felt, should be postponed till after the British plan for a West Indian Federation had been safely established. Attempts to interest West Indian governments in a bilateral agreement to control immigration failed.

In 1960 India withdrew its restrictions on emigration. In 1961 Jamaica withdrew its consent to a Federation. In early 1962 the Commonwealth Immigrants Bill was presented to parliament.

If the racial violence of Nottingham and Notting Hill had impressed on the West Indian community the need for greater organisation and militancy, the moves to impose 'coloured' immigration control strengthened the liaison between Asian and West Indian organisations. Already, in 1957, Claudia Jones, a Trinidadian and a communist, who had been imprisoned for her political activities in the US and then deported, had canvassed the idea of a campaigning paper. In March 1958 she, together with other West Indian progressives – Amy Garvey (the widow of Marcus Garvey) among them – brought out the first issue of what was to prove the parent Afro-Caribbean journal in Britain, the *West Indian Gazette*.[5] In 1959, after the Kelso Cochrane killing, Claudia Jones and Frances Ezzrecco (who had founded, in the teeth of the riots, the Coloured Peoples Progressive Association) led a deputation of West Indian organisations to the Home Secretary. And in the same year, 'to get the taste of Notting Hill out of their throats', the *West Indian Gazette* launched the first Caribbean carnival in St Pancras Town Hall.

At about the same time, at the instance of the High Commission of the embryonic West Indian Federation (Norman Manley, Chief Minister of Jamaica, had flown to London after the troubles), the more moderate Standing Conference of West Indian Organisations in UK was set up. Although its stress was on integration and multi-racialism, it helped to cohere the island groups into a West Indian entity.

Nor had the Asian community been unmoved by the 1958 riots, for soon afterwards an Indian Workers' Association was formed in Nottingham and, more significantly, all the local IWAs got together to establish a central IWA-GB. (Nehru had advised it on his visit to London a year earlier.)

Now, with immigration control in the offing, other organisations began to develop – among them the Pakistani Workers' Association (1961) and the West Indian Workers' Association (1961). And these, along with a number of other Asian and

Afro-Caribbean organisations, combined with sympathetic white groups to campaign against discriminatory legislation. The two most important umbrella organisations were the Coordinating Committee Against Racial Discrimination (CCARD) in Birmingham and the Conference of Afro-Asian-Caribbean Organisations (CAACO) in London. The former was set up in February 1961 by Jagmohan Joshi, of the IWA Birmingham, and Maurice Ludmer, an anti-fascist crusader from way back and later the founder-editor of *Searchlight*. CCARD itself had been inspired by a meeting at Digbeth called by the West Indian Workers' Association and the Indian Youth League to protest Patrice Lumumba's murder. That meeting had led to a march through Birmingham and other meetings against imperialism. In September 1961 CCARD led a contingent of blacks and whites through the streets of Birmingham in a demonstration against the Immigration Bill.

CAACO, initiated by the *West Indian Gazette* and working closely with the IWA and Fenner Brockway's Movement for Colonial Freedom, had its meetings and marches too, but it concentrated more on lobbying the High Commissions and parliament, particularly the Labour Party which had pledged to repeal the Act (if returned to power). But in August 1963, after the Bill had become Act and the Labour Party, with an eye to the elections, had begun to sidle out of its commitment, CAACO (with Claudia Jones at its head) organised a solidarity march from Notting Hill to the US embassy in support of 'negro rights' in the US and against racial discrimination in Britain – three days after Martin Luther King's People's March on Washington.

But international events also had adverse effects on black domestic politics. The Indo-China war in 1962 had split the communist parties in India. It now engendered schisms in the IWA-GB.

In April 1962 the Bill was passed and the battle lost. Racialism was no longer a matter of free enterprise; it was nationalised. If labour from the 'coloured' Commonwealth and colonies was still needed, its intake and deployment was going to be regulated not by the market forces of discrimination but by the regulatory instruments of the state itself. The state was going to say at the very port of entry (or non-entry) which blacks could come and which blacks couldn't – and where they could go and where they could live – and how they should behave and deport themselves. Or else... There was the immigration officer at the gate and the fascist within: racism was respectable, sanctioned, but with reason, of course; it was not the colour, it was the numbers – and for the immigrants' sakes – for fewer blacks would make for better race relations – and that, surely, must improve the immigrants' lot. It was a theme that was shortly to be honed to a fine respectability by Hattersley[6] and the Labour government. Evidently, hypocrisy too had to be nationalised. And in pursuit of that earnest, the Labour government of 1964 would make gestures towards anti-discriminatory legislation.[7]

Meanwhile, the genteel English 'let it all hang out'. In April 1963 the Bristol Omnibus Company discovered that it did not 'employ a mixed labour force as bus crews' – and freed from shame by the new absolution, it announced fearlessly 'a company may gain say fifteen coloured people and lose, through prejudice, thirty white people who decide they would sooner not work with them'.[8] But if Bristol – with three generations of black settlers and built on slavery – was only weighing up the statistics of prejudice, Walsall (with its more recent experience of blacks) made the more scientific pronouncement that 'coloureds can't react fast in traffic'. Bolton simply refused to engage 'riff-raff' any longer.[9]

The police felt liberated too. They had in the past appeared to derive only a vicarious pleasure from attacks on blacks; they had to be seen to be neutral. Now they themselves could go 'nigger-hunting' – the phrase was theirs – while officially polishing up on their neutrality. In December 1963 the British West Indian Association complained of increasing 'police brutality' stemming from the passing of the Commonwealth Immigrants Act. In 1964 the Pakistani community alleged that the wrists of Pakistani immigrants were being stamped with indelible ink at a police station in the course of a murder investigation: it was irrelevant that they had names and, besides, they all looked alike.[10] In 1965,

WISC (the West Indian Standing Conference, which replaced the more moderate Standing Conference of West Indian Organisations in UK after the fall of the West Indian Federation in 1962) documented police excesses in Brixton and surrounding areas in a report on *Nigger-hunting in England*.[11] And at the ports of entry immigration officers, given carte-blanche in the 'instructions' handed down by the government, were having a field day.

At the local level, tenants' and residents' associations were organising to keep blacks out of housing. The number of immigrants had increased considerably in the two years preceding the ban: they were anxious to bring in their families and dependants before the doors finally closed. Housing, which had always been a problem since the war, became a more fiercely contested terrain. The immigrants had, of course, been consigned to slum houses and forced into multi-occupation. Now there were fears that they would move further afield into the white residential areas. At the same time, public health laws were invoked to dispel multi-occupation.

Schooling, too, presented a problem, as more and more 'coloured' children began to enter the country and sought places in their local schools. In October 1963 white parents in Southall (which had a high proportion of Indians) demanded separate classes for their children because 'coloured' children were holding back their progress. In December the Commonwealth Immigrants' Advisory Council (CIAC), which had been set up to advise the Home Secretary on matters relating to 'the welfare and integration of immigrants', reported that 'the presence of a high proportion of immigrant children in one class slows down the general routine of working and hampers the progress of the whole class, especially where the immigrants do not speak or write English fluently'. This, it said, was bad for immigrant children too – for 'they would not get as good an introduction to British life as they would get in a normal school'. Besides, there was the danger of white parents removing their children and making some schools 'predominantly immigrant schools'.[12] In November Sir Edward Boyle, the avowedly liberal Minister of Education, told the House of Commons that it was 'desirable on education grounds that no one school should have more than about 30 per cent of immigrants'. Accordingly, in June 1965 Boyle's law enacted that there should be no more than a third of immigrant children in any school; the surplus should be bussed out[13] – but white children would not be bussed in.

As for West Indian children, whose difficulties were ostensibly 'Creolese English', low educability and 'behaviour problems', the solution would be found in 'remedial classes' and even 'special' schools.

None of these measures – or the various instances of discrimination – went without protest, however. The Bristol Bus Company, for instance, was subjected to a boycott and demonstrations for weeks until it finally capitulated. Police harassment, as already mentioned, was documented and publicised by West Indian organisations. The relegation of West Indian children into special classes and/or schools was fought – and continued to be fought – first by the North London West Indian Association and then by other local and national organisations.

But, by and large, the unity – between West Indians and Asians, militants and moderates – that had sprung up between the riots of 1958 and the Immigration Act of 1962 had been dissipated by more immediate concerns. Now there were families to house and children to school and dependants to look after: the immigrants were becoming settlers. And since it was Asian immigrants who, more than the West Indian, had come on a temporary basis – to make enough money to send to their impoverished homes – before the Immigration Act foreclosed on them, it was their families and relatives who swelled the numbers now. And their politics tended to become settler politics – petitioning, lobbying, influencing political parties, weighing-in on (if not yet entering) local government elections – and their struggles working-class struggles on the factory floor – and they, by virtue of being fought in the teeth of trade union racism, were to prove political too.

In May 1965 the first important 'immigrant' strike took place – at Courtauld's Red Scar Mill in Preston – over the management's decision to force Asian workers (who were concentrated, with a few West Indians, in one area of the labour process) to work more machines for (proportionately) less pay.[14] The strike failed, but not before it had exposed the active collaboration of the white workers and the union with management. A few months earlier, a smaller strike of Asian workers at Rockware Glass in Southall (London) had exposed a similar complicity. And the Woolf Rubber Company strike later in the same year, though fought valiantly by the workers, supported by the Asian community and in particular by the IWA, lost out to the employers through lack of official union backing.[15]

The Afro-Caribbean struggles of this period (post 1962) also reflected a similar community base, though different in origins. Ghana had become free in 1957, Uganda in 1962 and Jamaica and Trinidad and Tobago in the same year, but there were other black colonies in Africa and the Caribbean still to be liberated. And then there was the black colony in North America, which, beginning with Martin Luther King's civil rights movement, was revving up into the Black Power struggles of the mid-1960s.

King visited London on the way to receiving his Nobel prize in Oslo in December 1964. And at his instigation, a British civil rights organisation, the Campaign Against Racial Discrimination (CARD) was formed in February 1965 – federating various Asian and Afro-Caribbean organisations and sporting Labour Party 'radicals'.

More significant, however, was the visit of Malcolm X. Malcolm blitzed London in February 1965 and in his wake was formed a much more militant organisation, the Racial Action Adjustment Society (RAAS)[16] with Michael de Freitas, later Abdul Malik and later still Michael X, at its head. 'Black men, unite,' it called, 'we have nothing to lose but our fears.'

It is the fashion today, even among blacks, to see Michael X only as a criminal who deserved to be hanged for murder by the Trinidadian government (1975). (The line between politics and crime, after all, is a thin one – in a capitalist society.) But it was Michael and Roy Sawh (a Guyanese 'Indian') and their colleagues in RAAS who, as we shall see, more than anybody else in this period freed ordinary black people from fear and taught them to stand up for their rights and their dignity.[17] It was out of RAAS, too, that a number of our present-day militants have emerged.

It is also alleged, in hindsight and contempt, that RAAS had no politics but the politics of thuggery. But it was RAAS who descended on Red Scar Mills in Preston to help the Asian strikers (at their invitation). And the point is telling – if only because it marked a progression in the *organic* unity of the (Afro-) Asian, 'coolie', and (Afro-) Caribbean, slave, struggles in the diaspora, begun in Britain by Claudia Jones' *West Indian Gazette and Afro-Asian-Caribbean News* on which Abimanyu Manchanda, an Indian political activist and a key figure in the British anti-Vietnam war movement, was to work.

But RAAS, or black militancy generally, would not have had the backing it did but for the growing disillusion with the Labour Party's policies on immigration control and, therefore, racism. The 'coloured immigrants' still had hopes in the party of the working class and of colonial independence and sought to influence its policies. But after the 1964 general election, Labour's position became clearer. Peter Griffiths, the Tory candidate for Smethwick (an 'immigrant area' in Birmingham), had campaigned on the basis of ending immigration and repatriating 'the coloureds'. 'If you want a nigger for a neighbour, vote Liberal or Labour', he had sloganised – and won. But Labour won the election and Harold Wilson, the incoming Prime Minister, denounced Griffiths as 'a parliamentary leper'. However, Wilson's policies were soon to become leprous too: the Immigration Act was not only renewed in the White Paper of August 1965 but went on to restrict 'coloured immigration' further on the basis that fewer numbers made for better race relations. In pursuit of that philosophy, Labour then proceeded to pass a Race Relations Act (September 1965), which threatened racial discrimination in 'places of public resort' with conciliation. It was prepared, however, to penalise 'incitement to racial hatred' – and promptly proceeded to prosecute Michael X.

Equally off-target and ineffectual were the two statutory bodies that Labour set up, the National Committee for Commonwealth Immigrants (NCCI) and the Race Relations Board (RRB) – the one chiefly to liaise with immigrants and ease them out of the difficulties (linguistic, educational, cultural and so on) which prevented integration, and the other, as mentioned above, to conciliate discrimination in hotels and places through conciliation committees.

To ordinary blacks these structures were irrelevant: liaison and conciliation seemed to define them as a people apart who somehow needed to be fitted into the mainstream of British society – when all they were seeking were the same rights as other citizens. They (liaison and conciliation) were themes that were to rise again in the area of police–black relations – this time as substitutes for police accountability – and not without the same significance.

But if NCCI failed to integrate the 'immigrants', it succeeded in disintegrating 'immigrant' organisations – the moderate ones anyway and local ones mostly – by entering their areas of work, enticing local leaders to cooperate with them (and therefore government) and pre-empting their constituencies. Its greatest achievement was to lure the leading lights of CARD into working with it, thereby deepening the contradictions in CARD (as between the militants and the moderates). WISC and NFPA[18] disaffiliated from CARD and the more militant blacks followed suit, leaving CARD to its more liberal designs. The government had effectively shut out one area of representative black opinion. But an obstacle in the way of the next Immigration Act had been cleared.

When CARD finally broke up in 1967 the press and the media generally welcomed its debacle. They saw its sometimes uncompromising stand against racial discrimination as a threat to 'integration' (if not to white society), resented its outspoken and articulate black spokes-men and women, denouncing them as communists and maoists, and feared that it would emerge from a civil rights organisation into a Black Power movement. The 'paper of the top people', having warned the nation of 'The Dark Million' in a series of articles in the months preceding the August 1965 White Paper, now wrote, 'there are always heavy dangers in riding tigers – and these dangers are not reduced when the animal changes to a black panther' (*The Times*, 9 November 1967). And a *Times* news team was later to write that 'the ominous lesson of CARD… is that the mixture of pro-Chinese communism and American-style Black Power on the immigrant scene can be devastating'.[19] (International events were beginning to cast their shadows.)

The race relations pundits added their bit. The Institute of Race Relations (some of whose Council members and staff were implicated in CARD politics) commissioned a book giving the liberal version. Although an independent research organisation, replete with academics, the IRR had already been moving closer to government policies on immigration and integration – backing them with 'objective' findings and research.[20]

The race scene was changing – radically. The Immigration Acts, whatever their racialist promptings, had stemmed from an economic rationale, fashioned in the matrix of colonial-capitalist practices and beliefs. They served, as we have seen, to take racial discrimination out of the market-place and institutionalise it – inhere it in the structures of the state, locally and nationally. So that at both local and national levels 'race' became an area of contestation for power. It was the basis on which local issues of schooling and housing and jobs were being, if not fought, side-tracked. It was an issue on which elections were won and lost. It was an issue which betrayed the trade unions' claims to represent the whole of the working class, and so betrayed the class. It had entered the arena of politics (not that, subliminally, it was not always there) and swelled into an ideology of racism to be borrowed by the courts in their decision-making and by the fascists for their regeneration.[21]

Racial attacks had already begun to mount. In 1965, in the months preceding the White Paper but after Griffiths' victory, 'a Jamaican was shot and killed… in Islington, a West Indian schoolboy in Notting Hill was nearly killed by white teenagers armed with iron bars, axes and bottles… a group of black men outside a cafe in Notting Hill received blasts from a shot-gun fired from a moving car', hate leaflets appeared in Newcastle-upon-Tyne, crosses were burnt outside 'coloured citizens' homes' in Leamington Spa, Rugby, Coventry, Ilford, Plaistow and Cricklewood and 'a written warning (allegedly) from the Deputy

Wizard of the Ku Klux Klan was sent to the Indian secretary of CARD: "You will be burnt alive if you do not leave England by August 31st".'[22] The British fascists, however, denied any connection with the Klan – not, it would appear, on a basis of fact, but in the conviction that there was now a sufficient ground-swell of grassroots racism to float an electoral party. Electoral politics, of course, were not going to bring them parliamentary power, but they would provide a vehicle for propaganda and a venue for recruitment – and all within the law. They could push their vile cause to the limits of the law, within the framework of the law, forcing the law itself to become more repressive of democratic freedoms. By invoking their democratic right to freedom of speech, of association, etc. – by claiming equal TV time as the other electoral parties and by gaining 'legitimate' access to the press and radio – they would propagate the cause of denying others those freedoms and legitimacies, the blacks in the first place. They would move the whole debate on race to the right and force incoming governments to further racist legislation – on pain of electoral defeat. And so, in February 1967 the League of Empire Loyalists, the British National Party and local groups of the Racial Preservation Society merged to form the National Front (NF) – and in April that year put up candidates for the Greater London Council elections.

But they – and the government – reckoned without the blacks. The time was long gone when black people, with an eye to returning home, would put up with repression: they were settlers now. And state racism had pushed them into higher and more militant forms of resistance – incorporating the resistances of the previous period and embracing both shop floor and community. Asians and Afro-Caribbeans, sometimes in different areas of struggle, sometimes together.

RAAS, as we have seen, was formed in 1965. It was wholly an indigenous movement arising out of the opposition to native British racism but catalysed by Malcolm X and the Black Muslims. And so it took in, on both counts, the African, Asian, Afro-Caribbean and Afro-American dimensions of struggle and the struggles in the workplace and the community. It had, almost as

its first act, descended on the Red Scar Mills in Preston to help the
Asian strikers. It then set up office in a barber's shop in Reading
and worked and recruited in the North and the Midlands with
Abdulla Patel (one of the strikers from Red Scar Mills) and Roy
Sawh as its organisers there. In London, too, RAAS gathered a
sizeable following through its work with London busmen and
its legal service (Defence) for black people in trouble with the
police. It was written up in the press, often as a novel and passing
phenomenon, and appeared (in a bad light) on BBC's Panorama
programme. The disillusion with CARD swelled RAAS's numbers.
And the indictment of Michael X in 1967 for 'an inflammatory
speech against white people' – when white people indulged freely
in racist abuse – served to validate RAAS's rhetoric. At Speakers'
Corner Roy Sawh and other black speakers would inveigh
against 'the white devil' and 'the Anglo-Saxon swine', and find
a ready and appreciative audience. In June 1967 the Universal
Coloured Peoples' Association (UCPA) was formed, headed by
a Nigerian playwright, Obi Egbuna. It too arose from British
conditions, but, continuing in the tradition of the struggle against
British colonialism, stressed the need to fight both imperialism
and racism. The anti-white struggle was also anti-capitalist and
anti-imperialist – universal to all coloured peoples. And so its
concerns extended from racism in Britain and elsewhere to the
war in Vietnam, the independence of Zimbabwe, the liberation
of 'Portuguese Africa', the cultural revolution in China. It was,
of course, inspired and influenced by the Black Power struggle in
America and, more immediately, by Stokely Carmichael's visit to
London in July that year.

'Black Power', Egbuna declared at a Vietnam protest rally in
Trafalgar Square in October 1967, 'means simply that the blacks
of this world are out to liquidate capitalist oppression of black
people wherever it exists by any means necessary.' Black people
in Britain, the UCPA pointed out, though numerically small, were
so concentrated in vital areas of industry, hospital services (a
majority of doctors and nurses in the conurbations were black)
and transport that a black strike could paralyse the economy.
Some UCPA speakers at meetings in Hyde Park urged more

direct action. Roy Sawh (the members of one organisation were often members of another) 'urged coloured nurses to give wrong injections to patients, coloured bus crews not to take the fares of black people... [and] Indian restaurant owners to "put something in the curry"'.[23] Alex Watson, a Jamaican machine-operator, was reported to have exhorted coloured people to destroy the whites.[24] Ajoy Ghose, an unemployed Indian, pointed out that to kill whites was not murder and Uyornumu Ezekiel, Nigerian electrician, having derided the Prime Minister as a 'political prostitute', said that England was 'going down the toilet'.[25] They were all prosecuted; Ezekiel was discharged, the others fined.

But UCPA rhetoric was helping to stiffen black backs, its meetings and study groups to raise black consciousness, its ideology to politicise black people. The prosecution of its members showed up the complicity of the courts – 'protection rackets for the police', the secretary of WISC was to call them. And its example, like that of RAAS, encouraged other black organisations to greater militancy.

RAAS, it would appear, stressed black nationalism, while the UCPA emphasised the struggles of the international working class. But they were in fact different approaches to the same goals. RAAS's 'nationalism', stemming as it did from the West Indian experience, combined an understanding of how colonialism had divided the Asian and African and Caribbean peoples (coolie, savage and slave) with an awareness of how that same colonialism made them one people now: they were all blacks. Hence the Black House (and the cultural groups) that RAAS was briefly to set up in 1970 did not, like LeRoi Jones/Amiri Baraka's Spirit House which was its inspiration, exclude other 'coloureds'; the historical experience was different.

Meanwhile, the number of black strikes – mainly Asian, because it was they who were employed in the menial jobs in the foundries, the textile and paper mills, the rubber and plastic works – began to mount, and nearly all of them showed up trade union racism. Working conditions in the foundries were particularly unendurable. The job itself involved working with molten metal at 1,400 degrees centigrade. Burns and injuries were frequent.

The wage was rarely more than £14 a week and promotion to skilled white-only jobs was unthinkable. Every action on the part of the Asian workers was either unsupported or opposed by the trade union to which they belonged, for example in the strike at Coneygre Foundry (Tipton) in April 1967 and again in October 1968, at the Midland Motor Cylinder Co. in the same year and at Newby Foundry (West Bromwich) a year later. But the support from their communities and community organisations was unwavering. The temples gave free food to strikers, the grocers limitless credit, the landlords waived the rent. And joining in the strike action were local organisations and associations – IWAs and Pakistani Welfare Associations and/or other black organisations or individuals connected with them.

Some issues, however, embraced the whole community more directly. For, apart from the general question of wages, conditions of work, etc., quite a few of these strikes also involved 'cultural' questions, such as the right to take time off for religious festivals, the right to break off for daily prayer (among Muslims), the right of Sikh busmen to wear turbans instead of the official head-gear. And because of trade union opposition to such 'practices', the struggles of the class and the struggles of the community, of race, became indistinguishable.

These in turn were linked to the struggles back 'home' in the subcontinent – if only through family obligations arising from economic need predicated by under-development caused by imperialism. The connections were immediate, palpable, personal. Imperialism was not a thing apart, a theoretical concept; it was a lived experience – only one remove from the experience of racism itself. And for that reason, too, the politics and political organisations of the 'home' countries had a bearing on the life and politics of Indian and Pakistani settlers in Britain – now not in terms of electoral political parties so much as in terms of the resistance movements to the authoritarian state[26] – which, in turn, had resonances for them in Britain. Asian-language newspapers kept them in constant touch with events in the subcontinent, and the political refugees whom they housed and looked after not only involved them in their movements, but fired their own resistances. Reciprocally, their people back 'home' were keened to the mounting racism in Britain.

On all these fronts, then, blacks by 1968 were beginning to fight as a class and as a people. Whatever the specifics of resistance in the respective communities and however different the strategies and lines of struggle, the experience of a common racism and a common fight against the state united them at the barricades. The mosaic of unities observed earlier resolved itself, before the onslaught of the state, into a black unity and a black struggle. It would recede again when the state strategically retreated into urban aid programmes and the creation of a class of black collaborators – only to be forged anew by another generation, British-born but not British.

In March 1968 the Labour government passed the 'Kenyan Asian Act', this time barring free entry to Britain of its citizens in Kenya – because they were Asians. O.K. so they held British passports issued by or on behalf of the British government, but that did not make them British, did it? Now, if they had a parent or grandparent 'born, naturalised, or adopted in the UK' – like those chaps in Australia, New Zealand and places – it would be a different matter. But of course the government would set aside a quota of entry vouchers especially for them – for the British Asians, that is. The reasons were not 'racial', as Prime Minister Wilson pointed out to the Archbishop of Canterbury, but 'geographical'.[27]

Between conception and passage the Act had taken but a week. The orchestration of public opinion that preceded it had gone on for about a year, but it had risen to a crescendo in the last six months. In October Enoch Powell, man of the people, had warned the nation that there were 'hundreds of thousands of people in Kenya'[28] who thought they belonged to Britain 'just like you and me'. In January the press came out with scare stories, as it had done before the Immigration Act of 1962, except this time it was not smallpox but the clandestine arrival of hordes of Pakistanis. In February Powell returned to his theme – and other politicians joined in. Later in the month the *Daily Mirror*, the avowedly pro-Labour paper, warned of an 'uncontrolled flood of Asian immigrants from Kenya'. On 1 March the bill was passed.

Blacks were enraged. They had lobbied, petitioned, reasoned, demonstrated – even campaigned alongside whites in NCCI's Equal Rights set-up – and had made no impact. But the momentum was not to be lost. Within weeks of the Act Jagmohan Joshi, Secretary of the IWA Birmingham, was urging black organisations to form a broad, united front. On 4 April Martin Luther King was murdered...

'I have a dream.' They slew the dreamer.

Some two weeks later Enoch Powell spoke of his and the nation's nightmare: the blacks were swarming all over him, no, all over the country, 'whole areas and towns and parts of towns across England' were covered with them, they pushed excreta through old ladies' letter boxes; we must take 'action now', stop the 'inflow', promote the 'outflow', stop the fiancés, stop the dependants, 'the material of the future growth of the immigrant-descended population', the breeding ground. 'Numbers are of the essence.'

What Powell says today, the Tories say tomorrow and Labour legislates on the day after. Immediately, it was public opinion that was roused. The press picked up Powell's themes and Powell. The unspeakable had been spoken, free speech set free, the whites liberated; Asians and West Indians were abused and attacked, their property damaged, their women and children terrorised. Police harassment increased, the fascists went on a rampage and Paki-bashing emerged as the national sport. A few trade unionists made gestures of protest and earned the opprobrium of the rank and file. White workers all over the country downed tools and staged demonstrations on behalf of Powell. And on the day that even-handed Labour, having passed a genuinely racist Immigration Act, was debating a phoney anti-racist Race Relations Bill, London dockers struck work and marched on parliament to demand an end to immigration. Three days later they marched again, this time with the Smithfield meat-porters.

But the blacks were on the march too. On the same day as the dockers and porters marched, representatives from over fifty organisations (including the IWAs, WISC, NFPA, UCPA, RAAS, etc.) came together at Leamington Spa to form a national body, the Black People's Alliance (BPA), 'a militant front for Black Consciousness and against racialism'. And in that, the BPA was uncompromising from the outset. It excluded from membership immigrant organisations that had compromised with government policy or fallen prey to government hand-outs (Labour's Urban Aid programme was beginning to percolate through to the blacks) or looked to the Labour Party for redress. For, in respect of 'whipping up racial antagonisms and hatred to make political gains', there was no difference between the parties or between them and Enoch Powell. He was 'just one step in a continuous campaign' which had served to give 'the green light to the overtly fascist organisations... now very active in organising among the working class'.[29] Member organisations would continue to maintain their independent existence and function at the local level, in terms of the particular communities and problems; the BPA would operate on the national level, coordinating the various fights against state racism. And, where necessary, it would take to the streets en masse – as it did in January 1969 (during the Commonwealth Prime Ministers' Conference), when it led a march of over 7,000 people to Downing Street to demand the repeal of the Immigration Acts.

From Powell's speech and BPA, but nurtured in the Black Power movement, sprang a host of militant black organisations all over the country, with their own newspapers and journals, taking up local, national and international issues. Some Jamaican organisations marched on their High Commission in London, protesting the banning of the works of Stokely and Malcolm X in Jamaica, while others, like WISC, RAAS and the Caribbean Artists' movement, sent petitions. On the banning of Walter Rodney from returning to his post at the university, Jamaicans staged a sit-in at the High Commission. A 'Third World' Benefit for three imprisoned playwrights – Wole Soyinka in Nigeria, LeRoi Jones in America and Obi Egbuna in Britain – was held at the Round House with Sammy Davis, Black Eagles and Michael X. But Egbuna's imprisonment (with two other UPCA members), for uttering and writing threats to kill police, also stirred up black anger. 'Unless something is done to ensure the protection of our people,' wrote the Black Panther Movement in its circular of 3 October 1968, 'we will have no alternative but to rise to their defence. And once we are driven to that position, redress will be too late, Detroit and Newark will inevitably become part of the British scene and the Thames foam with blood sooner than Enoch Powell envisaged.'[30]

Less than six months after Powell's speech, Heath, the Tory leader, having sacked Powell from the Shadow Cabinet, himself picked up Powell's themes. Immigration, he said, whether of voucher-holders or dependants, should be 'severely curtailed' – and those who wished to return to their country of origin should 'receive assisted passage from public funds'. But Powell outbid him in a call for a 'Ministry of Repatriation' and 'a programme of large-scale voluntary but organised, financed and subsidised repatriation and re-emigration'. Two months later Heath upped the ante: the government should stop all immigration. Powell, who was on the same platform, applauded him. Callaghan, the Home Secretary, however, derided Heath's speech as 'slick and shifty'. Three days later Callaghan debarred Commonwealth citizens from entering Britain to marry fiancées and settle here, 'unless there are compassionate circumstances'. And in May 1969, in an even more blatant piece of 'even-handedness', Callaghan sneaked into the 'liberal' Immigration Appeals Bill[31] a clause which stipulated that dependants should henceforth have entry certificates before coming to Britain. And with that he set the seal on the prevarications, delays and humbug that British officials in the countries of emigration, mainly India and Pakistan now, subjected dependants to – till the young grew old in the waiting and old folk just gave up or died. It was a move in Powell's direction, but he meanwhile had moved on to higher things, like calculating the cost of repatriation. Before Callaghan could move towards him again, Labour lost the election (1970). It was now left to a Tory government under Heath to effect Powellite policies (on behalf of Labour) in the Immigration Act of 1971.

The new Act stopped all primary (black) immigration dead. Only 'patrials' (Callaghan's euphemism for white Commonwealth citizens) had right of abode now. Non-patrials could only come in on a permit to do a specific job in a specific place for a specific period. Their residence, deportation, repatriation and acquisition of citizenship were subject to Home Office discretion. But constables and immigration officers were empowered to arrest without warrant anyone who had entered or was suspected ('with reasonable cause') to have entered the country illegally or overstayed his or her time or failed to observe the rules of the Act in any other particular. Since all blacks were, on the face of them, non-patrials, this meant that all blacks were illegal immigrants unless proved otherwise. And since, in this respect, the Act (when it came into force in January 1973) would be retrospective, illegal immigrants went back a long way.

Entry of dependants of those already settled in Britain would continue to be made on the basis of entry certificates issued by the British authorities, at their discretion, in the country of emigration. Eligibility – as to age, dependency, relationship to the relative in the UK, etc. – would have to be proved by the dependant. Children would have to be under 18 to be eligible at all and parents over 65. But 'entry clearances' did not guarantee entry into Britain. It could still be refused at the port of entry by the immigration officer on the ground that 'false representations were employed or material facts were concealed, *whether or not to the holder's knowledge*, for the purpose of obtaining clearance' [emphasis added]. (When, in 1980, Filipino domestic workers who had entered legally were to ask to bring in their children, they would be deported – on the basis of this clause – for having withheld information (re children) which they were not asked for in the first place.) And as for those who wanted to be repatriated, every assistance would be afforded.

On the face of it, the Act appeared no more racist than its predecessors. Bans and entry certificates, stop and search arrests and 'Sus' (under section 4 of the 1824 Vagrancy Act anyone could be arrested 'on suspicion' of loitering with intent to commit an arrestable offence), detention and deportations were already everyday aspects of black life. Even the distinction that the Act made between the old settlers and the new migrants to make them all migrants again did not seem to matter much: they had never been anything but 'coloured immigrants'. But there was something else in the air. The 'philosophy' had begun to change, the raison d'être of racism. It was not that racism did not make for cheap labour any more, but that there was no need for capital to import it. Instead, thanks to advances in technology and changes in its own nature, capital could now move to labour, and did – the transnational corporations saw to that.[32] The problem was to get rid of the labour, the black labour that was already here. And racism could help there – with laws and regulations that kept families apart, sanctioned police harassment, invited fascist violence and generally made life untenable for the black citizens of Britain. And if they wanted to return 'home', assisted passages would speed their way.

To get the full flavour of the Immigration Act of 1971, however, it must be seen in conjunction with the Industrial Relations Act of the same year. For if the Immigration Act affected the black peoples (in varying ways), the Industrial Relations Act, which put strictures on trade unions and subjected industrial disputes to the jurisdiction of a court, the National Industrial Relations Court (NIRC), affected the black working class specifically. As workers, they were subject to the Industrial Relations Act's overall attack on the class (and later to the government's three-day week). As blacks, they were subject to the Immigration Act's threat of deportation – as illegal immigrants or for acting in ways not 'conducive to the public good'. As blacks and workers, they were subjected to the increasing racism of white workers and trade unions under siege – and more susceptible to being offered up to the NIRC for the adjudication of their disputes. Together, the Acts threatened to lock the black working class into the position of a permanent underclass. Hence, it is precisely in the area of black working-class struggles that the resistance of the early 1970s becomes significant.

But these were not struggles apart. They were, because they were black, tied up with other struggles in the community, which in turn was involved in the battles on the factory floor. The community struggles themselves had, as we have seen, become increasingly politicised in the Black Power movement and organised in black political groups. And they, after the failure of the white left to acknowledge the special problems of the black working class or the need for black self-help and organisation, began to address themselves to the problems of black workers – in the factories, in the schools, in their relationship with the police. Which in turn was to lead to more intense confrontation with, if not the state directly, the instruments of state oppression. But since these operated differentially in respect of the Asian and West Indian communities, the resistance to them was conducted at different levels, in different venues, with (often) different priorities.

The energies of the Asian community, for instance, were taken up with trying to get their families and dependants in – and once in, to keep them (and themselves) from being picked up as illegal immigrants. Since these required a knowledge of the law and of officialdom, it was inevitable that their struggles in this respect would be channelled into legal battles – mainly through the Joint Council for the Welfare of Immigrants (JCWI)[33] with its expertise and commitment – and into petitioning and lobbying. This aspect was further reinforced by the issue of the 'shuttlecock Asians', those British Asians in East Africa who (for one reason or another) were bandied about from country to country before eventually being imprisoned in Britain prior to admission.[34] From 1972 Asian leaders and organisation were also preoccupied with the resettlement of British Asian refugees from Amin's Uganda.

If the struggles to gain entry for their families and dependants drained the energies of the Asian community at one level, the abuse and the humiliation that those seeking entry were submitted to by immigration officials served to degrade and sometimes demoralise it. The instances are legion and have been documented elsewhere.[35] But the most despicable of them all was the vaginal examination of women for virginity – in itself an appalling violation but, for women from a peasant culture, a violation beyond violence. Further debilitating of the community was the police use of informers to apprehend suspected illegal immigrants individually and through 'fishing raids', generating thereby suspicion and distrust among families. In turn, the battles against them channelled the community's energies into getting the retrospective aspect of the Immigration Act regarding illegal immigrants repealed (and was finally 'rewarded' by the dubious amnesty of 1974 for all those who had entered illegally before 1973). But the police's Illegal Immigration Intelligence Unit (IIIU) remained in force.[36]

The Afro-Caribbean community, for its part (excepting the workplace, which will be treated separately), was occupied with fighting the mis-education of its children and the harassment of the police. Both problems had existed before, but they had now gathered momentum. West Indian children were consistently and right through the schooling system treated as uneducable and as having 'unrealistic aspirations' together with a low IQ. Consequently, they were 'banded' into classes for backward children or dumped in ESN (educationally subnormal) schools and forgotten. The fight against categorisation of their children as under-achieving, and therefore fit only to be an underclass, begun in Haringey (London) in the 1960s by West Indian parents, teachers and the North London West Indian Association (NLWIA) under Jeff Crawford, now spread to other areas and became incorporated in the programmes of black political organisations. An appeal to the Race Relations Board (1970) elicited the response that the placement of West Indian children in ESN schools was 'no unlawful act'. The Caribbean Education Association then held a conference on the subject and in the following year Bernard Coard (now Deputy Prime Minister of Grenada) wrote his influential work, *How the West Indian child is made educationally subnormal...* Black militants and organisations, meanwhile, had begun to set up supplementary schools in the larger conurbations. In London alone there was the Kwame Nkrumah school (Hackney black teachers), the Malcolm X Montessori Programme (Ajoy Ghose), the George Padmore school (John La Rose[37] and the Black Parents' Movement), the South-east London Summer School (BUFP: Black Unity and Freedom Party), Headstart (BLF:

Black Liberation Front) and the Marcus Garvey school (BLF and others).[38]

Projects were also set up to teach skills to youth. The Mkutano Project, for instance, started by the BUFP (in 1972), taught typing, photography, Swahili; the Melting Pot, begun about the same time by Ashton Gibson (once of RAAS), had a workshop for making clothes; and Keskidee, set up by an ex-CARD official, Oscar Abrams, taught art and sculpture and encouraged black poets and playwrights. For older students, Roy Sawh ran the Free University for Black Studies. And then there were hostels for unemployed and homeless black youth – such as Brother Herman's Harambee and Vince Hines' Dashiki (both of whom had been active in RAAS) – and clubs and youth centres. Finally, there were the bookshop cum advice centres, such as the Black People's Information Centre, BLF's Grassroots Storefront and BWM's Unity Bookshop,[39] and the weekly or monthly newspapers: *Black Voice* (BUFP), *Grassroots* (BLF), *Freedom News* (BP: Black Panthers), *Frontline* (BCC: Brixton and Croydon Collective), *Uhuru* (BPFM: Black People's Freedom Movement), *BPFM Weekly*, the *BWAC Weekly* (Black Workers' Action Committee) and the less frequent but more theoretical journal *Black Liberator* – and a host of others that were more ephemeral. Some of these papers took up the question of black women, and the BUFP, following on the UCPA's Black Women's Liberation Movement, had a black women's action committee.

RAAS's Black House was going to be a huge complex, encompassing several of these activities. But hardly had it got off the ground in February 1970 than it was raided by the police and closed down. And RAAS itself began to break up. Members of RAAS, however, went on to set up various self-help projects – as indicated above.

By 1971 the UCPA was also breaking up into its component groups, with the hard core of them going to form the BUFP. (National bodies were by now not as relevant to the day-to-day struggles as local ones and the former's unifying role could equally be fulfilled by ad hoc alliances.) The UCPA, RAAS, the Black Panthers and other black organisations had in the previous two years been increasingly occupied with the problem of police brutality and fascist violence. The success of Black Power had brought down on its head the wrath of the system. Its leaders were persecuted, its meetings disrupted, its places of work destroyed. But it had gone on gaining momentum and strength: it was not a party, but a movement, gathering to its concerns all the strands of capitalist oppression, gathering to its programme all the problems of oppressed peoples. There was hardly a black in the country that did not identify with it and, through it, to all the non-whites of the world, in one way or another. And as for the British-born youth, who had been schooled in white racism, the movement was the cradle of their consciousness. Vietnam, Guinea-Bissau, Zimbabwe, Azania were all their battle-lines, China and Cuba their exemplars. The establishment was scared. The media voiced its fears. There were rumours that Black Power was about to take over Manchester City Council.[40]

In the summer of 1969 the UCPA and the Caribbean Workers' Movement were documenting and fighting the cases of people beaten up and framed by the police – in Manchester and London. In August the UCPA held a Black Power rally against 'organised police brutality' on the streets of Brixton. In April 1970 the UCPA and the Pakistani Progressive Party staged a protest outside the House of Commons over 'Paki-bashing' in the East End of London. And the Pakistani Workers' Union called for citizens' defence patrols: a number of Asians had been murdered in 1969 and 1970. A month later over 2,000 Pakistanis, Indians and West Indians marched from Hyde Park to Downing Street demanding police protection from skinhead attacks. In the summer of 1970 police attacks on blacks – abuse, harassment, assaults, raids, arrests on 'Sus', etc., in London, Manchester, Bristol, Birmingham, Leeds, Liverpool, etc. – put whole black communities under siege. In July and August there were a series of clashes between black youth and the police in London and on one occasion over a hundred youth surrounded the Caledonian Road police station demanding the release of four blacks who had been wrongfully arrested. Things finally came to a head in Notting Hill on 9 August, when police broke up a demonstration against the proposed closure of the

Mangrove restaurant with unprecedented violence. The blacks fought back, a number of them were arrested and nine of the 'ringleaders' subsequently charged with riot, affray and assault.

The Mangrove was a meeting place and an eating place, a social and welfare club, an advice and resource centre, a black house for black people, a resting place in Babylon. And if only for this reason, the police could not leave it alone. They raided it and raided it, harassed its customers and relentlessly persecuted its owner, Frank Critchlow. They made it the test of police power; the blacks made it a symbol of resistance. The battle of the blacks and the police would be fought over the Mangrove.

The trial of the Mangrove 9 (October–December 1971) is too well documented to be recounted here, but, briefly, they won. They did more: they took on what the defence counsel called 'naked judicial tyranny' – some by conducting their own defence – and won. Above all, they unfolded before the nation the corruption of the police force, the bias of the judicial system, the racism of the media – and the refusal of black people to submit themselves to the tyrannies of the state. Other trials would follow and even more bizarre prosecutions be brought, as when the alleged editor of *Grassroots* was charged with 'encouraging the murder of persons unknown' by reprinting an article from the freely available American Black Panther paper on how to make Molotov cocktails. But they would all be defended – by the whole community – and become another school of political education.[41]

If the Mangrove marked the high-water mark of Black Power and lowered the threshold of what black people would take, it also marked the beginnings of another resistance: of black youth condemned by racism to the margins of existence and then put upon by the police. 'Sus' had always laid them open to police harassment, but the government's White Paper on Police–Immigrant Relations in 1973, which warned of 'a small minority of young coloured people... anxious to imitate behaviour amongst the black community in the United States', put the government's imprimatur on police behaviour. The previous year the press and the police had discovered a 'frightening new strain of crime' and 'mugging' was added to 'Sus' as an offence on which the police could go on the offensive against West Indian youth.[42] The courts had already nodded their approval – by way of an exemplary 20-year sentence passed on a 16-year-old 'mugger'. From then on, the lives of black youths in the cities of Britain were subject to increased police pressure. Their clubs were attacked on one pretext or another, their meeting places raided and their events – carnivals, bonfires, parties – blanketed by police presence. Black youths could not walk the streets outside the ghetto or hang around streets within it without courting arrest. And apart from individual arrests, whole communities were subjected to road blocks, stop and search and mass arrests. In Brixton in 1975 the paramilitary Special Patrol Group (SPG) cruised the streets in force, made arbitrary arrests and generally terrorised the community. In Lewisham the same year the SPG stopped 14,000 people on the streets and made 400 arrests. The pattern was repeated by similar police units in other parts of the country.[43]

The youth struck back and the community closed behind them at Brockwell Park fair in 1973, for instance, and at the Carib Club (1974) and in Chapeltown, Leeds, on bonfire night (1975), and finally exploded into direct confrontation, with bricks and bottles and burning of police cars, at the Notting Hill Carnival of 1976 – when 1,600 policemen took it on themselves to kill joy on the streets.

Clearly the politics of the stick had not paid off – or perhaps needed to be stepped up to be really effective. But by now a Labour government was in power and the emphasis shifted to social control.

Meanwhile, the struggles in the workplace were throwing up another community, a community of black class interests – linking the shop-floor battles of Pakistanis, Indians and West Indians, sometimes directly through roving strike committees, sometimes through black political organisations, while combating at the same time the racism of the trade unions, from within their ranks. Where they were not unionised, black workers first used the unions, who were rarely loath to increase their numbers, however black, to fight management for unionisation – and then took on the racism of the unions themselves. Unions, after all, were the organisations of their class and, however vital their struggles as blacks, to remain a people apart would be to set back the class struggle itself. They had to fight simultaneously as a people and as a class – as blacks and as workers – not by subsuming the race struggle to the class struggle but by deepening and broadening class struggle through its black and anti-colonial, anti-imperialist dimension. The struggle against racism was a struggle for the class.

A series of strikes in the early 1970s in the textile and allied industries in the East Midlands and in various factories in London illustrate these developments. In May 1972 Pakistani workers in Crepe Sizes in Nottingham went on strike over working conditions, redundancies and pay. They composed the lowliest two-thirds of the workforce, were subjected to constant racial abuse by the white foreman and worked, without adequate safety precautions and toilet and canteen facilities, an 84-hour week for £40.08. And yet five of their number had been made redundant – after the workers had joined the Transport and General Workers' Union (TGWU). There was no official support from the union, however, till a Solidarity Committee composed of the wives and families of the strikers and of other Asian workers, community organisations and the Nottingham-based BPFM forced the TGWU to act. In June the management capitulated, agreeing to union recognition and the re-instatement of the workers who had been made redundant.

The strike of Indian workers at Mansfield Hosiery Mills in Loughborough in October 1972 was for higher wages and against the denial of promotion to jobs reserved for whites. The white workers went along with the wages claim but not promotion, and the union, the National Union of Hosiery and Knitwear Workers, first prevaricated and then decided (after the strikers had occupied the union offices) to make the strike official, but not to call out the white workers. Once again, community associations, Asian workers at another company factory and political organisations like the BPFM and the BWM provided, in the Mansfield Hosiery Strike Committee, the basis for struggle.

So that when strikes by Asian workers at the Courtauld-owned Harwood Cash Lawn Mills in Mansfield and E.E. Jaffe and Malmic Lace in Nottingham broke out in the middle of 1973, the Mansfield Hosiery Strike Committee was at hand to give them support. More importantly – from a long-term view – the Strike Committee, pursuing its policy of pushing the trade union movement to fight racism not just in word but in deed, now called for a Conference of Trade Unions against Racialism. Accordingly, in June 1973 350 delegates from all the major unions and representatives from black community groups and black political organisations[44] came together at a conference in Digbeth Hall, Birmingham. From this emerged the Birmingham Conference Steering Committee, which in turn led to the setting up of the National Committee for Trade Unions against Racialism (NCTUAR).

Meanwhile, in the London area in June 1972, West Indian workers at Stanmore Engineering Works struck work demanding wage increases recommended by their union, the Amalgamated Union of Engineering Workers (AUEW). They went further – they staged a sit-in. But although the union was prepared to award strike pay, it was not prepared to bring its national weight to bear on the strike – by, for instance, getting workers and unions in the motor industry to 'black' products from Stanmore Engineering. The strikers were eventually removed by a court injunction and sacked.

Trade union racism showed up again a year later in the strike at Standard Telephone and Cables (New Southgate), a subsidiary of ITT, over promotion of West Indians to 'white-only jobs'. The craft unions, like the Metal Mechanics, remained stubbornly craft/race oriented. The Electrical Trades Union (ETU) opposed the strike as detrimental to its (white) members, into whose ranks blacks sought promotion. The local AUEW shop steward, though supporting the strikers, could not get the support of his union on a national basis. The NCTUAR called on the trade unions and trade unionists to back the workers in their official strike action against racial discrimination – and leafleted the annual Trades Union Congress (TUC) Conference at Blackpool. Once again, all the black political organisations, the London-based BUFP, BCC, BWCC and the BWM, along with the BWAC and the BPFM from the East Midlands, came to the aid of the strikers. The BWAC sent a cable to the Non-Aligned Conference in Algiers pointing out the international depredations of ITT. But all to no avail.

In November 1973, in a strike at Perivale Gütermann, a yarn factory in Southall, over the question of wages and productivity, Indian and Pakistani workers struck work and were sacked. The TGWU branch supported the strike but gave no strike pay till February the following year. Management tried to introduce their version of the Indo-Pakistan war into the factory, but failed to inflame communal passions. The workers once again turned to the communities for help and were assisted by Indian and Pakistani workers' associations, *gurdwaras* and local shops, who between them collected money and supplied the men on strike with free sugar, flour, oil and essential groceries. The TGWU, which, like most unions, had hitherto refused to cooperate with the government's restrictive Industrial Relations Act, now referred the case of the dismissed workers to the NIRC – which of course ruled against the men. The strike was defeated.

The apotheosis of racism, however, and therefore the resistance to it, was reached in 1974 at the strike in Imperial Typewriters (in Leicester), a subsidiary of the multinational Litton Industries. For here the white workers, management and unions worked hand in glove and were backed up by the violent presence of the National Front at the factory gates. Over a thousand of the 1,500 workforce were Asians, a large section of them women, most of them refugees from Uganda, and the strike itself arose from the usual practices of racial discrimination and exploitation. The TGWU refused to support the strikers with the hoary excuse that they had not followed correct negotiating procedures, and even prevailed on some of the Asian workers to remain at work by insisting that 'the tensions are between those Asians from the subcontinent and those from Africa'. By now, of course, there was virtually a standing conference of black strike committees in the Midlands and a network of community associations and groups plus a number of black political organisations, all of which came to the aid of the strikers. And money came in from, amongst others, the Southall IWA, Birmingham Sikh temple, a women's conference in Edinburgh, the Birmingham Anti-Racist Committee and the European Workers' Action Committee. The strikers won, but the firm was closed down shortly afterwards by the multinational parent company.[45]

By the middle of the 1970s, the youth had begun to emerge into the vanguard of black struggle. And they brought to it not only the traditions of their elders but an experience of their own, which was implacable of racism and impervious to the blandishments of the state. The daily confrontations with the police, the battles of Brockwell Park and Chapeltown and Notting Hill and their encounters with the judicial set-up had established their hatred of the system. And they were now beginning to carve out a politics from the experiences of their own existence. Already by 1973, 'marginalised' young West Indians in the ghettos of Britain were being attracted to the popular politics of Rastafari. Bred in the 'gullies' of Jamaica, the Rastas were mortally opposed to consumer-capitalist society and saw in their own predicament the results of neo-colonial and imperialist intervention.[46] And in their locks and dress and music they signified their deadly opposition. They were the 'burning spear' of the new resistance. The police took note, the state also.

The Labour government's White Paper of September 1975 and the Race Relations Act that followed it in February 1976 spelt out between them the anxieties of the state. Having noted that 'about two out of every five of the coloured people in this country now were born here and the time is not far off when the majority of the coloured population will be British born', the government warned that it was 'vital to our well being as a society to tap these reservoirs of resilience, initiative and vigour in the racial minority groups and not to allow them to lie unused or to be deflected into negative protest on account of arbitrary and unfair discriminatory practices'. Hence the government would pass a Race Relations Act which would encompass whole areas of discrimination and vest the new Commission for Racial Equality (CRE), a merger of the CRC[47] and the RRB, with a few more powers to deal with it – and develop in the process a class of collaborators who would manage racism and its social and political fall-out. At the same time, it would hand out massive sums of money from its Urban Aid programme to key black self-help groups and so stamp out the breeding-grounds of resistance.[48]

The strategy worked in the short run. But even within a year, it was showing signs of failing in the long term. In September 1975 three West Indians (two of them youngsters), in the hope of financing black political groups that had refused to be corrupted by state benefice and of setting up black schools and self-help groups, held up the Spaghetti House, a restaurant in Knightsbridge. At the end of a five-day siege, they were arrested and charged and received sentences from seventeen to twenty-one years. For Sir Robert Mark, Metropolitan Police Commissioner, 'the Spaghetti House case... was the most difficult and potentially explosive of all the various problems' he had to deal with in his career,[49] but it was also one in which his strategy to by-pass his political masters and go direct to the media for the legitimation of police practice had paid off. It was an entente that, given the endemic racism of the media and the police, operated naturally vis-à-vis the black population, but would now be extended to other areas of society and substitute legitimation for accountability.[50]

Among the Asians, too, it was the youth who were moving into the forefront of struggle. Like their Afro-Caribbean peers, they had been bred in a culture of racism and, like them, were impatient though not dismissive of the forms of struggle that their elders conducted. The fascist attacks in their community had gone on mounting, the police afforded no protection against them, condoned them, even, by refusing to recognise them as racially motivated. And the police themselves subjected the community to racial abuse, arbitrary arrest and 'fishing raids' for 'illegal immigrants'. And then, in June 1976, opposite IWA's Dominion Cinema, Southall, a symbol of Asian self-reliance and security, 18-year-old Gurdip Singh Chaggar was set upon by a gang of white youths and stabbed to death. (The motive, announced Sir Robert Mark, was not necessarily racial.)

A few months earlier, the government (Labour) had announced a Green Paper on Nationality (on the lines of the present Tory Act) which would 'rationalise' the law which they themselves had fouled up in 1968. (Of course they had, as was their wont, balanced it with an anti-discriminatory Race Relations Bill which was just then, March, going through parliament.) In April the NF staged a march through the black areas of Bradford under police protection, but were beaten back by the people of Manningham, Asians and Afro-Caribbeans, young and old. In May the press started a concerted campaign against immigration with the revelation that a homeless British Asian family expelled from Malawi was being housed in a four-star hotel at a cost of £600 per week to the British tax-payer. Later that month, Enoch Powell announced that he had secret information from a 'suppressed' government report which said that bogus dependants and wives from India were making their way into the country. The press picked up Powell as Powell had picked up the press. And the attacks on the 'Asian invaders' became more intense through the days of May. On 4 June Chaggar was killed.[51]

The community was stunned. A meeting was held and the elders went about it in the time-honoured way, passing resolutions, making statements. The youth took over – marched to the police station, demanding redress, stoning a police van en route. The police arrested two of them. They sat down before the police station and refused to move – until their fellows were released. They were released. The following day the Southall Youth Movement (SYM) was born.

Various Asian youth movements sprang from this initiative – whenever and wherever there was need and in response to specific circumstances. But since these circumstances were invariably connected with fascist attacks and murders and/or police inability either to protect or apprehend (an inability so massive that it had taken a qualitative leap into connivance),[52] the youth movements tended to centre largely around the defence of their communities, and their organisations to reflect that purpose. (Their intervention in the campaigns against deportation would come later.) In the course of the next couple of years a number of youth organisations and defence committees sprang up, in London, Manchester, Leicester, Bradford, several of them in London alone – in Brick Lane after the murders of Altab Ali and Ishaque Ali, in Hackney after the murder of Michael Ferreira, in Newham after the murder of Akhtar Ali Baig. And, like the strike committees earlier, the youth groups moved around aiding and supporting each other – joining and working with West Indian youth groups in the process, sometimes on an organisational basis (SYM and Peoples Unite, Bradford Blacks and Bradford Asian Youth Movement), sometimes as individuals, often coalescing into political groups (Hackney Black People's Defence Organisation and Bradford's United Black Youth League).

At another level, political groups were consciously formed by Afro-Caribbeans, Asians and Africans who had been active in white left movements but had left them because they did not speak to the black experience. And they took on not only the black condition in Britain, but that of black peoples everywhere. They were anti-racist and anti-imperialist; and they were active in their communities. Their publications showed these concerns and helped further to politicise black people. *Samaj in'a Babylon*, in Urdu and English, and the group that produced the paper, came out of Chaggar's murder (June 1976), the Notting Hill riots (August 1976) and Soweto (June 1976). *Black Struggle* was its theoretical but accessible counterpart, *Mukti* its successor. Black Socialist Alliance (BSA) would comprehend them all for a while and shift the emphasis to campaigning material. Blacks Against State Harassment (BASH) would later address itself specifically to state racism. Other papers and journals and defence committee sheets and newsletters came and went, like their organisations, as the struggle rose and fell, moved and shifted, re-formed – but moving always in one direction: against the police, the government, racism. And the sheep/goat distinction that the state had hoped, by selective openings in higher education, to achieve, had broken down: the educated gave of their skills to the community and the community grounded them in the realities of political struggle.

Stop at Heathrow a minute, at the airport, as you are coming in or, if you are lucky, going out. Look around you, and you will see the division of labour that characterises the workforce of Britain. Cleaning and sweeping the (women's) lavatories, the halls, the stairways are Asian women from nearby Southall. Among the porters you will find a scattering of Asian and West Indian men. In the catering section, white women pack the food on the trays, while Asian women pack the same trays with cutlery (for £10 less per week). The menials in the kitchen are invariably Asian women – plus a few men, perhaps, for the heavier work.

And, of course, there is no question of promotion. Indeed they are lucky if the agency that employs them does not sack them and re-employ them at some other terminal, at the same wage if not a lower one. Their union, the TGWU, has been indifferent to their demands and in 1975, when 450 Asian workers walked out on their own initiative, the union declared the strike unofficial. The women managed, though, to elicit a few concessions on their own – and went back to work.[53]

The strike at Grunwick Film Processing plant in North London in August 1976 is, of course, more celebrated – not only because the Asian workers, most of them women from East Africa, sustained it in wet and snow and police harassment of pickets for over a year, but also because the whole force of the unions and of government appeared to be gathered at last on behalf of black workers. Not only were the strikers given strike pay by their union, but were also supported by the national unions – TGWU, TUC and UPW (Union of Post Office Workers) – and by local union branches, shop stewards committees, trade councils, the lot. And cabinet ministers appeared on the picket lines. The basic issue for the strikers was the question of racist exploitation with which union recognition was involved, but, in the course of accepting union support, they also accepted the union line that union recognition by management was really the basic issue, losing in the process the lasting support of the black community. Union recognition would not have of itself got the vast backing of the unions, let alone that of cabinet ministers – it had never happened before – but there was now a deal between the government and unions (the Social Contract) which in exchange for workers not striking ensured, through the Employment Protection Act, that employers did not prevent unionisation. And that put Grunwick in the middle of it.

As the strike dragged on into a year and the media and the management and its supporters threatened to involve more fundamental political issues such as the closed shop and the mass picket, the unions lost interest and left. In November 1977 four Asian strikers, two of them women, started a hunger strike outside the TUC headquarters. They were immediately suspended by their union and their strike pay withdrawn. Len Murray, General Secretary of the TUC, suggested that they take up their hunger strike at the factory gates and not outside his office.[54]

The lessons of the earlier strikes – that black workers needed to rally the community behind them and from that base force the unions to their side – had been temporarily unlearnt by workers who had not had the benefit of that tradition. On the other hand, the persistence of Asian women in going on the picket lines, month after month, against the pressure of their husbands and their fathers, the deception of the union and the attacks of the SPG – supported consistently by women's groups – had established the strength of the emerging black women's movement.

In 1977 the National Front, encouraged by their performance (in terms of the percentage of votes cast) in previous local elections, staged several marches through black city areas, with the police ensuring for them the freedoms of speech and assembly. They were closely attended by anti-racist groups – and black youth took the opportunity to stone both police and fascists alike.

In January 1978 Judge McKinnon ruled that Kingsley Read's pronouncement on Chaggar's death – 'One down, one million to go' – did not constitute incitement to racial hatred. 'In this England of ours,' the Judge observed, 'we are allowed to have our own views still, thank goodness, and long may it last.' Kingsley Read was the head of the fascist National Party.

In the same month, in the run-up to the local elections, itself a run-up to the general election of the following year, Margaret Thatcher assured the nation that her party would 'finally see an end to immigration', for 'this country might be rather swamped by people with a different culture'. Since primary immigration had ended with the 1971 Act, she was clearly referring to dependants. Shortly afterwards, the House of Commons (all-party) Select Committee on Race Relations and Immigration, sounding a similar note, went on to recommend 'new procedures to tighten up identity checks' and 'the consideration of a system of internal control on immigration'. The Tories promised to go further: they would 'improve' existing 'arrangements... to help those who are really anxious to leave this country'. The existing 'arrangements', such as the SPG and the IIIU, the immigration officials, and the Home Office, the courts and the media, were obviously not enough; the Tories would reverse policies of 'reverse discrimination' and amend the law on incitement to racial hatred, requiring it to prove 'an intent to offend'.

The media quickly tuned into Thatcher's warning about 'swamping'. The *Daily Mail*, in a series of articles on immigration, with headlines such as 'They've taken over my home town', gave real life stories of 'culture swamping'. A BBC television discussion programme on immigration afforded Enoch Powell enough latitude to enlarge on his theme of 'induced repatriation'. In the local elections that followed in May, Tory candidates reiterated and justified Tory proposals.

Hardly had the orchestration ceased than white fascist maggots began to crawl out of the decaying capitalist matter. Whole communities were terrorised. Three Asians were murdered in London within a period of three months, a shot-gun attack was mounted on West Indians in Wolverhampton, places of worship were desecrated and properties damaged and vandalised. And Tory-controlled local councils, mandated by their victory at the polls, set out to pursue Thatcherite policies in preparation for her victory.[55]

Emboldened by these events, but also wishing to show the country that they were the true party of fascism, the NF in April the following year requested permission from the local council to hold an election meeting at Southall Town Hall. Permission had been refused elsewhere and, even in Ealing, refused by the previous Labour-controlled council. Now, however, the Tory majority, after little prevarication, granted permission. Five thousand people demonstrated before the Ealing Town Hall the previous day, demanding that the meeting be called off, but to no avail. Instead the council flaunted the Union Jack, the NF's symbol, from the roof of the town hall. It was St George's day, a day celebrated by the NF. The Southall community planned a peaceful protest. 'But on the day, 2,756 police, including SPG units, with horses, dogs, vans, riot shields and a helicopter, were sent in to crush the protest' – and the whole town centre declared a 'sterile' area.[56] People were penned in, unable to get to the town hall or go back home – and began milling around. The police went berserk. Police vans were driven at crowds of people and when they scattered and ran, officers charged after them, hitting out at random. Blair Peach, a relentless anti-racist campaigner and teacher, was beaten to death and hundreds of others injured, many seriously. The offices of Peoples Unite (an Afro-Caribbean-Asian meeting centre) were vandalised by police in readiness for the Tory council to demolish them – years before the scheduled date. Asian newspapers recalled the Amritsar massacre of that other April in 1919.

The trials of the Southall 342 were held twenty-five miles away, far from the eye of the community, in Thatcher country. The magistrates rushed rapidly through the cases, convicting with abandon – 80 per cent in the first weeks of the trials – before the community could alert public opinion and the conviction rate was brought down to 50 per cent. The SPG officer who had bludgeoned Blair Peach to death remained unidentified and untried. The (Tory) government refused to hold an inquiry. The Home Secretary tut-tutted the SPG and, despite a massive public outcry against the unit (in which even the media was caught up), let it go back to its former devices. The Metropolitan Police Commissioner, Sir David McNee, summed it all up in an epigram: 'If you keep off the streets in London and behave yourselves, you won't have the SPG to worry about.' But Southall, Southall knew, would not lightly be invaded again, as the third of July was to prove.[57]

The Tory government of 1970, with its Immigration Act and Industrial Relations Act, its White Paper on Police–Immigrant Relations and other bits and pieces of policy, had begun the moves from the control of blacks at the gates to their control within. The Labour government had continued in the same vein, and not always by default: there was the Child Benefit law[58] and the Green Paper on Nationality – and, of course, there was their unwavering support for the police and their practices. The Tory government of 1979 now sought to perfect these measures, carry them to a logical conclusion, a final solution, within an overall attack on the working class and the welfare state in the framework of a law-and-order society. In articulating and clarifying the ideology of British racism in the run-up to the elections, Thatcher had established a climate in which officials in the health service, employment, education, housing, social and welfare services would, without benefit of edict, insist on passports and identity checks before affording a service to black citizens. Her Nationality Bill, by providing for various classes of (black) citizenship, would tend to regularise these practices.[59] Britain was effectively moving to a pass-law society.

The resistance of the black community went up a notch and, as so often before, threw up new types of struggle and new leaderships – this time in the form of the black women's movement, which would encompass all the struggles and add its own particular perspective to the resistance of the late 1970s. A few Afro-Caribbean women's groups had been in existence for over a decade, taking up issues that neither the white women's movement nor the black parties would concern themselves with. Asian women had begun to support their sisters through industrial strikes, on the Grunwick picket line, for instance, and outside Heathrow Airport. By 1978 black women's groups, Asian and Afro-Caribbean, had sprung up all over Britain and came together to form one powerful national body, the Organisation of Women of Asian and African Descent (OWAAD), with its paper *FOWAAD*. OWAAD would hold national conferences and work with other national black groups, whilst allowing its constituent groups autonomy of work in their communities. Through OWAAD, the Asian and Afro-Caribbean experiences and campaigns could cross-fertilise and develop particular lines of struggle that would benefit the whole black community. For they were taking up issues of discrimination against class, race and gender at once – in the face of harassments which, under the new Tory regimen, went deep into community life, into households, into children's welfare.

It was naturally Asian women's groups which first became aware of issues such as the discrimination in new Child Benefit provisions – since it was mainly their community's children which were kept out by immigration law. But they were soon joined in their campaigning by Afro-Caribbean women who were already exposing other state attacks on black family life. Together they worked on issues of black child care, black prisoners' rights, the enforced use of Depo-Provera and abortion law (without recourse to abortion, black women would be subjected increasingly to dangerous contraception methods such as the use of Depo-Provera). Asian women joined the campaigns against 'Sin-bins' (special 'adjustment units' which replaced ESN schooling for West Indian children), which the United Black Women's Action Group in North London had started. Brixton Black Women's Group launched the first Black Women's Centre (1979).

In fighting for educational and social and welfare services for the whole community, Asian and Afro-Caribbean women pinpointed the parallel histories of a common racism. In health care, for example, black women fought against the neglect of 'black disease'. Simultaneous campaigns were mounted in Brent against sickle-cell anaemia (affecting West Indians) and Vitamin D deficiencies causing rickets (affecting Asians). And issues such as forcible sterilisation, arising from the health services' obsession with black fertility, or the easy consignment of black women to mental hospitals, arising from its stereotyped understanding of 'black psyches in captivity', were fought by black women from both communities.

Asian women in *AWAZ* (Voice) and Southall Black Sisters (set up in the wake of 23 April 1979) continued to lead the protest against the virginity testing and X-raying of immigrants. Here they gave the lead not only to other women, but to long-established, male-dominated Asian organisations such as the IWA, which eventually joined them. And when Asian youth groups began to campaign in the community over specific immigration cases, it was the black women that helped keep the names of Anwar Ditta and Nasira Begum in the public consciousness.

Black women have also been active in working-class struggles, as in the strike of Asian women at Futters (March–May 1979) and at Chix (1979–80), worked in local community self-defence groups and combined in national black campaigns such as BSA and BASH. And from the richness of their struggles – at the factory gate, on the streets, in the home, at the schools, in the hospitals, at the courts – and from their joint initiative with IWA and BASH arose the first national black demonstration against state brutality (June 1979), when blacks, with the violence of virginity tests, the fascists and the SPG still fresh in their minds, marched in their outraged thousands through the heart of London.[60]

The loom of British racism had been perfected, the pattern set. The strands of resistance were meshed taut against the frame. The frame had to give. Instead, it was screwed still tighter in the unexplained death of Rasta 'Cartoon' Campbell in Brixton prison[61] (March 1980), the murder of Akhtar Ali Baig on the streets of Newham (July 1980) and the burning to death of thirteen young West Indians in a fire in New Cross (January 1981).

It was clear to the black community from the evidence of a black witness, if not the evidence of their whole history in Britain, that the fire had been started by the fascists. But even before the investigation was concluded, the police, with the aid of the press, had put it about that it was the work of a disaffected black party-goer, or a prank that went wrong or maybe an accident. Finally they 'proved' through forensic expertise that the fire had been self-inflicted one way or another. Just nine months earlier, the police had 'raided' a black meeting place in St Pauls Bristol, only to be beaten back by the youth and routed by the community. Now the community closed ranks again. From all over the country they gathered at meetings in New Cross. A day of action was planned. The Race Today Collective[62] took over its organisation. And on 2 March over 10,000 blacks downed tools and marched through the heart of London, past the halls of imperial finance, past the portals of the yellow press, past the Courts of Justice, past the proud shopping centre of consumer society, past Broadcasting House and into the anointed place of free speech – Speakers' Corner.

It had been, for its size and length and spread of time, a peaceful march. There had been a few skirmishes, a window or two broken and a few arrests made. But the banner headlines in the people's press spoke of 'mob violence', 'blacks on the rampage', the invasion of privacy, the damage to property. The quality press mourned the breakdown of police–black relations, the frustration of the blacks, even at times white insensitivity to 'black problems' – and went back to sleep again. The Home Secretary muttered something about an inquiry into racial violence. White society ensconced itself in its goodness and thanked God for the British 'bobby'. And, heartened, the bobbies went back to baiting Brixton, the fascists to baiting Southall.

In April, Brixton exploded in rebellion, in July, Southall – for blacks, Afro-Caribbean and Asian alike, all distinction between police and fascist had faded – and in the days following, Liverpool, Manchester, Coventry, Huddersfield, Bradford, Halifax, Blackburn, Preston, Birkenhead, Ellesmere Port, Chester, Stoke, Shrewsbury, Wolverhampton, Southampton, Newcastle, High Wycombe, Knaresborough, Leeds, Hull, Derby, Sheffield, Stockport, Nottingham, Leicester, Luton, Maidstone, Aldershot and Portsmouth, black and white – rebellion in slum city – for the deprived, the state was the police.

Nowhere have the youth, black and white, identified their problems with unemployment alone. That has been left to the social analysts of a past age. The youth know, viscerally, that there will be no work for them, ever, no call for their labour: it was not just a matter of the recession (the rich were doing all right), technology was taking over and the recession just gave 'them' the chance to get rid of the workers and bring in the robots. Society was changing, and they didn't need the secretary of the British Association for the Advancement of Science to tell them that it was 'a fundamental and irreversible change'. But they do not want to be pushed into artificial work schemes or institutionalised leisure or receive hand-outs from the enemy state. There is enough to go round and they want a part of it, a say in its giving. Or they will get it by thieving and 'loitering' and hustling – those things which pass for normalcy in a slum but threaten established society.

They are not the unemployed, but the never employed. They have not, like their parents, had jobs and lost them – and so become disciplined into a routine and a culture that preserves the status quo. They have not been organised into trade unions and had their politics disciplined by a labour aristocracy. They have not been on the marches of the dis-employed, so valiantly recalled by Labour from the hunger marches of the 1930s. Theirs is a different hunger – a hunger to retain the freedom, the life-style, the dignity which they have carved out from the stone of their lives.

The police are not an intrusion into that society but a threat, a foreign force, an army of occupation – the thick end of the authoritarian wedge, and in themselves so authoritarian as to make no difference between wedge and state.

That authoritarianism had been perfected in the colonies, in Ireland, in the fields of British racism, and, as it grew, it found ways to by-pass its political masters and become accountable to no one but itself – by obtaining legitimation for its actions from the silent majority through its cultivated liaison with the media.

It was once held that the British police were governed more by popular morality than by the letter of the law. They have now become the arbiters of that morality. There is no criticism of them they would brook, no area of society they do not pronounce on (with the shadow of force behind them). Look at the ferocity with which they attack their critics (even the parliamentary tribunes of the people),[63] their refusal to be accountable to elected local police authorities, their pronouncements on the jury system, the unemployed, homosexuality, etc.,[64] the press campaign mounted by their PRO, the Police Federation, for increased police powers (in various submissions to the Royal Commission on Criminal Procedure for instance) or the bon mots of their police chiefs[65] to understand how the police have moved from accountability to legitimation.

But then a government which is not accountable to the people – a government which governs with the politics of the stick and the policies of a thousand cuts, which is anti-working class and anti-women and anti-youth – must have a police force that is accountable to it and not to the people. In turn, the government itself needs to be legitimated by an ideology of repression. And it is not merely that a free market economy requires a law and order state but that, even in its passing, it leaves only the option of a mixed economy with a corporate state maintained by surveillance. They are but two shades of the same authoritarianism, the one more modern than the other, but neither speaking to the birth of a new society that waits in the wings of the new industrial revolution.

6

RAT AND THE DEGRADATION
OF BLACK STRUGGLE*

There is a class war going on within Marxism as to who – in
the period of the de-construction of industrial capitalism and
the re-composition of the working class – are the real agents
of revolutionary change: the orthodox working class, which is
orthodox no more, or the 'ideological classes' who pass for the
new social force or forces. It is a war that was engendered, on
the one hand, by the growing disillusion with Soviet communism
and, on the other, by the receding prospect of capturing state
power in late capitalist societies where such power was becoming
increasingly diffuse and opaque. The solution to both, on the
ground, pointed to a variant of social democracy under the
rubric of Eurocommunism. The solution, for theory, pointed to
a re-reading of Marx, a re-hashing of Gramsci and a return to
intellectual rigour accompanied by activist mortis. The working
class, as a consequence, was stripped of its richest political seams
– black, feminist, gay, green, etc. – and left, in the name of anti-
economism, a prey to economism. Conversely, the new social
forces, freed from the ballast of economic determinism (and class
reductionism), have been floated as the political and ideological
'classes' of the new radicalism. But that flight from class has served
only to turn ideological priorities into idealistic preoccupations,
and political autonomy into personalised politics and palliatives
which, for all that, have passed into common left currency and
found a habitation and a name in Labour local authorities. The
clearest expression of these tendencies and the mortality they bring

---

* This essay was written in April 1985.

140

to the new social movements are to be seen in the philosophy and practice of Racism Awareness Training (RAT), the blight of the black struggle – itself a result of the flight of race from class.

Hitherto the interests of the class were woven into the concerns of the communities – and black denoted the colour of their politics, not of their skins. And in this they were guided by the understanding that any struggle against racism which deepened and extended the class struggle was the right struggle. Conversely, any struggle that led to the cul de sac of reactionary nationalism was the wrong one.

But the continued threat of black struggle, however limited its success, led to state strategies to break up black into its constituent nationalities on the one hand and to heavy-handed policing of the young on the other – and culminated in the youth rebellions of 1981.

The trajectories of this history have been detailed elsewhere. Here it is important to note that 1981 marked a change in state strategy – from suppressing black struggle to buying it off – and Lord Scarman was its (unwitting) architect.

The rise and rise of ethnicity

It was his report on the Brixton 'riots' that pointed to a new ethnic strategy. The foundation for that strategy, however, had already been intimated in the report of the Home Affairs Committee on Racial Disadvantage (1981) – which was itself informed by a whole school of ethnicity that had emerged (at Bristol University's Social Science Research Council Unit on Ethnic Relations) to take on the 'problem' of British-born blacks.

Whereas multiculturalism, addressing itself to the revolt of the first-generation 'immigrant', diagnosed the problem as one of cultural misunderstanding, the ethnicists, in trying to relate to the ongoing revolt of British-born blacks, connected it with the cultural limbo to which racism had ostensibly condemned them. Neither Asian/Afro-Caribbean nor British but afflicted by both, the second generation was adrift of its moorings and rudderless, caught in a cross-current of emotion in its search for identity – not least, to fight racism with. And in that search, it kept returning to its ethnicity and, redefining it, found refuge therein. Ethnicity refers, therefore, to the creation of a new reactive culture on the part of British-born Asians and West Indians alike. But where Asians tended to go into their cultures to make the new ethnicity, West Indian ethnicity came out of a mixture, a 'creolisation', of Afro-Caribbean culture with the 'host' culture. 'Those who were born in Britain', states Watson, 'are caught between the cultural expectations of their parents (the first-generation migrants) and the social demands of the wider society. Young Sikhs and Jamaicans, for instance, often feel that they do not "fit" in either culture... Largely in response to racism, these two minorities have begun a process of ethnic redefinition – or "creolisation"...'[1] Or, in Weinreich's language: 'West Indian boys have conflicted identifications with the general representatives of their own ethnicity and the native white population.' Hence, the 'changes' in the second generation should be seen as 'redefinition of their ethnic distinctiveness'.[2] It is racism, however, according to the Ballards, that has 'precipitated a reactive pride in their separate ethnic identity'.[3] Ethnicity itself, for Wallman, is a 'perception' of difference, a 'sense' of it, something that was 'felt', a clue to identity.[4]

By acknowledging the resistance to racism on the part of the second generation only to banish it to 'conflicted identification' and 'ethnic redefinition', the ethnicists deny the connection between race and class and between racism and imperialism – and reincarcerate the second generation in the castle of their skin. Identity is all. The Home Affairs Committee then takes on the ethnic theme and, making ethnicity official, signs up institutional racism as racial disadvantage – leaving it to Scarman to tie it up with ethnic need.

Like the Race Relations Act of 1976, the main planks of the Scarman report were racial discrimination (direct and indirect) and racial disadvantage. Racial discrimination Scarman, too, was prepared to leave to the 'existing law', and presumably the Commission for Racial Equality (CRE). But racial disadvantage, which the 1976 Act – steering its way gingerly between the Scylla of institutional racism and the Charybdis of inherent inferiority – had left (undefined) to the vagaries of Equal Opportunity, was in Scarman to be (specifically) treated in terms of special ethnic needs and problems.* And it is here at the point of cure, in the act of applying the ethnic poultice to the ethnic wound, that racial disadvantage begins to smell of inherent disability.

The West Indian family, implies Scarman, is comparatively unstable, 'doubtless because of the impact of British social conditions on the matriarchal extended family structure of the West Indian immigrants'.[5] For instance, 'the percentage of children in care and of single-parent families in the black community is noticeably higher than one would expect in relation to the proportion of black people in the community as a whole. Fifty percent of single parent families in... Lambeth in 1978 were non-white.' Besides, 'the two wards where the April disorders were centred – Tulse Hill and Herne Hill – contain some 22% of all the single-parent households in Lambeth and 2.1% of the 0–18 group in those wards are in care. Of the 185 children in care of those two wards on 10 September 1980, 112 (61%) were black.' In addition, it was estimated that '200–300 young blacks are homeless, sleeping rough or squatting in Brixton'.

Young West Indians, for Scarman are 'a people of the street... They live their lives on the street, having often nothing better to do: they make their protest there: and some of them live off street crime.' Inevitably, they must come into conflict with the police, 'whom they see as pursuing and harassing them on the streets'. And this hostility of black youth to the police has '*infected* older members of the community' (emphasis added). The street-corners are 'social centres' for old people too, and 'young and old, good and bad have time on their hands and a continuing opportunity... to engage in endless discussion of their grievances', so that 'in Brixton even one isolated instance of misconduct can foster a whole legion of rumours which rapidly become beliefs firmly held within the community'.

---

* 'The special problems and needs of the ethnic minorties', is how Scarman put it.

If this is not as elaborate as Moynihan's 'tangled pathology' of the American 'Negro family',* it is because Scarman's brief was to investigate the 'Brixton disorders' not the West Indian community. But, given his determination to acquit the state of institutional racism, it was inevitable that he should find the West Indian community guilty of inherent disability and so give racial disadvantage a meaning which even the Home Affairs Committee report on the subject (July 1981) had been careful to avoid. But the committee, since its brief was racial disadvantage as such, also referred to the disadvantage suffered by the Asian community and located it in language, religion, custom and (peasant) illiteracy. (Only the 'East African Asians' were an exception.) Between them, the two reports set out the terms of West Indian and Asian ethnic need and provided the criteria on which the government based its (ethnic) programmes and allocated its (ethnic) funds.

The ensuing scramble for government favours and government grants (channelled through local authorities) on the basis of specific ethnic needs and problems served, on the one hand, to deepen ethnic differences and foster ethnic rivalry and, on the other, to widen the definition of ethnicity to include a variety of national and religious groups – Chinese, Cypriots, Greeks, Turks, Irish, Italians, Jews, Muslims, Sikhs – till the term itself became meaningless (except as a means of getting funds). This 'vertical mosaic' of ethnic groups, so distanced from the horizontal of class politics, then became even more removed by the policies of 'left' Labour councils who, lacking the race-class perspective which would have allowed them to dismantle the institutional racism of their own structures, institutionalised ethnicity instead. And it was left to a handful of genuinely anti-racist programmes and/or campaigns, such as those against deportation, police harassment and racial violence (sustained largely by GLC funding), to carry on the dwindling battle for community and class.

The other cure for racial disadvantage propounded by Scarman was 'positive action', which meant no more than a determined

---

* 'Once or twice removed, it [the weakness of the family structure] will be found to be the principal source of most of the aberrant, inadequate or anti-social behaviour that did not establish, but now serves to perpetuate the cycle of poverty and deprivation.'[6]

effort at promoting equal opportunity or, more precisely, reducing unequal opportunity for ethnic minorities, but backed up this time by a system of monitoring. And this, too, was taken up avidly by inner-city administrations who, having set up their own race relations units (to administer ethnic programmes and ethnic funds), required now an ethnic staff – not least, to keep an eye on jobs for ethnics.

Underlying the whole of Scarman's report is a socio-psychological view of racism, resonant of the ideas of the ethnic school, which, when coupled with his views on racial disadvantage, verges on the socio-biological. Institutional racism, for Scarman, is not a reality of black life but a matter of subjective feelings, perceptions, attitudes, beliefs. Ethnic minorities have a 'sense' of 'concealed discrimination'. Young blacks have a 'sense of rejection' and 'a sense of insecurity'. They do not 'feel' secure socially, economically or politically. They 'see' policemen 'as pursuing and harassing them on the streets' and the older generation have come to share this 'belief'. (The 'belief' in the Asian community is that the police do not protect them against 'alleged' racist attacks.) Community 'attitudes and beliefs' (caused by a lack of confidence in the police) underlay the disturbances. 'Popular attitudes and beliefs' themselves 'derive their strength' from the 'limbo of the half-remembered and the half-imagined'. The 'image' of a hostile police force is 'myth' and 'legend'.[7]

Equally, if the police force was guilty of anything, it was not institutional racism but racial prejudice which 'does manifest itself occasionally in the behaviour of a few police officers on the street'. And the breakdown of police–community relations was, on the part of the police, due to the fact that their 'attitudes and methods' had not quite caught up with 'the problem of policing a multicultural society'. Part of the policeman's training, therefore, should be directed to 'an understanding of the cultural backgrounds and attitudes of ethnic minorities'.

Racism, for Scarman, was in the mind – in attitudes, prejudices, irrational beliefs – and these were to be found on both sides of the divide – black and white. Institutional racism was a matter of black perception, white racism was a matter of prejudice. Or that, on the face of it, was what Scarman seemed to be saying – and at worst, it was even-handed, liberal even. But what he had effectively done was to reduce institutional racism to black perception and replace it with personal prejudice and so shift the object of anti-racist struggle from the state to the individual, from changing society to changing people, from improving the lot of whole black communities, mired in racism and poverty, to improving the lot of 'black' individuals.

It was a plan that the nascent 'black' petit-bourgeoisie, nourished on government (and local government) aid for ethnic need and positive action for ethnic equality, leapt to embrace. By and large, the ethnics were content to fight each other in their quest for office. And it was only when there was a white blockage in the system, preventing them from going up further, that the ethnics turned 'black' and pulled out all their oppressed 'black' history to beat the whites with. Hence the demand for Black Sections in the Labour Party; the rise and fall of the Black Media Workers' Association (BMWA) (the fall coming after the white media made room for them in ethnic slots – since when, they have gone back to being Afro-Caribbeans and Asians respectively); and the emergence of a black trade union aristocracy, the Black Trade Union Solidarity Movement (BTUSM). None of these give a fart for ordinary black people, but use them and their struggles as cynically as any other bourgeois class or sub-class.

Ironically enough, most of the support for these groups has come from the 'left wing' of the Labour Movement which, having failed to incorporate black working-class struggles and black working-class leadership into its own history and organisation, now feels compelled to accommodate black sects in its vaunted broad church. Taking black out of the context of the struggles in which it was beaten into a political colour, the white left now believes that any self-seeking middle-class group that calls itself black has an automatic right to appropriate that history and is automatically political or progressive. What is even more ironical is that this should be happening at a time when, in the rush for office, even such reconstituted blackness is breaking up into Afro-Caribbean and Asian, with the Afro-Caribbeans claiming a prior right to black history on the basis, simply, of a darker colour – thereby emptying 'black' of politics altogether.* Black Sections are no more representative of black working people than the Labour Party is of white. In fact, black politics has to cease to be political for blacks to get into politics. The BTUSM is no more interested in the lot of the rank and file than their lordships Chapple and Murray were as erstwhile leaders of their unions. The BMWA, in the short period of its fight-to-get-into-Channel 4 existence, never did anything for the lower ranks of black workers or, for that matter, demanded to make political black plays or programmes that would have improved the lot of ordinary Afro-Caribbeans or Asians – unless exposing the foibles and manners of one's own people to white voyeurs, but from the inside this time, can be considered funny or political. But then, an ethnic media can only reproduce the cult of ethnicity. And a culture of ethnicity, unlike a culture of resistance, has no community and has no class.

And to undergird it all, undergird the efforts of the new ethnics to move up and away – up through the white blockages in the system and away from the black communities and their troubles – there is a whole school of thought and enterprise which promises to change white minds and white attitudes so that a thousand black flowers can bloom in the interstices of the white structure. Felicitously, it calls itself RAT (Racism Awareness Training) and it is to this final degradation of black struggle that I now turn my attention.

The birth of RAT

RAT began life in HAT (Human Awareness Training) on a military base in Florida at the end of the 1960s, when the reverberations of black rebellion in American cities began to resonate in the military installations in the US and Japan and drove the Defense Department to a Human Goal Proclamation upholding individual

---

* This degradation of 'black' has now passed into vulgar usage and separated Afro-Caribbeans from Asians – as in 'black and Asian', which is itself a nonsense, as one refers to colour (not politics) and the other to geography.

dignity, worth and equal opportunity in its ranks. The training of human relations instructors at the Defense Race Relations Institute (DRRI), therefore, was meant to inculcate a knowledge of minority cultures and history, together with an understanding of personal racism.

HAT, of course, had formed part of human relations training for some time, but the race relations element came into prominence only after the Kerner Commission (1968) declared that racism in America was a white problem and that it inhered in the very structures of society. 'What white Americans have never fully understood – but what the Negro can never forget – is that white society is deeply implicated in the ghetto. White institutions created it, white institutions maintain it and white society condones it.'[8] On the face of it, the Kerner report looked like a radical statement (as radical as Scarman appeared liberal), and though it connected racism with white institutions, nowhere did it connect the institutions themselves with an exploitative white power structure. So that oppression was severed from exploitation, racism from class and institutional racism from state racism.

The US Commission on Civil Rights (1970) echoed the Kerner Commission and went on to define racism (which Kerner had left undefined) as 'any attitude, action or institutional structure which subordinates a person or group because of his or their color', adding that an 'institutional structure was any well-established, habitual or widely accepted pattern of action' (i.e., behavioural) or 'organizational arrangements whether formal or informal' (i.e., administrational). The Commission also made a distinction between 'overt racism' and 'indirect institutional subordination' (which was to become direct and indirect discrimination in the British context). And combating racism, stated the Commission, involved 'changing the behavior of whites' and 'increasing the capabilities of non-white groups' (which in Britain was to become known as tackling racial disadvantage). But the principal responsibility was 'with the white community rather than within the non-white communities'.[9]

Following the two reports, a whole host of literature sprang up in education, psychology and the churches, rescuing racism from structural taint and interiorising it within the white psyche and white behaviour – and formulating programmes for combating racism on that basis. The New York-based Council for Interracial Books, Integrated Education (Chicago), the Foundation for Change and the Detroit-centred New Perspectives on Race were particularly active in the educational field. Writing in *Integrated Education*, Paul Goldin formulated a 'Model for racial awareness training of teachers in integrated schools' which 'pushes one (through inter-racial confrontation) into an identification with the minority position'.[10] In *Developing New Perspectives on Race*, however, Michigan's school superintendent, Patricia Bidol, advocated a more cognitive approach, emphasising that 'only whites can be racists because it is whites that have control over the institutions that create and enforce American cultural norms and values' – and it is whites who benefit from it. She distinguished, therefore, between overt (Archie Bunker type) racism and covert (unintentional) racism – and defined racism itself as 'prejudice plus institutional power'. And it was Bidol and Detroit's New Perspectives on Race who pioneered in the development of racism awareness training for educators.[11]

But the work of the Detroit Industrial Mission following the burning of the city (1967) and the rise of black militancy in DRUM (Dodge Revolutionary Union Movement) and FRUM (Ford Revolutionary Union Movement) pointed to the need to create a 'new white consciousness' through both attitudinal and behavioural change. The emphasis hitherto, wrote its Associate Director Robert W. Terry in *For Whites Only*, had been on changing attitudes to change behaviour or changing behaviour (through law, for instance) in order to change attitudes. But though both attitudes and behaviour were critical and both needed to be changed, 'attitudes will be misplaced and behavior misdirected if consciousness remains untouched'. For even the most well-intentioned person, argues Terry, taking on from where the Civil Rights Commission had left off, without being 'personally involved in overt acts of racial injustice', can perpetuate racism in institutions merely by the way the American 'cultural or belief

system... sets his orientation in the decision-making process'.
Hence, it was important to be conscious of cultural (historical,
linguistic, etc.), institutional (direct and indirect) and individual
racism all at once.[12] Cultural racism had to be examined wherever
it occurred (language, textbooks, media), 'confrontation' was a
good way of challenging personal racism and, for institutional
racism, Terry provided a model checklist designed by the Chicago
Campaign for One Society: 'Inventory of racism: how to look for
institutional racism'.*

The elements of the RAT credo were already set by the time
Judy Katz came to write her D.Ed. thesis: *Systematic Handbook
of Exercises for the Re-education of White People with Respect to
Attitudes and Behaviorisms* (1976) – except that by now she could
also draw on the Women's Movement for an even more personal
interpretation of oppression and the need for consciousness-
raising. That perspective would, in addition, also allow her (and
her followers) to distort the language, style and analysis of the
black movement and further remove racism from its exploitative
context and render it class-less.

Racism, states Katz, is indeed a white problem, and white
people had better take conscience of it – for the sake of their
own mental health. As far back as 1965, she points out, the
Commission on Mental Health described racism as the number
one mental health problem in the United States. 'Its destructive
effects severely cripple the growth and development of millions
of our citizens, young and old alike.'[13] Even before that, the
Myrdal 'report' on 'The American Dilemma' (1944) had drawn
attention to the hiatus, the schism, the rupture in the (white)
American psyche: between 'American ideals of equality, freedom,
God-given dignity of the individual, inalienable rights' and
'the practices of discrimination, humiliation, insult, denial of
opportunity to Negroes and others in a racist society'.[14] New
research had sprung up to show that racism was a 'psychological
problem... deeply imbedded in white people from a very early
age both on a conscious and an unconscious level'. And even

* This same checklist is reproduced in Katz's handbook.

black commentators, according to Katz, confirmed the diagnosis, pointed to a cure – like Whitney Young, for instance, head of the National Urban League:

> ... most people are not conscious of what racism really is. Racism is not a desire to wake up every morning and lynch a black man from a tall tree. It is not engaging in vulgar epithets... It is the day to day indignities, the subtle humiliations that are so devastating... The Kerner Commission has said that if you have been an observer; if you have stood by idly, you are racist.

Katz even rallies radical blacks like DuBois to her cause: 'Am I, in my blackness, the sole sufferer? I suffer. And yet, somehow, above the suffering, above the shackled anger that beats the bars, above the hurt that crazes, there surges in me a vast pity – pity for a people imprisoned and enthralled, hampered and made miserable for such a cause.' And more recent black militants, like Stokely Carmichael, taken out of the context of struggle: 'if the white man wants to help, he can go home and free his own people',[15] or Malcolm X: 'whites who are sincere should organize themselves and figure out some strategies to break down race prejudice that exists in white communities'.[16]

Racism, for Katz, is an 'essence' that history has deposited in the white psyche, like sexism is an 'essence' deposited in the male: oppressors oppress themselves. It is a part of the psychosocial history of white America, part of its collective unconscious. It is in American customs, institutions, language, mores – it is both conscious and unconscious at the same time, both overt and covert. There is no escaping it. And because the system is loaded in their favour, all that whites can be, even when they fight racism, is anti-racist racists: if they don't, they are just plain, common or garden racists.

Hence, any training programme that intends to bring individual whites to a consciousness of themselves should also take conscience of American culture and institutions. And it should be done at two levels at once – the cognitive or informative and the affective or emotional – at the level of thinking and at the level of feeling. The techniques that had hitherto been used in human relations training erred on one side or the other; or, like multicultural or ethnic studies, they were too other-oriented, not self-aware enough; or they were, like inter-racial encounters, too exploitative, once again, of Third World peoples. Only white on white techniques promised any success, and it was on that basis that Ms Katz had devised a systematic training programme which was influenced as much by the shift in psychotherapy towards a teaching role as the shift in education towards a counselling role. The point, after all, was not to change attitudes, but to change behaviour to change the world.

Since then (1976), the Katz technique of racism awareness training – an intensive six-stage programme of forty-eight exercises crammed into two weekends but adaptable 'to many different settings' – has become widely used in the United States, 'in school systems, with teachers, counselors and administrators, as part of Affirmative Action Programs with managers; at university communities with students, faculties, and administrators...'[17]

Part of its appeal lay, of course, with the American penchant for therapy, but part of it was also due to the political climate in which it grew: the collapse of the Black Power movement into culturalism and theological liberation, the personalisation of power in the Women's Movement and the diaspora of guilt broadcast by Israel in the wake of its imperial adventures.

Taking a leaf out of the Black Power book, Ms Katz defines racism as a 'white problem'. But whereas the white problem in Black Power ideology referred to the white capitalist power structure, in Ms Katz it is reduced to a personal one, a problem of individuals who, because they are white, have power – over non-whites. Having so established white guilt as irreversible, almost inborn, Ms Katz takes infinite pains to warn whites that they should not feel guilty, for guilt is 'a self-indulgent way to use up energy'.* On the other hand, whites suffer from racism – as much as men suffer from sexism. And 'we have learnt from the Feminist Movement that men as well as women are adversely

---

* In one of the exercises in the Handbook, Ms Katz advises the 'facilitator' that 'one way to manage feelings of guilt is to emphasize that racism is deeply ingrained in our system and that we are clearly products of our system' and then proceeds illogically to demand that one changes oneself rather than the system.

affected by oppressive sex roles'. Her programme of anti-racist sensitivity training, therefore, promises through a 'process of self-examination, change and action that we will someday liberate ourselves and our society'.

It is the sort of psychospiritual mumbo-jumbo which, because it has the resonances of the political movements of its time – capitalists have changed the world, our business is to interpret it – and, by reducing social problems to individual solutions, passes off personal satisfaction for political liberation, and then wraps it all up in a Madison Avenue sales package promising instant cure for hereditary disease, claimed the attention not just of Middle America but of a grateful state. For what better way could the state find to smooth out its social discordances while it carried on, untrammelled, with its capitalist works?

The spread of RAT

It was not, on the face of it, a package that would have appealed to the British 'character', but it seemed the logical extension to the work of a group of teachers and community workers (mostly black) whose campaign against racial symbols in children's books had derived its message and method directly from the Council for Interracial Books in the US – who were themselves proponents of RAT. Accordingly, in 1978, the group founded the Racism Awareness Programme Unit (RAPU) on the rock of Katzian teaching and was joined soon after by renegades (mostly black) from the multicultural faith, disaffected by its inability to speak to white racism. In the following year, some of the RAPU people, along with others, set up the National Committee on Racism in Children's Books and began to produce a quarterly magazine, *Dragons Teeth*. The journal's aim of investigating (and challenging) racial bias in children's books, however, was centred around black images and stereotypes. And this, over the next two years, led to a preoccupation with black identity and reclaiming the past and found its obverse in white identity and RAT.

RAT, by now, had begun to make inroads into the public sector. Some interest in human relations training (including race relations) had been evinced in official circles with the rise of black youth militancy in the mid-1970s. But these, where they did obtain – principally in education, police and probation services – took the form of the occasional conference or seminar or lecture. Industry paid a little more attention to race relations, but strictly for O and M purposes, and was therefore limited, as in the work of the Industrial Language Training Centres (ILTCs), to things like difficulties in communication between employers and employees because of language and culture.

By 1980, Nadine Peppard, who as Race Relations Adviser at the Home Office was responsible for developing race relations training, and advising the police, prison and probation services, was arguing for the type of affective techniques that had been developed in the US – at the DRRI in Florida, among others, and by the Council for Interracial Books. Although a more conscious effort, she felt, had recently been made in the 'practitioner services' to include 'the general question of attitudes and the psychology of prejudice', group work techniques, such as role-playing and training games, were still restricted to the industrial field (in the work of the ILTCs, for instance). 'A practical analysis of what is required', urged Ms Peppard, 'clearly shows that those attitudes or beliefs which underlie actual behaviour must be seen as the heart of the matter and that to construct a training scheme which tries to ignore them is to beg the question.'[18] An essential aspect of group work, she suggested, was the type of 'sensitivity training', 'consciousness-raising' or 'awareness training' that was 'a standard aspect of training' in the US. As a reference point and guide, she cited the 'experimental training programme' mounted at the University of Oklahoma by Professor Judy Katz.

In education too, the end of the 1970s saw a general shift of emphasis, often within multicultural teaching itself, from imparting information to challenging attitudes. Before students could understand other people's customs, they would, it appeared, have to be opened up to such understanding, made receptive to it, emotionally and mentally. Hence, a psychological or affective approach was necessary – for the 'affective component "leads" the cognitive in attitude change'.[19] Information, in other words, did not change people's attitudes and behaviour. On the other hand, if you changed people's attitudes and behaviour, they would be more receptive to the information. The sociological approach of multiculturalism was yielding to the psychological approach of racism awareness training.

But not till after the riots of 1981 and Scarman did either the official race relations courses or RAPU take off seriously into RAT. For one thing, Scarman had changed the terms of debate from the material effects of racism on poor blacks to the cultural effects on and the job prospects of middle-class ethnics. For another, he had, in his recommendations on local authority spending and police training, provided a breeding-ground for RAT and the reproduction of 'imagined communities'[20] and their ethno-psychological struggles for identity against ethno-centrism.*

A flurry of reports, working groups and conferences on local authority strategies to combat racial disadvantage ensued.[21] The Minister of State for Home Affairs, declaring that 'it cannot be unfair to give help to those with a special handicap',[22] pledged central government support for local authority endeavours. Race relations subcommittees, ethnic advisers, RAT courses – and even (elected) black councillors – began to spring up – in every inner-city borough in London and the conurbations. The GLC, Brent, Haringey, Hackney, Camden, Islington, Lambeth, Newham, Northants, Coventry, Bradford, Nottingham, Leicester, Sheffield, Birmingham, Greater Manchester, Liverpool – they all had their ethnic units and ethnic officers and ethnic projects, their ethnic monitoring units and, above all, as an investment in an ethnic future, their RAT courses, some of them even compulsory for local authority staff, some of them with their own RAT inspectorate. (They were also, not fortuitously, the areas that had 'rioted' or were ripe for 'riot' in 1981.)

And yet, in terms of the material conditions of the workless, homeless, school-less, welfare-less blacks of slum city, all this paroxysm of activity has not made the blindest bit of difference. The GLC Housing Committee Chairman admitted in 1984

* Identity is the personalisation of nationalism, ethnicity its group expression – all points in the same continuum.

that racial harassment on some East London estates was 'on a scale not seen in this country for 40 to 50 years'.[23] In the same year, the Policy Studies Institute survey concluded: 'the quality of the housing of black people is much worse than the quality of housing in general in this country'.[24] And unemployment for blacks, already twice the average for whites at the end of 1982, has worsened considerably.

All that has happened is that the centre of gravity of the race relations industry has moved from the central government and the CRE to the local state and with it, the black struggle, not for community and class any more, but for hand-outs and position. And racism awareness, not black power, was the new ideology.

The same tendencies to ethnicising and RATifying racism were observable in education. In 1981, the Rampton Committee of Inquiry into the Education of Children from Ethnic Minority Groups, though acknowledging racism in the teaching profession, identified racism with 'a set of attitudes and behaviour towards people of another race which is based on the belief that races are distinct' and went on to repeat the shibboleths of the American school. Racism could be 'both intentional and unintentional' and 'a well intentioned and apparently sympathetic person, may, as a result of his education, experiences or environment, have negative, patronising or stereotyped views about ethnic minority groups which may subconsciously affect his attitude and behaviour towards members of those groups'.[25] And Rampton, like Scarman, emphasised 'the particular educational needs' of particular ethnic groups – which doubtless helped the National Association of Schoolmasters and the Union of Women Teachers to pass off their 'negative, patronising or stereotyped' view of West Indian children for 'educational need': 'many West Indian children suffer from the fact they belong to a sub-culture of British culture with no readily identifiable distinctiveness' – in contrast, that is, to Asian children who are 'largely the products of a stable cultural background'.[26]

But Rampton also gave a fillip to RAT in schools. The Birmingham Education Department even got its 'multicultural outreach worker', David Ruddell, to devise its own teaching kit

– on Katzian lines, of course, but adapted to British needs (as Katz had said one could do). So that although the basic 'philosophy' remained the same ('white racism is a white problem', 'racism = prejudice plus power' and all that stuff), the reality in British inner-city schools also demanded that some attention was paid to the racist violence of the National Front (NF), at whose instigation ('intentional or unintentional') innumerable black kids had been attacked and quite a few killed. But Ruddell gets over the difficulty with his opening salvo. 'One of the barriers to the recognition and tackling of racism today', he writes in his introduction to 'Recognising racism: a filmstrip, slide and cassette presentation for racism awareness training',[27] 'is the equating of racism with strong personal prejudice, with violence and the National Front. This is a vision of racism no less widespread among the teaching and caring professions than among the rest of the public. And it is a convenient and restrictive vision, for it allows the vast majority of racist thought and action to go unchecked.' Not all black people come face to face with 'this most extreme expression of racism', but 'all black people suffer the effects of the subtle but endemic institutional racism that permeates our society and our culture'. And then, as though catching himself in the act of too brazenly writing off the experience of a whole class, Ruddell attempts to bring it back through culture – 'cultural racism comes as the luggage of our history, our language and probably our class structure' – but is baulked by the opposing culture of Scarmanite ethnicity and the cult of RAT. From there on, his pamphlet takes off into the higher reaches of psychologism to reach a screeching crescendo in Brenda Thompson's 'I am a white racist – but willing to learn'.

Another school of thought, emanating from the Inner London Education Authority, however, feel that there is an anti-racist element in multicultural education which they, as radicals, can exploit. Accordingly, they call themselves the Anti-Racist Strategies Team. But their 'Pilot Course' for teachers, for all its political posturing and anti-RAT rhetoric, has the same RAT outlook and even some of its training methods such as 'Concentric Circles: an exercise to help participants to get to know each other',

'Simulation Game', 'Brainstorming and commitments to changing institutions and practices – a sharing of ideas' (and this under 'Strategies for Action'!) and 'a heavy video' of Salman Rushdie's 'Viewpoint on Racism' for Channel 4 (which, because it errs on the side of rhetoric, as opposed to analysis, has become meat for RAT courses).[28]

The Language Training Centres for industry, on the other hand, have gone over to psychological and affective techniques without necessarily espousing the Katz philosophy. They have, for instance, moved away 'from a narrow definition of language to one which encompasses all aspects of effective communication training and probes behind the actual words used to the attitudes beneath'.[29]

The churches fell for RAT much more easily and as of second nature: its credo, after all, was no different from theirs: you must change yourself before you can change the world. Racism, in RAT eyes besides, had the look of original sin. And there was a certain set ritual and ceremony about RAT exercises, even a RAT confessional and a RAT priesthood to facilitate your entry into a raceless heaven, and an aura of piety surrounding it all. But, of course, the different church groups stress different aspects of RAT, as churches are wont to do. The Methodist Leadership Race Awareness Workshop (MELRAW), for instance, speaks of the need for 'becoming aware of the sin of racism and seeking forgiveness so that we can begin truly to work for reconciliation'.[30] On the other hand, the Ecumenical Unit for Racism Awareness Programmes (EURAP) sees 'Racism Awareness Workshops' as 'designed to help people to get free of the clutter of upbringing, of misinformation and prejudice in order to be equipped to tackle the abuse of power'. EURAP also stresses the need for periodical assessment 'to see whether effective practices have emerged'.[31] If tackling the abuse of power is the goal, the churches have the example of the World Council of Churches' material support (albeit short lived) of revolutionary movements in Africa. By comparison, they have had one-thousand nine-hundred and eighty-five years to assess whether or not changing minds changes society. But then, that is why RAT belongs in the church, but not, necessarily, the church in RAT.

Where RAT afforded immediate sanctuary to racism, however, was in the police force. The 1981 rebellions against the police and their state had discredited the police force on all counts and at every level. The Brixton 'disorders', in particular, had shown up the endemic and unrelenting racism of the force in its entirety. Scarman, in rescuing them and the state from such public and universal opprobrium, had let them off with a reprimand for 'racially prejudiced attitudes' (in the lower ranks) and a severe course of multiculturalism and attitude-training. Gratefully, the police accepted the sentence.

They had, immediately after the inner-city 'riots', made a stab at multicultural studies at the Hendon Police Training College and even appointed a black lecturer, John Fernandes, to carry it off. But, after Scarman, the police were threshing around for a training programme that would change attitudes and behaviour rather than educate and inform. A Police Working Party was set up the following year, but even before it could report (February 1983), the Metropolitan Police Force, influenced by the work of the DRRI in Florida, went off into HAT, with all its attendant simulation games, 'experiential exercises' and role-playing. At the same time it entered into a joint study and experiment in RAT with the ILTC.

Multiculturalism, meanwhile, had died at Hendon: Fernandes' attempt to find an anti-racist strain in multi-culture had brought him up against the hard rock of police racism, both at the recruit level and the senior officers' – and put paid both to Fernandes and multiculturalism. But RAT was waiting in the wings and, no sooner had Fernandes been suspended, found its way into the Police Training College – through RAPU, whose leading black light was also a member of the Police Working Party and Ethnic Adviser to Haringey all at once. The Fernandes case had, by then, blown up into an important political issue for blacks – leading to a campaign highlighting the racism not only of the police force but of the unions.[32] But RAPU and its black facilitators gave no thought or mind to dividing black struggle or placating the police with RAT placebos – reputedly for £600 a throw.*[34] But then, that is the type of commerce that RAT lends itself to.

RAT also abounds in the voluntary sector – among youth workers, community theatres, housing groups, advice centres, community workers, nursery managers, who, because of the sense of vocation and commitment that have brought them to their jobs, are particularly susceptible to RAT potions.[35] And lest their commitment should let the voluntary sector stray from their particular briefs, the Home Office has made it a point (through Voluntary Service Unit funding) to corral them into umbrella organisations in Leicestershire, West London and Manchester.

Then there is black RAT for black people – as in RAPU and LRATU (Lewisham Racism Awareness Training Unit), for instance – concerned with recovering black identity and raising black consciousness and, in the stated case of the Lewisham Unit, with enhancing and strengthening 'practices that lead to power acquisition particularly within the confines of white dominated organizations and society in general'.[36] Inter-racial RAT (not advocated in Katz) has tended to dwindle of late, but still holds sway in bodies like URJIT (Unit for Racial Justice in Tooting), whose confused thinking and flagellatory rhetoric, as expressed in Tuku Mukherjee's *I'm Not Blaming You: an anti-racist analysis*, would border on the risible but for the seriousness with which they take themselves.

Finally, there are the professional RAT operators who appear to have come out of management training and business rather than from an involvement with black issues – and make a business of RAT. Foremost among them is Linda King and Associates: Anti-Racist Consultants in Public Relations, Management and Staff Development. Founded by a black American woman, the firm has

---

* The police have gone into all sorts of RAT experiments since this, but a recent Home Office assessment on 'RAT for the police' has doubts whether RAT fits into the 'traditional culture of police training'. 'What the trainers were offering... were courses bearing upon the relationship between black people and white people. What the participants were expecting were courses dealing not just with this, but with the relationship between black people and the police.' Clearly, the police did not want to be treated as whites suffering from racism but as police suffering from blacks. And RAT did not seem to be able to help them there, but a revised RAT, it was expected, has possibilities.[33]

a leaning towards American concepts and American terminology such as 'internalised oppression', 'peoples of colour', 'parenting', etc. It even has courses for 'parenting in an anti-racist way' – for mixed couples, that is. It also has cut-price courses, and gets written up in up-market (and sexist) journals like *Cosmopolitan*, where you might be surprised to come across words like 'slavery' and 'colonialism', but not after they have been treated to RAT. 'People can't help being racist', Linda King is quoted as saying. 'It is a form of conditioning which comes from our history of slavery and colonialism and present inequalities in the economic structure. But we can unlearn it.' And, of course, you must then 'choose to put into practice what you have learned'.[37]

The business propensities of RAT have also begun to be recognised in RAPU, the first and true church. Riven by schisms and sects and internal quarrels, its missionary zeal blunted by heresies and tainted by consorting with the police, and disappointed at seeing the moneychangers arrive in their temple (when they themselves were being funded by the GLC), RAPU has fallen from grace. But its (black) high priestess, taking note of the times, has set herself up as 'Affirmata', a 'Race and Sex Equality Training and Consultancy' in the manner of King. White racism, it appears, is no longer a white problem, but a business proposition.

RAT fallacies and falsehoods

The confusion and fallacies of RAT thinking, as well as its metaphysics, have come through in the presentation. Thus racism is not, as RAT believes, a white problem, but a problem of an exploitative white power structure; power is not something white people are born into, but that which they derive from their position in a complex race/sex/class hierarchy; oppression does not equal exploitation; ideas do not equal ideology; the personal is not the political, but the political is personal;* and personal liberation is not political liberation.

---

* Changing society and changing oneself is a continuum of the same commitment – else, neither gets changed.

Some of the confusion arises from the wrong use of terms. Racism, strictly speaking, should be used to refer to structures and institutions with power to discriminate. What individuals display is racialism, prejudiced attitudes, which give them no intrinsic power over non-whites. That power is derived from racist laws, constitutional conventions, judicial precedents, institutional practices – all of which have the imprimatur of the state. In a capitalist state, that power is associated with the power of the capitalist class and racial oppression cannot be disassociated from class exploitation. And it is that symbiosis between race and class that marks the difference between the racial oppressions of the capitalist and pre-capitalist periods.

The fight against racism is, therefore, a fight against the state which sanctions and authorises it – even if by default – in the institutions and structures of society and in the behaviour of its public officials. My business is not to train the police officer out of his 'racism', but to have him punished for it if, that is, he is meant to be accountable to the community he serves. Nor does changing the attitude of an immigration officer stop him from carrying out virginity tests – but changing immigration law (or merely the instructions from the Home Office) would. Nor can (middle-class) housing officers who have undergone RAT change housing conditions for the black working class, as long as the housing stock is limited. Nor, finally, does disabusing the minds of the owners and editors of the yellow press of their 'racism' prevent them from propagating their poisonous ideology of racism (when it sells papers); only a concerted continuing, public and political campaign can do that.

RAT, however, professes to change attitudes and behaviour, and thereby power relations not in reality, but by sleight of definition: by defining personal relations as power relations.

That is not to say that RAT does not act as a catharsis for – guilt-stricken whites – or as a catalyst, opening them out to their own possibilities and those of others, leading even to a change in their individual treatment of blacks. (The unit of oppression for RAT is the abstract individual.) It might even, for a rare few, open up a path to political activism, but such people will have already had such a potential, anyway and all that RAT could have done was to catalyse it. But its pretentiousness to do more is at once a delusion of grandeur and a betrayal of political black struggle against racism and, therefore, the state.

More importantly, in terms of strategy, the distinction between racialism and racism – the distinction between power relationships between individuals (however derived) and the power relationships between classes (however mediated) – helps to distinguish between the lesser fight (because attitudes must be fought too) and the greater, and allows of different tactics for different fights, while clarifying at the same time the different strands of the same fight – so that the state does not play one against the other.

But then, the use of the term 'racism' to mean both (personal) racialism and (structural) racism – influenced partly by the use of the term sexism, which itself arose from the tendency in the Women's Movement to personalise politics by personalising power (there is no 'sexualism' in the Women's Movement)* – has passed into common usage, itself a sign of the decline of black struggle. And it would be pedantic not to accept it as such – till, that is, struggle again changes the terminology.

In the meantime, RAT has to be hoist with its own petard – it invites that sort of metaphor to explain itself, mixed and confused. Racism, for RAT, is a combination of mental illness, original sin and biological determinism (which, perhaps, explains its middle-class appeal). It is 'the number one health problem in America', according to Katz – and if her disciples in Britain have not proclaimed it as clearly for this country (they have had no Mental Health Commission to back up such a view), they have, in their therapy, certainly treated racism on that basis.

Racism, according to RAT, has its roots in white culture, and white culture, unaffected by material conditions or history, goes back to the beginning of time. Hence, racism is part of the collective unconscious, the pre-natal scream, original sin. That

---

*   The Women's Movement (in the West) personalised power – legitimately – to mean the immediate, direct and personal physical power of men over women, but then extrapolated it illegitimately to black and Third World struggle, which are connected more immediately and directly to economic exploitation and political power.[38]

is why, in the final analysis, whites can never be anything more than 'anti-racist racists'. They are racist racists to begin with, born as they are to white privilege and power; but if they do nothing about it, 'collude' (consciously or unconsciously) in the institutional and cultural practices that perpetuate racism, then they are beyond redemption and remain racist racists. If, on the other hand, they 'take up arms' – or, in this case, RAT, against such privileges – 'and opposing, end them', in their own lives, at least, they could become 'anti-racist racists'. Racists, however, they remain in perpetuity. It is a circular argument bordering on the genetic, on biological determinism: racism, in sum, is culture and culture is white and white is racist. And the only way that RAT can break out of that circle is to acknowledge the material conditions that breed racism. But then, it would not be RAT.

For that same reason, RAT eschews the most violent, virulent form of racism, the seed bed of fascism, that of the white working class – which, contrary to RAT belief, is racist precisely because it is powerless, economically and politically, and violent because the only power it has is personal power. Quite clearly, it would be hopeless to try and change the attitudes and behaviour of the poorest and most deprived section of the white population without first changing the material conditions of their existence. But, at that point of recognition, RAT averts its face and, pretending that such racism is extreme and exceptional, teaches teachers to avert their faces too. And that, in inner-city schools, where racism affords the white child the only sport and release from its hopeless reality, is to educate it for fascism. David Ruddell, Antoinette Satow and even blacks like Basil Manning and Ashok Ohri specifically deny the importance of the battles against the NF on the basis that such an extreme form of racism is not necessarily the common experience of most blacks and, in any case, lets off the whites with fighting overt racism out there and not covert racism in themselves, in their daily lives and in their institutions (meaning, really, places of work, leisure, etc.).[39] But that is because they, like the activists of the Anti-Nazi League, but for different reasons, do not see the organic connection between racism and fascism. Martin Webster, the National Activities Organiser of the

NF, saw it, though, when he declared that 'the social base of the NF is made up of the desperate and the dispossessed among the white working class'.[40]

Nor does RAT, because it ignores all but the middle class, make a distinction between the different racisms of the different classes – the naked racism of the working class, the genteel racism of the middle class and the exploitative racism of the ruling class – if only to forge different strategies and alliances to combat the different racisms.

But then, to ask RAT to do anything so political is, as a Tamil saying has it, like trying to pluck hairs from an egg. RAT plays at politics, it is a fake, a phoney – a con trick that makes people think that by moving pebbles they would start an avalanche, when all it does is to move pebbles, if that, so that the avalanche never comes.

And because, in Britain, black people have been involved in this con trick – in introducing it, practising it, reproducing it – RAT has been able to mis-appropriate black politics and black history – and degrade black struggle. For if black struggle in Britain has meant anything, it has meant the return of politics to a working-class struggle that had lost its way into economism, the return of community to class, the forging of black as a common colour of colonial and racist exploitation, and the opening out of anti-racist struggles to anti-fascism and anti-imperialism both at once.

Equally, if black and Third World feminism has meant anything, it has meant, on the one hand, a corrective to the personalisation of politics and the individualisation of power in the white Women's Movement and, on the other, an attempt to forge a unity of struggle between race, gender and class. RAT (which in Britain boasts black women in its ranks, some of them one-time activists) not only works in the opposite direction on both counts, but, in dividing the women on race lines reflects and reinforces the opposing feminist tendency to divide the 'race' on sex lines, and further disaggregates the struggle. Such fragmentation of struggle, while helping perhaps to overcome the personal paranoia that capital visits on different groups differentially, sends them off in search of their sectional identities, leaving capital itself unscathed.

Which is why even if there is no longer a classic working class to carry on a classic class struggle, the struggles of the new social forces must, for that very reason, focus on the destruction of the ruling class – for that there is, under whatever guise or name it appears before the respective movements: patriarchy, white racism, nuclearism, or is conjured up by the 'new marxists': power blocs, hegemonies, dominant factions. And particularly now, when the technological revolution has given capital a new lease of life and allowed the ruling class to disperse and dissimulate its presence – in so many avatars – while centralising and concentrating its power over the rest of us.

7

RACE, TERROR AND CIVIL SOCIETY*

White racial superiority is back on the agenda – in the guise, this
time, not of a super-race but of a super-nation, a super-people,
a chosen people on a mission to liberate the world. The Iraqi
people have to be saved from themselves – by force, necessarily,
because they know no better. And who better to do it than the
US of A, 'the land of the free and the home of the brave'? Its
stated mission? Regime change, pre-emptive strike, full-spectrum
dominance – the Bush doctrine, written in tablets of stone and
conveyed to the nation through the metaphysics of fear and the
politics of deceit, wrapped up in the vision of a Manichaean
world polarised between good and evil: Us (of A) and Them (the
sub-homines), based now on the myth that 'our way of life, our
freedom, our democracy' is the *sine qua non* of all civilisation.
'Post-modern imperialism' is how Robert Cooper, adviser to the
EU and one-time adviser to Blair, describes it. Thus, the real war,
not the phoney war, is not between civilisations, as Huntington
would have it, but against the enforced hegemony of western
civilisation. But Bush and Blair cleave to these notions despite all
the evidence to the contrary that the war has increased divisions
in the country, led to insurgency on all sides, attracted terrorists in
Iraq and furnished the basis of terrorism at home. And they still
insist that it is their values, their prosperity, their civilisation, that
the lesser beings want to destroy out of sheer envy. It is that notion
of a superior civilisation that marks out the racism of the twenty-
first century and 'embeds' it in America's imperial project.

But there are other racisms, apart from this 'civilisational
racism', that globalisation has thrown up through its displacement

* This essay was written in October 2005.

of peoples. The racism meted out to asylum seekers and migrants, even when they are white, for instance – which is passed off as xenophobia, the (natural) fear of strangers. But the other side of the 'fear or hatred of strangers' is the preservation and defence of 'our people', 'our culture', our race – nativism. If it is xenophobia, it is, in the way it denigrates and reifies people before segregating and/or deporting them, a xenophobia that bears all the marks of the old racism, except that it is not colour coded. It is racism in substance, though xeno in form. It is xeno-racism, a racism of global capital.

Then, there is the racism directed at Muslims on the basis of religion, signified this time not just by race or immigration status (refugee, asylum seeker, and so on), but by dress and appearance as well – combining the characteristics of both asylum seeker and terrorist, reflecting the combined 'war' on asylum and on terror.

The war on asylum in fact pre-dates the events of 11 September. But after the London bombings of 7 July, the two trajectories – the war on asylum and the war on terror – have converged to produce a racism which cannot tell a settler from an immigrant, an immigrant from an asylum seeker, an asylum seeker from a Muslim, a Muslim from a terrorist. We are, all of us blacks and Asians, at first sight, terrorists or illegals. We wear our passports on our faces or, lacking them, we are faceless.

Now anyone whose face is not quite the right shade, who does not walk in exactly the right way, who does not wear the right clothes for the season, can be taken as a potential suicide bomber – as law-abiding Brazilian electrician Jean Charles de Menezes learnt to his cost. And, if you are recognisably Muslim (or just believed to be Muslim), you will be subjected to official stops and searches by the police and to unofficial racial attacks and harassment in the community. The Muslim community is being driven into a siege mentality, reinforcing the very segregation that the government wants to prevent. To make matters worse, Blair is now proposing to set up a commission on integration to see whether multiculturalism has, as he thinks, been instrumental in breeding terrorists by steeping them in their own culture and so alienating them from British society. But it is precisely because

Blair refuses to accept that the war in Iraq could have played a part in breeding home-grown suicide bombers, that multiculturalism has become the whipping-boy. And the generality of commentators have gone along with him because they fail to distinguish between the multicultural society as a fact of Britain's national make-up, arrived at through the anti-racist struggles of the 1960s and 1970s, and multiculturalism as a cure-all for racial injustice, promoted by successive governments. The first, pluralism, envisages a culturally diverse society; the second, culturalism, engenders a culturally divisive society. Multiculturalism as such did not create separatism or ethnic enclaves. Culturalism did.

Culturalism, or ethnicism, as policy, was Thatcher's and Scarman's answer to the racism that in 1981 had ignited the major cities of Britain. Lord Scarman in his investigations into the Brixton riots denied point blank the existence of institutional racism, and located the cause of the riots in 'racial disadvantage', the cure for which was pouring money into ethnic projects and strengthening ethnic cultures. But, as the Institute of Race Relations pointed out at the time, the fight against racism cannot be reduced to a fight for culture. Nor does it require the state to give people their cultures; they already have them, however attenuated these cultures may be by racism. Nor is culture a commodity to be sponsored. Conversely, to sponsor culture is to reify it, reduce it to its rituals. Hence the apt description of government policies on multiculturalism as of 'the steel-band, sari, samosa' variety. Nor does learning about other people's cultures make the racists less racist. Besides, the racism that needs to be contested is not personal prejudice (which has no authority behind it) but institutionalised racism, the racism woven, over centuries of colonialism and slavery, into the structures of society and into the instruments and institutions of government, local and central. And that is why Macpherson, in his landmark report on racism, passed over the shibboleth of cultural compensation as the antidote to racism and established institutionalised racism instead as the problem that needed to be tackled. Alas, this proposal had hardly become policy before it was virtually killed off by the tabloids and the Right.

The multiculturalism, then, as practised by governments – both Labour and Conservative – was instrumental in creating ethnic enclaves. Whereas the multicultural society that has grown up in large parts of the country came out of the struggles of the black communities against racism – struggles for equal pay and against discrimination on the shop floor, struggles to make the police protect communities from racial attack, struggles for children not to be streamed or bussed out of schools, struggles to include other histories in educational curricula, struggles against the Sus laws that criminalised black youth not for an actual offence, but for being likely to commit one (just like the anti-terror laws today) and many more. And it is this multicultural Britain that needs to be defended against the Labour government's attempts to ride roughshod over those hard-won anti-racist victories which established the UK as an exemplar to the rest of Europe on integration. Instead, Britain is now showing all the signs of reducing its policies to the lowest common denominators of those in Europe: core values, enforced language classes, citizenship lessons and the like. These will all shift the UK towards the standard European model of monoculturalism.

But the Blair government, which has itself parodied anti-racism in its own culturalist policies, seems determined to undermine the fundamentals of the diverse society that has been created in this country on the basis of a segregation theory conjured up to explain the alienation of Muslim youth. This, however, is not borne out by the facts. In the first place, the segregation theory would apply, by and large, to their parents' generation. That arose from racial segregation in public housing and white flight combined with the post-industrial collapse of the factories and foundries they had manned. So when the government held out ethnic compensation, they grabbed it with both hands, creating in the process ethnic enclaves in places like Oldham and Burnley and Bradford. And the result of that segregation was the riots of 2001, not the terrorist attacks of 7/7.

Second, none of the suicide bombers could be said not to have been integrated into British society. Abdullah Jamal (formerly Jermaine Lindsay) was married to a white, English woman,

Mohammad Sidique Khan was a graduate teacher who helped children of all religions with learning difficulties, Shehzad Tanweer was also a graduate and often helped out in his father's fish-and-chip shop and Hasib Hussain was sent to Pakistan because he had fallen into the English culture of drinking and swearing.

You can't get more integrated than that, not within a couple of generations. And yet, they were prepared to take their lives and the lives of their fellow citizens in the name of Islam. One reason, therefore, must be as Mohammad Sidique Khan stated it: the invasion and destruction of Iraq. Even by a process of elimination, it is clear that whatever the prize for martyrdom in the hereafter, its cause must be sought in the degradation and hopelessness of Muslim life in the here and now – in Afghanistan, Iraq, Palestine, Bosnia, Chechnya.

Hence, the more Blair goes on denying his complicity in the destruction of Iraq and its part in the terrorist cause, the more he has to find other causes to blame 7/7 on and the more he engages in the politics of fear the more to erode democratic rights and civil liberties. Conversely, the sooner he owns up to the Iraq debacle, the sooner he will be able to address himself to the most important element in the apprehending of terrorists: intelligence, intelligence, intelligence. The trouble is that he even tailors intelligence to the cut of his political coat, and substitutes authoritarian measures in its stead.

The latest anti-terrorist bill (October 2005) bears out this point. This is the fourth counter-terrorist measure in five years and it has expanded the definition of terrorism and created new terrorist offences. The Terrorism Act 2000 had already proscribed 'terrorist organisations' which had been resisting tyrannies in their home countries or been involved in liberation movements. The Anti-Terrorism Crime and Security Act 2001, hurried through parliament after 11 September, went even further than this in that it effectively abolished *habeas corpus* and brought in detention without trial, but for foreign nationals only. Thus every refugee and asylum seeker (meaning Muslim) was not only suspected of being linked to 'international terrorism' but subject also to the stop and search powers granted by the previous Act.

The fact that the 2001 legislation applied only to foreign nationals made it open to legal challenge. So when, in December 2004, the Law Lords ruled that the indefinite detention of foreign nationals was discriminatory, Home Secretary Charles Clarke rushed through the Prevention of Terrorism Act 2005 which introduced control orders legislation (that is, house arrest and electronic tagging) to replace detention without trial.

In the event, the anti-terrorist laws net in not just Muslims who are foreign nationals, but Muslims who are British (the enemy at the gate and the enemy within). Hence, while control orders are currently invoked against foreign nationals only, the government has signalled that it will extend them to British nationals under the new counter-terror measures. And as for the proposal to hold suspects for three months without trial, this is simply internment by another name.

Then there is the Home Secretary's intended use of immigration law to set new guidelines for deportation, specifying a list of 'unacceptable behaviour' which would merit deportation, even to countries that practise torture such as Jordan and Algeria – on the undertaking, of course, that they will not torture these particular deportees ('memoranda of understanding', they call it). And there are similar counter-terrorism measures that the government is proposing to bring in through the back-door of administrative edict, by-passing parliament and open debate. The danger here is not just that a criminal justice system based on equal rights to justice is under threat from measures that corral Muslims into a separate and more punitive system, but that the very foundations of democracy are being eroded by an overbearing executive. When the executive arrogates more and more power to itself (it is after all the Home Secretary and not the courts who decides who will be detained, who will be subject to control orders and who will be returned to face torture) and expects the judiciary merely to rubber-stamp its decisions, the role of the judiciary and the respect in which it is held are undermined. Besides, the separation of powers, which silently characterises Britain's unwritten constitution and is therefore the more to be cherished and safe-guarded, is being systematically undone.

It is here, though, that the government faces its biggest challenge, because the judiciary, mindful of the constitutional settlement that accords it jurisdiction over its separate sphere, is fighting back. It is, for instance, by no means certain that the judges will accept the 'memoranda of understanding' being negotiated with countries that practise torture. If this happens, the government threatens to go over the heads of the judiciary by amending or withdrawing from the Human Rights Act so as to by-pass Article 3 of the European Convention on Human Rights which forbids the return of people to countries that practise torture and 'inhuman or degrading treatment or punishment'.

But if this is how the country's liberties are being eroded at the national level, the clause in the Terrorism Bill 2005 which makes it an offence to 'glorify' any 'act of terrorism' anywhere in the world if this 'indirectly' encourages others to emulate it, undermines liberation movements and struggles for democracy at the international level. Apart from the ambiguous use of words (and legal language should be precise), the law itself is a catch-all law, a blanket law, which does not distinguish between a liberation fighter for whom terrorism is the tactic of the last resort and a terrorist for whom terrorism is a categorical imperative.

Not to make that distinction is also not to make the distinction between state terrorism and individual terrorism. It is to absolve the state terror of an occupying power like Israel while blaming the individual terrorism of the occupied for liberation. Besides, Palestinian suicide bombers do not emerge from Islamic fundamentalism, but from the hopelessness of freeing their people any other way. The first arises from choice, the second from choicelessness. Not to distinguish between them is not only to play into the hands of Israel and justify state terror, but to avoid seeking a solution to the Palestinian question.

Israel already sets the agenda for the US and Britain on counterterrorism. It can now under the rubric that terrorism is terrorism – except when undertaken by an occupying power (on the 'four legs good, two legs bad' logic) – continue to determine the future of Palestine and the Palestinians. And the Palestinians and those who support them in their struggle for liberation will be condemned, if not prosecuted, as glorifiers and celebrants of terror.

Blair's reasoning behind all this is that 'the rules of the game have changed'. But the game is democracy and not one part of it can be changed without starting a chain reaction that damages the whole and debases British values.

And yet Blair exhorts ethnic minorities to live up to them. Aye, there's the rub. For when our rulers ask us old colonials, new refugees, desperate asylum seekers – the *sub-homines* – to live up to British values, it is not the values they exhibit that they refer to, but those of the Enlightenment which they have betrayed. Whereas we, the *sub-homines*, in our very struggle for basic human rights not only hold up basic human values, but challenge Britain to return to them. We are the litmus test of British values. The Enlightenment project, in other words, is not over till its remit of liberty, equality and fraternity is extended to include the non-white peoples of the world. That is the challenge our presence in Europe signifies.

Nor has the task of the Reformation been completed – not so long as there is a connection between Church and State (as in Britain) – which, in practice, is bound to privilege the state religion over all others. That, again, is the challenge that Islam, Hinduism, Sikhism, etc., signify.

On the other hand, states that pretend to secularism, like France, are still to distinguish between rites and rights. The religious symbols that people exhibit (like the cross and the hijab) may in their view be a rite, but from the view of the secular state, it is a right. For what, in the final analysis, defines a secular state is the paramountcy of individual liberty: my freedom is only limited by yours.

The greatest threat to western values, however, arises from globalisation and market fundamentalism – changes that affect personal morality, which, after all, is the transliteration of abstract Enlightenment values into living practice. For, the market reduces everything to a cash nexus, even personal relationships. And the transition of the welfare state to the market state, as a categorical imperative of globalisation, has altered the priorities of government from the social welfare of the people to the economic welfare of corporations, which in turn replaces moral values with commercial values: caring with indifference, altruism with selfishness, generosity with greed; and, on another level, imagination with fantasy, music with noise, art with artifice. In the absence of such values, of idealism even, young British Muslims have turned to Islam not just as a belief system but as a movement.

Once there were great movements, concerted struggles, within countries and/or internationally, against poverty and exploitation and all sorts of injustice – against capitalism and imperialism. Today there are no great working-class movements, no Third World revolutions. There is no cohering ideology that transcends national boundaries, like socialism. Hence the struggles against immiseration, against dictatorships, against foreign occupation grow up around religion, 'the sigh of the oppressed', and take on the characteristics of millenarian movements. And in the interstices of these movements arise their distortions: fundamentalism.

But Islamic fundamentalism is a passing phase, certainly in its intensity. First, because 7/7 has also blown up in the faces of the Muslim leadership and clergy in this country and demands that they take conscience of what is being done in the name of the Qur'an. Second, because it demands that Islam lives in this world and not in the next. And in the soul-searching that must follow, I see the first stirrings of the Islamic Reformation – which in the process would divert the anti-imperialist struggles of the Muslim world from individual acts of terror to mass collective action that finds common cause with the anti-globalisation, anti-imperialist movement.

Addendum: Seven theses on multiculturalism

1. In itself multiculturalism simply means cultural diversity. But, in practice, that diversity can either be progressive leading to integration, or regressive leading to separatism.

2. The force that drives multiculturalism in either direction is the reaction to racism and, in particular, the racism of the state which sets the seal on institutional and popular racism.
3. The reaction to racism is either resistance (struggle) or accommodation. (Submission is not an option, nor is terrorism.)
4. Resistance to, or struggle against, racism engenders a more just society, enlarges the democratic remit and provides the dynamics of integration that leads to a pluralist society.
5. Accommodating to racism engenders a retreat from mainstream society into the safety of one's own ethnicity and leads to separatism.
6. Anti-racism is the element that infuses politics into multiculturalism and makes it dynamic and progressive. (Note that the Race Relations Acts of 1965, 1968 and 1976 were the result of anti-racist struggles of the '60s and '70s.)
7. Remove the anti-racist element and multiculturalism descends into culturalism/ethnicism. (Witness the post-Scarman settlement that reduced the fight against racism to a fight for culture and led to ethnic enclaves.)

PART III

GLOBALISATION AND DISPLACEMENT

If racism does not stay still, neither does imperialism. With changes in the productive forces – especially the revolution in micro-technology – imperialism has taken on a new lease of life. Capital can now move to labour, seeking out at will the cheapest pool of workers and most conducive investment climate moving from one labour pool to another leaving devastation and dislocation in its wake. Development, if any, is not organic to the country, but serves the need of global capital and, at best, benefits its comprador elite, as revealed in 'Imperialism and disorganic development in the silicon age'.

The technological revolution has had enormous worldwide impact: shifted the centre of gravity of production from industrial to the service sector; pointed to the end of the nation state as an economic unit; jolted 'socialist' states into modernising; created global assembly lines and a new hierarchy of production.

These 'new circuits of imperialism' are being facilitated by a globalising mass culture, war (low intensity or direct invasion) and the imposition of conducive regimes. Today's migrants and asylum seekers are the casualties, political and economic at once, of the new imperium. 'There is no such thing as illegal immigrants, only illegal governments.'

Two of the essays, 'A black perspective on the [first] Gulf war' and 'Poverty is the new black' (which were to prove only too prophetic in terms of the later war on terror and the demonisation of the enemy within) address the domestic fall-out of globalisation – Islamophobia and rebellion of the dispossessed – and point activists towards new parameters of struggle.

8

IMPERIALISM AND DISORGANIC DEVELOPMENT IN THE SILICON AGE*

One epoch does not lead tidily into another. Each epoch carries with it a burden of the past – an idea perhaps, a set of values, even bits and pieces of an outmoded economic and political system. And the longer and more durable the previous epoch the more halting is the emergence of the new.

The classic centre–periphery relationship as represented by British colonialism – and the inter-imperialist rivalries of that period – had come to an end with the Second World War. A new colonialism was emerging with its centre of gravity in the United States of America; a new economic order was being fashioned at Bretton Woods. Capital, labour, trade were to be unshackled of their past inhibitions – and the world opened up to accumulation on a scale more massive than ever before. The instruments of that expansion – the General Agreement on Tariffs and Trade, the International Monetary Fund and the World Bank – were ready to go into operation.[1] Even so, it took the capitalist nations of Western Europe, Japan and the United States some twenty-five years to rid themselves of the old notions of national boundaries and 'lift the siege against multinational enterprises so that they might be permitted to get on with the unfinished business of developing the world economy' (Rockefeller). The Trilateral Commission was its acknowledgement.

Britain, hung up in its colonial past, was to lag further behind. It continued, long after the war, to seek fresh profit from an old

---

* This essay was written in October 1979, and is a development and reformulation of a paper originally given at the 'Three Worlds or One?' conference, Berlin, June 1979.

relationship – most notably through the continued exploitation of colonial labour, but this time at the centre. So that when the rest of Europe, particularly Germany, was reconstructing its industries and infrastructure with a judicious mix of capital and labour (importing labour as and when required), Britain, with easy access to cheap black labour and easy profit from racial exploitation, resorted to labour-intensive production. And it was in the nature of that colonial relationship that the immigrants should have come as settlers and not as labourers on contract.

The history of British immigration legislation including the present calls for repatriation is the history of Britain's attempt to reverse the colonial trend and to catch up with Europe and the new world order.

That order, having gone through a number of overlapping phases since the war, now begins to emerge with distinctive features. These, on the one hand, reflect changes in the international division of labour and of production, involving the movement of capital to labour (from centre to periphery) which in turn involves the movement of labour as between the differing peripheries. On the other hand, they foreshadow a new industrial revolution based on microelectronics – and a new imperialism, accelerating the 'disorganic' development of the periphery. And it is to these new developments in capitalist imperialism that I want to address myself, moving between centre and periphery – and between peripheries – as the investigation takes me, bearing in mind that these are merely notes for further study.

The early post-war phase of this development need not detain us here, except to note that the industrialisation undertaken by the newly independent countries of Asia and Africa (Latin America had begun to industrialise between the wars) put them further in hock to foreign capital, impoverished their agriculture and gave rise to a new bourgeoisie and a bureaucratic elite.[2] The name of the game was import substitution, its end the favourable balance of trade, its economic expression state capitalism, its political raison d'être bourgeois nationalism. Not fortuitously, this period coincided with the export of labour to the centre.

Capital and labour migration

By the 1960s, however, the tendency of labour to move to capital was beginning to be reversed. The post-war reconstruction of Europe was over, manufacturing industries showed declining profit margins and capital was looking outside for expansion. The increasing subordination of Third World economies to multinational corporations made accessible a cheap and plentiful supply of labour in the periphery, in Asia in particular. Advances in technology – in transport, communications, information and data processing and organisation – rendered geographical distances irrelevant and made possible the movement of plant to labour, while ensuring centralised control of production. More importantly, technological development had further fragmented the labour process, so that the most unskilled worker could now perform the most complex operations.

For its part, the periphery, having failed to take off into independent and self-sustained growth through import substitution,[3] turned to embrace export-oriented industrialisation – the manufacture of textiles, transistors, leather goods, household appliances and numerous consumer items. But capital had first to be assured that it could avail itself of tax incentives, repatriate its profits, obtain low-priced factory sites and, not least, be provided with a labour force that was as docile and undemanding as it was cheap and plentiful. Authoritarian regimes, often set up by American intervention, provided those assurances – the Free Trade Zones provided their viability.[4]

The pattern of imperialist exploitation was changing – and with it, the international division of production and of labour. The centre no longer supplied the manufactured goods and the periphery the raw materials. Instead the former provided the plant and the know-how while the latter supplied primary products and manufactures.

The parameters of that new economic order are best expressed in the purpose and philosophy of the Trilateral Commission. Founded in 1973, under the sponsorship of David Rockefeller of the Chase Manhattan Bank, the Commission brought together representatives of the world's most powerful banks, corporations, communications conglomerates, and international organisations plus top politicians and a few 'free' trade unions and trade union federations (from North America, Europe and Japan) to reconcile the contradictions of transnational capital, while at the same time checking 'the efforts of national governments to seize for their own countries a disproportionate share of the benefits generated by foreign direct investment'.[5] As Richard Falk puts it: 'The vistas of the Trilateral Commission can be understood as the ideological perspective representing the transnational outlook of the multinational corporation' which 'seeks to subordinate territorial politics to non-territorial economic goals'.[6]

And for the purpose of that subordination, it was necessary to distinguish between the differing peripheries: the oil-producing countries and the 'newly industrialising' countries, and the under-developed countries proper (which the Commission terms the 'Fourth World').

The implications of this new imperial ordinance for labour migration – not, as before, between centre and periphery but as between the peripheries themselves – are profound, the consequences for these countries devastating. The oil-rich Gulf states, for instance, have sucked in whole sections of the working population, skilled and semi-skilled, of South Asia, leaving vast holes in the labour structure of these countries. Moratuwa, a coastal town in Sri Lanka, once boasted some of the finest carpenters in the world. Today there are none – they are all in Kuwait or in Muscat or Abu Dhabi. And there are no welders, masons, electricians, plumbers, mechanics – all gone. And the doctors, teachers, engineers – they have been long gone – in the first wave of post-war migration to Britain, Canada, USA, Australia, in the second to Nigeria, Zambia, Ghana. Today Sri Lanka, which had the first free health service in the Third World and some of the finest physicians and surgeons, imports its doctors from Marcos' Philippines. What that must do to the Filipino people is another matter, but all that we are left with in Sri Lanka is a plentiful supply of unemployed labour, which is now being herded into the colony within the neo-colony, the Free Trade Zone.

The first countries to industrialise in South East Asia were Taiwan in the 1950s and, in the 1960s, South Korea, Singapore and Hong Kong. Taiwan and South Korea were basically offshore operations of the USA and Japan – and, by virtue of their strategic importance to America, were able to develop heavy industry (ship-building, steel, vehicles) and chemicals in addition to the usual manufacture of textiles, shoes, electrical goods, etc. And by the middle of the 1970s, these two countries had gone over from being producers of primary products to producers of manufactured goods. Singapore's industrialisation includes ship repair (Singapore is the fourth largest port in the world) and the construction industry. Hong Kong, the closest thing to a 'free economy', is shaped by the world market.

What all these countries could offer multinational capital, apart from a 'favourable climate of investment' (repatriation of profit, tax holidays, etc.), was authoritarian regimes with a tough line on dissidence in the workforce and a basic infrastructure of power and communications. What they did not have was a great pool of unemployed workers. That was provided by the neighbouring countries.

Hong Kong uses all the migrant labour available in the region, including workers from mainland China, and is currently negotiating with the Philippines government for the import of Filipino labour. South Korea's shortage of labour, by the very nature of its development, has been in the area of skilled workers. But it is Singapore which is the major employer of contract labour – from Malaysia mostly (40 per cent of the industrial workforce) and also from Indonesia, the Philippines and Thailand – and that under the most horrendous conditions. For apart from the usual strictures on *Gastarbeiters* that we are familiar with in Europe, such as no right of settlement, no right to change jobs without permission and deportation if jobless, Singapore also forbids these workers to marry, except after five years, on the showing of a 'clean record', and then with the permission of the government – and that on signing a bond that both partners will agree to be sterilised after the second child is born. Lee Kuan Yew, with a nod to Hitler, justifies the policy on the ground that 'a multiple replacement rate right at the bottom' leads to 'a gradual lowering of the general quality of the population'.[7] Their working conditions too are insanitary and dangerous and makeshift shacks on worksites (like the bidonvilles) provide their only housing.

And yet the plight of the indigenous workers of these countries is not much better. The economic miracle is not for them. Their lives contrast glaringly with the luxury apartments, automobiles and swinging discos of the rich. To buy a coffee and sandwich on a thoroughfare of Singapore costs a day's wage, in South Korea 12- and 13-year-old girls work 18 hours a day, 7 days a week, for £12 a month, and Hong Kong is notorious for its exploitation of child labour.[8]

How long the repressive regimes of these countries can hold down their workforce on behalf of international capital is a moot point – but multinationals do not wait to find out. They do not stay in one place. They gather their surplus while they may and move on to new pastures their miracles to perform.

The candidates for the new expropriation were Indonesia, Thailand, Malaysia and the Philippines whose economies were primarily based on agriculture and on extractive industries such as mining and timber. Like the first group of countries they too could boast of authoritarian regimes – ordained by the White House, fashioned by the Pentagon and installed by the CIA – which could pave the way for international capital. Additionally, they were able to provide the cheap indigenous labour which the other group had lacked – and the Free Trade Zones to go with it. What they did not have, though, was a developed infrastructure.

Multinationals had already moved into these countries by the 1970s and some industrialisation was already under way. What accelerated that movement, however, was the tilt to cheap labour, as against a developed infrastructure, brought about by revolutionary changes in the production process.

To that revolution, variously described as the new industrial revolution, the third industrial revolution and the post-industrial age, I now turn – not so much to look at labour migration as labour polarisation – between the periphery and the centre, and within the centre itself, and its social and political implications in both.

Capital and labour in the silicon age

What has caused the new industrial revolution and brought about a qualitative leap in the level of the productive forces is the silicon chip or, more accurately, the computer-on-a-chip, known as the microprocessor. (You have already seen them at work in your digital watch and your pocket calculator.)

The ancestry of the microprocessor need not concern us here, except to note that it derives from the electronic transistor, invented by American scientists in 1947 – which in turn led to the semi-conductor industry in 1952–3 and in 1963, to the integrated circuit industry. Integrated circuits meant that various electronic elements such as transistors, resistors, diodes, etc. could all be combined on the tiny chip of semi-conductor silicon, 'which in the form of sand is the world's most common element next to oxygen'.[9] But if industrially the new technology has been in existence for sixteen years, it is only in the last five that it has really taken off. The periodisation of its development is important because it is not unconnected with the post-war changes in the international division of production and of labour and the corresponding movements and operations of the multinational corporations.

The microprocessor is to the new industrial revolution what steam and electricity was to the old – except that where steam and electric power replaced human muscle, microelectronics replaces the brain. That, quite simply, is the measure of its achievement. Consequently, there is virtually no field in manufacturing, the utilities, the service industries or commerce that is not affected by the new technology. Microprocessors are already in use in the control of power stations, textile mills, telephone-switching systems, office-heating and typesetting as well as in repetitive and mechanical tasks such as spraying, welding, etc. in the car industry. Fiat, for instance, has a television commercial which boasts that its cars are 'designed by computers, silenced by lasers and hand-built by robots' – to the strains of Figaro's aria (from Rossini). Volkswagen designs and sells its own robots for spot welding and handling body panels between presses. Robots, besides, can be re-programmed for different tasks more easily than personnel can be re-trained. And because microprocessors can be re-programmed, automated assembly techniques could be introduced into areas hitherto immune to automation, such as batch production (which incidentally constitutes 70 per cent of the production in British manufacturing). From this has grown the idea of linking together a group of machines to form an unmanned manufacturing system, which could produce anything from diesel engines to machine tools and even aeroengines. And 'once the design of the unmanned factory has been standardised, entire factories could be produced on a production line based on a standard design'.[10] The Japanese are close to achieving the 'universal factory'.

A few examples from other areas of life will give you some idea of the pervasiveness of microelectronics. In the retail trade, for instance, the electronic cash register, in addition to performing its normal chores, monitors the stock level by keeping tabs on what has been sold at all the terminals and relays that information to computers in the warehouse which then automatically move the necessary stocks to the shop. A further line-up between computerised check-outs at stores and computerised bank accounts will soon do away with cash transactions, directly debiting the customer's account and crediting the store's. Other refinements such as keeping a check on the speed and efficiency of employees have also grown out of such computerisation – in Denmark, for instance (but it has been resisted by the workers).

There are chips in everything you buy – cookers, washing machines, toasters, vacuum cleaners, clocks, toys, sewing machines, motor vehicles – replacing standard parts and facilitating repair: you take out one chip and put in another. One silicon chip in an electronic sewing machine for example replaces 350 standard parts.

But it is in the service sector, particularly in the matter of producing, handling, storing and transmitting information, that silicon technology has had its greatest impact. Up to now automation has not seriously affected office work which, while accounting for 75 per cent of the costs in this sector (and about half the operating costs of corporations), is also the least productive, thereby depressing the overall rate of productivity. One of the chief reasons for this is that office work is divided into several tasks (typing, filing, processing, retrieving, transmitting and so forth) which are really inter-connected. The new technology not only automates these tasks but integrates them. For example, the word processor, consisting of a keyboard, a visual display unit, a storage memory unit and a print-out, enables one typist to do the work of four while at the same time reducing the skill she needs. Different visual display units (VDUs) can then be linked to the company's mainframe computer, to other computers within the company (via computer network systems) and even to those in other countries through satellite communication – all of which makes possible the electronic mail and the electronic funds transfer (EFT) which would dispense with cash completely.

What this link-up between the office, the computer and telecommunications means is the 'convergence' of previously separate industries. 'Convergence' is defined by the Butler Cox Foundation as 'the process by which these three industries are coming to depend on a single technology. They are becoming, to all intents and purposes, three branches of a single industry'.[11] But 'convergence' to you and me spells the convergence of corporations, horizontal (and vertical) integration, monopoly. A 'convergence' of Bell Telephones and IBM computers would take over the world's communication facilities. (Whether the anti-trust laws in America have already been bent to enable such a development I do not know, but it is only a matter of time.)

Underscoring the attributes and applications of the microprocessor is the speed of its advance and the continuing reduction in its costs. Sir Ieuan Maddock, Secretary of the British Association for the Advancement of Science, estimates that 'in terms of the gates it can contain, the performance of a single chip has increased ten thousandfold in a period of 15 years'. And of its falling cost, he says, 'the price of each unit of performance has reduced one hundred thousandfold since the early 1960s'.[12]

'These are not just marginal effects,' continues Sir Ieuan, 'to be absorbed in a few per cent change in the economic indicators – they are deep and widespread and collectively signal a fundamental and irreversible change in the way the industrialised societies will live... Changes of such magnitude and speed have never been experienced before.'[13]

I am not arguing here against technology. Anything that improves the lot of mankind is to be welcomed. But in capitalist society such improvement redounds to the few at cost to the many. That cost has been heavy for the working class in the centre and heavier for the masses in the periphery. What the new industrial revolution predicates is the further degradation of work where, as Braverman so brilliantly predicted, thought itself is eliminated from the labour process,[14] the centralised ownership of the means of production, a culture of reified leisure to mediate discontent and a political system incorporating the state, the multinationals, the trade unions, the bureaucracy and the media, backed by the forces of 'law and order' with microelectronic surveillance at their command. For in as much as liberal democracy was the political expression of the old industrial revolution, the corporate state is the necessary expression of the new. The qualitative leap in the productive forces, ensnared in capitalist economics, demands such an expression. Or, to put it differently, the contradiction between the heightened centralisation in the ownership of the means of production – made possible not only by the enormous increase in the level of productivity but also by the technological nature of that increase – and the social nature of production (however attenuated) can no longer be mediated by liberal democracy but by corporatism, with an accompanying corporate culture, and state surveillance to go with it.

But nowhere is there in the British literature with the exception of the CIS report,[15] any hint of a suggestion that the new industrial revolution, like the old, has taken off on the backs of the workers in the peripheries – that it is they who will provide the 'living dole' for the unemployed of the West. For, the chip, produced in the pleasant environs of 'Silicon Valley' in California, has its circuitry assembly in the toxic factories of Asia. Or, as a Conservative Political Centre publication puts it, 'while the manufacture of the chips requires expensive equipment in a dust-free, air-conditioned environment, little capital is necessary to assemble them profitably into saleable devices. And it is the assembly that creates both the wealth and the jobs.'[16]

Initially the industry went to Mexico, but Asia was soon considered the cheaper. (Besides 'Santa Clara was only a telex away'.) And even within Asia the moves were to cheaper and cheaper areas: from Hong Kong, Taiwan, South Korea and Singapore in the 1960s, to Malaysia in 1972, Thailand in 1973, the Philippines and Indonesia in 1974 and soon to Sri Lanka. 'The manager of a plant in Malaysia explained how profitable these moves had been: "one worker working one hour produces enough to pay the wages of 10 workers working one shift plus all the costs of materials and transport".'[17]

But the moves the industry makes are not just from country to country but from one batch of workers to another within the country itself. For, the nature of the work – the bonding under a microscope of tiny hair-thin wires to circuit boards on wafers of silicon chip half the size of a fingernail – shortens working life. 'After 3 or 4 years of peering through a microscope,' reports Richael Grossman, 'a worker's vision begins to blur so that she can no longer meet the production quota.'[18] But if the microscope does not get her ('grandma where are your glasses' is how electronic workers over 25 are greeted in Hong Kong), the bonding chemicals do.[19] And why 'her'? Because they are invariably women. For, as a Malaysian brochure has it, 'the manual dexterity of the oriental female is famous the world over. Her hands are small and she works fast with extreme care. Who, therefore, could be better qualified by nature and inheritance to contribute to the efficiency of a bench assembly production line than the oriental girl?'[20]

To make such intense exploitation palatable, however, the multinationals offer the women a global culture – beauty contests, fashion shows, cosmetic displays and disco dancing – which in turn enhances the market for consumer goods and western beauty products. Tourism reinforces the culture and reinforces prostitution (with package sex tours for Japanese businessmen), drug selling, child labour. For the woman thrown out of work on the assembly line at an early age, the wage earner for the whole extended family, prostitution is often the only form of livelihood left.[21]

A global culture then, to go with a global economy, serviced by a global office the size of a walkie-talkie held in your hand[22] – a global assembly line run by global corporations that move from one pool of labour to another, discarding them when done – high technology in the centre, low technology in the peripheries – and a polarisation of the workforce within the centre itself (as between the highly skilled and unskilled or de-skilled) and as between the centre and the peripheries, with qualitatively different rates of exploitation that allow the one to feed off the other – a corporate state maintained by surveillance for the developed countries, authoritarian regimes and gun law for the developing. That is the size of the new world order.

Disorganic development

But it is not without its contradictions. Where those contradictions are sharpest, however, are where they exist in the raw – in the peripheries.[23] For what capitalist development has meant to the masses of these countries is increased poverty, the corruption of their cultures, and repressive regimes. All the GNP they amass for their country through their incessant labour leaves them poorer than before. They produce what is of no real use to them and yet cannot buy what they produce – neither use value nor exchange value – neither the old system nor the new.

And how they produce has no relation to how they used to produce. They have not grown into the one from the other. They have not emerged into capitalist production but been flung into it – into technologies and labour processes that reify them and into social relations that violate their customs and their codes. They work in the factories, in town, to support their families, their extended families, in the village – to contribute to the building of the village temple, to help get a teacher for the school, to sink a well. But the way of their working socialises them into individualism, nuclear families, consumer priorities, artefacts of capitalist culture. They are caught between two modes, two sets, of social relations, characterised by exchange value in the one and use value in the other – and the contradiction disorients them and removes them from the centre of their being. And not just the workers, but the peasants too have not escaped the capitalist mode. What it has done is to wrench them from their social relations and their relationship with the land. Within a single life-time, they have had to exchange sons for tractors and tractors for petrochemicals. And these things too have taken them from themselves in space and in time.

And what happens to all this production, from the land and from the factories? Where does all the GNP go – except to faceless foreign exploiters in another country and a handful of rich in their own? And who are the agents but their own rulers? In sum, what capitalist development has meant to the masses of these countries is production without purpose, except to stay alive; massive immiseration accompanied by a wholesale attack on the values, relationships, gods that made such immiseration bearable; rulers who rule not for their own people but for someone else – a development that makes no sense, has no bearing on their lives, is disorganic.

To state it at another level. The economic development that capital has super-imposed on the peripheries has been unaccompanied by capitalist culture or capitalist democracy. Whereas, in the centre, the different aspects of capitalism (economic, cultural, political) have evolved gradually, organically, out of the centre's own history, in the periphery the capitalist mode of production has been grafted on to the existing cultural and political order. Peripheral capitalism is not an organised body of connected, inter-dependent parts sharing a common life – it is not an organism. What these countries exhibit, therefore, is not just 'distorted' or 'disarticulated' development (Samir Amin), but disorganic development: an economic system at odds with the cultural and political institutions of the people it exploits. The economic system, that is, is not mediated by culture or legitimated by politics, as in the centre. The base and the superstructure do not complement and reinforce each other. They are in fundamental conflict – and exploitation is naked, crude, unmediated – although softened by artefacts of capitalist culture and capitalist homilies on human rights. And that contradiction because of capitalist penetration, runs right through the various modes of production comprising the social formation. At some point, therefore, the political system has to be extrapolated from the superstructure and made to serve as a cohesive – and coercive – force to maintain the economic order of things. The contradiction between superstructure and base now resolves into one between the political regime and the people, with culture as the expression of their resistance. And it is cultural resistance which, in Cabral's magnificent phrase, takes on 'new forms (political, economic, armed) in order fully to contest foreign domination'.[24]

But culture in the periphery is not equally developed in all sectors of society. It differs as between the different modes of production but, again as Cabral says, it does have 'a mass character'. Similarly at the economic level, the different exploitations in the different modes confuse the formal lines of class struggle but the common denominators of political oppression make for a mass movement. Hence the revolutions in these countries are not necessarily class, socialist, revolutions – they do not begin as such anyway. They are not even nationalist revolutions as we know them. They are mass movements with national and revolutionary components – sometimes religious, sometimes secular, often both, but always against the repressive political state and its imperial backers.

9

NEW CIRCUITS OF IMPERIALISM*

Imperialism is still the highest stage of capitalism – only, the circuits of imperialism have changed with the changes wrought in capital by the revolution in the production process. The magnitude of that revolution, as fundamental as that of the Industrial Revolution, and as comprehensive and cumulative, can only be quantified when it finally comes to rest. But even its initial tremors, like those of the Industrial Revolution, have challenged the social order, shifted the gravitational pull of employment from one sector (industrial this time) to another (the service sector) and pointed to the end of the existing polity (today, the nation state) as a viable economic unit. And it has jolted the 'socialist' states of the Soviet Union and China into modernising their economies, into putting economics back in command. What beggars comparison, however, is that where once steam and subsequently electricity replaced muscle power, today microelectronics, in Sir Ieuan Maddock's grand metaphor, replaces the brain.[1] Hitherto it has largely been the energy component of labour that was being replaced, today it is more the skill component. The 'dead labour' that goes into computers is not so much labour by hand as labour by brain.

And Prometheus is unbound again. Capital is freed from the exigencies of labour. Not only can it do with less labour now – but with less variety of labour – with the unskilled or semi-skilled at one end of the production process and the highly skilled at the other. The skills have been taken into the machines, leaving it to the unskilled to operate them and the highly skilled to programme them. Different skills, besides, can be combined and fed into the same computer – as in the diagnostic machines used in medicine.

* This essay was written in April 1989.

Different crafts can be merged as in the newspaper industry, where the arts of the compositor, the typesetter and the printer have been collapsed into a VDU and computer – thereby also reducing the space required to house them from a factory floor to a desktop. Faced with labour 'troubles', TV companies are resorting to news-gathering equipment which can combine the functions of sound, lighting and camera into one unit, and so do away with 'the crew system'.

The heavy labour-intensive industries of the period of industrial capitalism – iron, steel, ship-building – are dead or dying or have passed on to the 'newly industrialising countries' of the Third World where labour is still cheap and plentiful or could be made to be so. Coal is a-dying. Industries, that is, which employed thousands of workers on the factory floor and in the pits and bound them in communities of resistance to capital are gone or going from the centre – and traditional labour organisations rendered ineffectual and effete.

Even in those industries that are left behind, such as ship-building, computer-aided design (CAD) and computer-aided manufacture (CAM) have taken over a considerable part of the work of construction. Some of the construction, in fact, takes place not in the dock but in the factory. At the Harland and Wolff shipyard various parts of the ship are pre-constructed before being welded together in the dock. In coalmining face-workers' skills are now being built into machines and the supervision of these machines then transmitted to the surface via MINOS (mine operating system) and MIDAS (machine information display and automation system). And in the car industry robots are taking over much of the assembly line work of factory production. In Japan robots make robots.

The factories themselves can now be broken down into smaller units and scattered all over the world – in global assembly lines – stretching (in the microelectronics industry, for instance) from Silicon Valley in California or Silicon Glen in Scotland to the Export Processing Zones (EPZs) of Taiwan, Singapore, Malaysia, Sri Lanka. Or, in the car industry, different parts of a single motor can be made in different factories spread over Europe across the Atlantic through to the Pacific before being assembled and re-assembled and pre-assembled in any given city of the world. 'The Ford Fiesta assembled at Dagenham', wrote Robin Murray in 1987, 'used transmissions from Bordeaux, road wheels from Genk, body panels from Spain and suspension components from West Germany.'[2] And Mitsubishi cars assembled as Lancers in Thailand, with transmissions from the Philippines, doors from Malaysia and sundry other parts from Indonesia, are rebadged as Dodge and Plymouth Colts for delivery to Chrysler in Canada.[3]

The growing use of flexible manufacturing systems (FMS), whereby plants can be orientated from one type of product to another without re-tooling, allows capital to gear production to the needs of the market. In Pirelli's new electric-wire-making factory in Wales, for instance, FMS has enabled production to be switched from one type of wire to another or one colour casing to another within minutes.[4] And the introduction of FMS in Boeing's Renton plant in Seattle has enabled it to turn out a 737 every one and a half days.[5]

Changes in the production process, that is, have freed industrial capital (industrial, banking, they are all one now[*] except in the way they are deployed) from spatial strictures, given it mobility of plant and flexibility of production, enabling it to move the factory to the market, custom-build the product for the consumer or, as in the garment industry, come back to its home-base when the design, layout and cutting techniques have become incorporated into a computer and do not need the cheap labour of the periphery any more. *Machina volente*, capital can take up its factory and walk any time labour gives it trouble or proves costly. Ford has recently moved its Sierra plant out of Dagenham, with its culture of trade union militancy, to the folding colliery town of 'quiet, conservative, Catholic' Genk to produce twice the number of cars with less than a fourth the number of shop stewards and twice the

---

[*] 'Some large MNCs develop and control their own transnational banking networks... There are large Swiss banks which are subsidiaries of US MNCs (Dow Banking, Bank Firestone, Bankinvest, Transinfer Bank, Philip Brothers)... The Schnieder group has shares in Belgian, West German and Italian banks, and its own bank, BUE, has subsidiaries in Switzerland, Luxembourg and the USA... Dow Chemical has a network of eight banks covering nine countries.'[6]

number of robots.[7] And in the Midlands Asian garment-makers have combined new manufacturing techniques with cheap Asian female labour to undercut garment imports from Asia.

Hierarchies of production

It is not enough to understand these changes in terms of the globalisation of production and the new international division of labour any more without also examining the hierarchies of production in which these are set – with the developed countries (DCs) holding on to the new high-technology industries while 'devolving' the older industries of steel manufacture, ship-building and the like to the newly industrialising countries (NICs) and relegating light industries (textiles, toys, footwear) and the unskilled, 'back-end' work of assembling and testing chips to the under-developed countries proper (UDCs). It is not, of course, a fixed water-tight division: there is constant movement and overlap, especially as between the DCs and the NICs, in terms of the commodities produced and, to that extent, of their respective functions. But the gap between them never closes. Today's NICs do not become tomorrow's DCs – and if they do, it will be only because the DCs have moved on to higher things, become HDCs (highly developed countries) – and the chances of the UDCs becoming NICs are even more remote. A country or two might escape its particular category – especially those that are into an industry as escalating as electronics – but the category itself cannot move out of its appointed station in the hierarchy of capital. If there is movement, it is no more than the movement of a conveyor belt that runs on fixed stations. It is the belt that moves, not the stations; if they did, the whole system would collapse. There cannot, in other words, be a world of classless capitalism, where all the nations are equally capitalist.

'Unrealistic aspirations'...

Countries like South Korea and Taiwan, for instance – even after long years of proving themselves relatively stable, reliable, hospitable (to American capital) and cast in America's image – have not been able to break out of the impasse of low and medium technology because of American and Japanese refusal to forgo technological superiority and/or market control. South Korea, the more advanced of the two countries, has been into wafer fabrication,* 'the front-end' of the industry, for some time, but the memory chips it produces do not have the range or the market that the Japanese have – and South Korea is not going to be given them because of 'intellectual property problems, trade barriers and a reluctance to talk about exchanging ideas, not to mention technology'.[8] Similarly, America has refused to countenance South Korea's ambitions to take off into the aerospace industry and has suggested it sticks to making components instead.[9]

Taiwan set up a whole science park seven years ago to woo 'high-tech' entrepreneurs into helping it 'leapfrog' from a low- to a medium- and hi-tech economy. But, despite enticing seventy-three research-based companies (most of them in electronics, most of them American) into the park and 'allaying the fears of US companies about having their designs or technology, or both, being ripped off' by bringing in a 'US semi-conductor industry veteran' to run the company, Taiwan seems to have leapfrogged into making chips 'imitating animal sounds – barks, bleats, miaows and roars – in toys'.[10]

Singapore, after twenty years of assembling and testing chips in the 'back-end' of the industry (and twenty years is a long time in electronics), has just about made it into wafer fabrication – as has Hong Kong. But they are both alleged to lack the expertise and the market to inveigle sizeable foreign investment on which to take off.

Brazil and India are the other two NICs that are said to be headed for the big time – because of their export capacity in heavy industry such as iron, steel, ship-building and machine tools. But Brazil is strangled by debt ($115 billion) and inflation (934 per cent),[11] while India, though comparatively debt-free and

---

* Wafer fabrication or 'fab' is the etch-printing of integrated circuits (ICs) on to a wafer of silicon.

in advance of other NICs in terms of traditional industry, is still to enter the silicon age.

And Mexico, though it has shown sustained growth over the past thirty years, seems to have owed much of its success to the discovery of oil, on the one hand, and its border economy (based on in-bond assembly plants, *maquiladoras*, literally 'golden mills'), on the other – neither of which can be counted on for permanent prosperity, one being subject to the vagaries of nature, the other to the vagaries of American car production. For although the *maquiladoras* – an EPZ by any other name... – also host the manufacture of various electronic goods such as TVs and air-conditioners, their real importance is that, by providing access to a cheap off-shore labour reserve in-shore ('just 1,546 miles from Detroit'), they help to maintain the competitive edge of the American car industry. 'The bottom line is this,' declared Rex Maingot of American Industries Inc. to a conference of business executives at Expo Maquila '86, 'your cost per Mexican worker is 69 cents an hour versus at least $9 an hour in the States – a saving of $15,000 a year per worker. You can see how down here a GM car can be made competitive with the Japanese.'[12] And judging from Mexico's slow death by debt ($104 billion) and negative growth (–0.5 per cent in 1988),[13] it is more likely that the country instead of ascending to the DCs is sinking into the UDCs.

... and realistic development

But 'unrealistic aspirations' apart, the DCs do not mind the NICs excelling them in yesterday's industries. Brazil, Mexico, South Korea and Taiwan have all become major exporters of steel in the last fifteen years and Brazil today is the third largest in the world. Over half the EEC's iron ore needs, besides, is met by Brazil – at 'banana prices', it might be added. South Korea has recently overtaken Japan as the foremost ship-building nation, with Taiwan following close behind. Mexico, Brazil, Korea, Singapore, Hong Kong, Taiwan are all manufacturers and exporters of electrical goods and transport equipment. And almost all the NICs have taken off, and are able to fall back on, textile and garment manufacture – a fact curiously reminiscent of Britain's own take-off into the Industrial Revolution on cotton.

'In 1960', comments Nigel Harris, 'the old-established core of the world system in North America and Western Europe produced 71 per cent of the world's products and 78 per cent of manufacturing output. Twenty-one years later, those respective shares had fallen to 60 and 59 per cent. The shares of the United States and Britain – 49 and 53 per cent in 1960 – were by 1981 down to 35 and 33 per cent.' The World Bank, he concludes, 'estimates that the trend will reduce the share of Western Europe and North America in manufacturing to under half by 1990'.[14]

Judged on the basis of industrialisation, the NICs of Latin America and South East Asia have doubtless leapt into the twentieth century in a bound. But to argue that they are in competition with the DCs is to overlook the fact that the DCs, having entered into a whole new ball game, have willingly ceded their old ball-park to the NICs.

Judged on the basis of their export capacity in manufactured goods, the NICs could even be seen as 'fast closing the gap with the more developed countries'.[15] The point, however, is that the DCs have moved into a whole new era, a whole new realm of production – with electronics and lasers and bio-genetics and nuclear power, and synthetic 'raw' materials replacing cotton and steel and copper – and the gap between them (the DCs) and the NICs is become epochal.

Judged on the basis of their GDPs,* the NICs, of South East Asia in particular, may be seen as displaying accelerated growth. But how has that growth benefited the mass of people? Where has it lifted them from the morass of poverty and hunger and hopelessness in which previous centuries of subjugation had sunk them? Where (with apologies to Eliot) is the development we have lost in growth?

---

*   Between 1973 and 1984 the annual growth rate of GDP for South Korea for instance, was 7.2 per cent, Taiwan 8.5 per cent, Hong Kong 9.1 per cent, Singapore 8.2 per cent.[16]

Debt and dependency

The path of capitalist 'development' brings us 'nearer to death... no nearer to God'. Because it is a dependent capitalist development – a development that subjects itself to the demands of metropolitan capital, the exigencies of metropolitan need. It is tied development – tied to the purse-strings of the multinational corporations, the transnational banks and, in the final analysis, to the directions and directives of the International Monetary Fund and the World Bank. So that even when it advances in its own cause, it is led into advances for the few at the expense of the many. It is a development that creates a species of mutant capitalism that has to consume its own environment to survive.

Brazil's rapid industrialisation owes not a little to what Peter Evans calls the 'triple alliance' of multinational capital, state capital and 'elite local capital',[17] but it is also to the same combination of forces that it owes its people's poverty, its ecological devastation and its slow death by debt (at $115 billion, the highest in the world). A case in point is the proposed construction of the Kararao hydro-electric dam in the Amazon, which, while providing badly needed power to run the industries that will provide the exports to pay off debt, will also mean the wholesale destruction of the country's rainforests and the annihilation of its Indian peoples.

Already vast areas of Amazonia have been ravaged and moon-scaped by the search for gold (Brazil is the fourth largest producer), the mining of iron ore (on which the EEC and Japan rely for their steel) and the cutting down of trees that have taken 500 years to grow (to provide hardwood for the First World). South Africa's ConsGold, Britain's Rio Tinto Zinc and a number of Japanese and American corporations are involved in the mining projects (which also extend to bauxite and manganese) along with local big-time capitalists, small-time land speculators and sundry parasites such as money-lenders and *garimpeiros* (gold-diggers). And the Brazilian government, having got into debt to get into development, can only get out of debt by getting further into 'development'. But that 'development' – in the Xingu river dam – has now come up against the united resistance of the

Indian peoples across Brazil and into North America, the Green Movement and, strangely enough, the World Bank (ostensibly in the interests of ecology, but probably in the hope that the plans of the Indians and the environmentalists to raise funds to buy off the Brazilian government and pull it out of debt will also help to keep the Bank from throwing good money after bad).[18]

Mexico's industrialisation, like Brazil's, also took off on the basis of alliances between foreign and local capital (state and private). By 1980, the amount of foreign capital (mostly American) invested in the country (mostly in manufacture) totalled $27 billion. 'Foreign companies were said to control over half the output of private mining... 84 per cent of the rubber industry, 80 per cent of tobacco, 67 per cent of chemicals, 62 per cent of machinery and 79 per cent of electrical equipment.'[19] And although the country's emergence as an oil producer should have kept it economically afloat, it only served to drown it in debt – since most of the money borrowed to develop the oil industry ended up in the Swiss bank accounts of corrupt officials and (allegedly) ex-President Lopez-Portillo,[20] while most of the oil revenue went into the coffers of the right-wing Oil Workers' Union and its leader, Joaquin Hernandez Galicia. And Mexico has had to borrow again to recover from its debt crisis.

In South East Asia industrialisation was (with the obvious exception of Hong Kong) fostered and fashioned by the state before being 'handed over' to private capital. The state occupied 'the commanding heights' of the economy, controlling the banking system, public spending, investment – and the labour market. And it provided the infrastructure and climate that would attract foreign capital. It was the sort of combination of central planning and robber baron enterprise that seemed particularly suited to the specifically export-oriented industrialisation of the South East Asian NICs.

Today there is hardly an industry (and a lot of them are in electronics) in these countries which is not a joint venture with multinationals or is not controlled by them. To a certain extent, this is predicated by the nature of the electronics industry itself – with its convergences, integrations and mergers – but it largely stems from metropolitan capital's need to keep both the technology and the markets within its own domain. And the only way that NICs can keep on 'growing' is by toeing the MNC line. Hyundai's repeated attempts to produce more sophisticated memory chips, for instance, were able to take off only on the basis of a joint venture with Texas Instruments.[21] Over half the companies in Taiwan's science-based industrial park are either subsidiaries of US companies ('such as the telecoms giant AT&T, the semi-conductor equipment manufacturer Varian and the disk-drive maker Priam') or joint ventures.[22] The first wafer-fabrication plant to be set up in Singapore five years ago was SGS-Thomson Microelectronics, a private joint venture between Italian and French conglomerates.[23] Hong Kong is all joint venture.

There is nothing independent about these countries. There is no autonomous growth, no development that speaks to the needs of the people. But then, export-oriented industrialisation is metropolitan-governed industrialisation. Domestic capital is constrained by metropolitan capital, is servile to metropolitan capital. It owns but does not control, it produces but cannot sell; both production and market are in the gift of the centre.

Whereas the NICs of Latin America have been tied to dependency through debt, the NICs of South East Asia accept dependency as a 'mode' of production, a way of life.

Hierarchies of labour

The trajectory of the UDCs is different and is set not so much by capital's design for production as by its drive for accumulation. We are dealing here with the crude, nasty end of capital, not with the refined, urbane aspect of its NIC adventures. It is not here in the UDCs to woo lesser capital but to gobble up resources. If capital inveigles the NICS into the deathly embrace of its own purpose, it lays waste the UDCs, with all its pristine voracity.

And what changes in the production process have done is to deliver these countries up to such exploitation in different and more absolutist ways than before – not least in the labour-intensive 'back-end' of the electronics industry itself. Capital does not have to import cheap labour any more, with all its attendant social cost. It can move instead to the captive labour pools of the Third World and from one pool to another, choosing its locale of exploitation, its place of greatest profit, grading it according to the task in hand – which itself is a variable given the exponential changes in the electronics industry and the market-bound fate of an ever depressing light industry (the only industries that the UDCs can claim as their own). Thus there is a hierarchy of labour stretching from the centre to the outer periphery, not as between the highly skilled and the unskilled only but as among the unskilled themselves – so that the arduous, toxic work of bonding, for instance, tiny, hair-thin wires to circuit boards on wafers of silicon is done by the unskilled female labour of South East Asia, while the cleaner, safer, more straightforward task of operating the machinery into which the integrated circuits go is done by the de-skilled workers at the centre. Capital is still dependent on exploiting workers for its profit, only now the brunt of that exploitation has shifted to the under-developed countries of the Third World, and the increasing intensity of exploitation there more than compensates for its comparative loss at the centre. Only the blind chauvinism of Eurocentric marxism which mistakes its working class for the whole working class could bid the class farewell.

To put it differently, the technological revolution has allowed capital to shift the burden of extracting surplus value from the workers at the centre to the workers at the (outer) periphery. And that surplus value is not relative, as at the centre, but absolute. Capital does not need to pay peripheral labour a living wage to reproduce itself: it does not need labour on a long-term basis when technology is all the time catching up to replace it and, unlike at the centre, there is no social wage below which labour cannot fall, and what there is is readily abrogated by the government to let foreign capital in. And, in any case, there are enough cheaper and captive labour reserves in the periphery for capital to move around in, discarding each when done.[24]

And the governments of the UDCs, desperate not for development as such but to end the unemployment that threatens their regimes, enter into a Dutch auction with each other, offering the multinational corporations cheaper and cheaper labour, de-unionised labour, captive labour, female labour and child labour – by removing whatever labour laws, whatever trade union rights have been gained in the past from at least that part of the country, the EPZ, which foreign capital chooses for its own.* These are the only terms on which capital will come in and, once it is allowed in, it makes other demands – infrastructural demands, to begin with, such as unencumbered land, electric power. And if the power generated is insufficient to work its factories and/or takes away from the power available to the civilian population, it will dam up the rivers for you and develop hydro-electric schemes – and lend you the money to do it with, treat you to foreign experts (who know everything about damming-up rivers but damn-all about your country) – and irrigation schemes to open out your dry zones to landless peasants. And before you know where you are, it has taken over your land for agribusiness, to grow sugar cane and pineapple where once you grew rice, and transformed the ordinary fare of the people, the fish from the seas and the fruit from the trees, into tourist delicacies to be fed into the maws of the Hiltons, the Intercontinentals and the Holiday Inns. In the meantime, you are in hock to the gills, everything you own is in pawn: your land, labour, raw materials, mineral reserves, the lot.

This is not a fanciful scenario, but one that obtains in Sri Lanka today. Admittedly, Sri Lanka – despite its previously high literacy rate (83 per cent), previously free education and health service and previously high turn-out at general elections (70–80 per cent) (previously meaning before the World Bank got to it) – is somewhere near the bottom of the UDC table. But even countries at the top, like Malaysia and Thailand, have scarcely graduated out of labour-intensive semi-conductor assembly and light industry. Malaysia's plan to lift off into heavy industry with car manufacture and iron and steel production has since had to be 'rationalised' due to 'the prevailing weak financial position of local assemblers as well as the declining market for motor

---

* The Dominican Republic has put La Romana Zone under the control of foreign capital for thirty years.[25]

vehicles'.[26] And its attempts to move up into wafer fabrication from integrated circuit assembly – which it is being priced out of by Thailand's cheaper labour force – have been 'hobbled by infrastructural constraints'.[27] The government is now falling back on traditional manufacture in palm oil, rubber, tin, etc., and even in these has had to renege on its *bumiputra* (Malayanisation, literally 'sons of the soil') policies and permit foreign ownership and investment.[28]

Thailand has also got an edge (not only on Malaysia but other South East Asian countries) in the matter of joint venture car assembly and export, but it is currently being challenged by the Philippines' Car Development Programme, an all-Japanese affair. Indonesia is now catching up with Malaysia and Thailand (but being rich in oil has fallen into debt!).[29]

All these countries are, of course, involved in the 'back-end' of the electronics industry and in garments manufacture to one extent or another, but Thailand now leads the way in agribusiness and food-processing. Pineapple and tomato plantations and 'agro-food' industries (such as animal feed for chickens for export) have taken over from 'traditional' agriculture; tuna and shrimp farming have become big business, and processed meats (such as sausage and ham) are being re-directed from local consumption to export markets. For the Thai middle class there is instant noodles, frozen meat balls, processed dim sums and Indonesian satays 'on tap'. And all this with the help of agribusiness and food-processing conglomerates from the USA, Japan, Europe and even Taiwan. Dole has the largest pineapple plantation and canning operation in the country. Mitsubishi is involved in pineapple canning and prawn farming. Oscar Meyer has joint ventures in processed meats. Arbor Acres Farm Inc. has been a long time in the business of breeding and feeding and freezing chickens for export.

Thailand is today the world's largest exporter of canned pineapple and tuna – and frozen food, it is estimated, will soon be a multi-billion dollar export earner. In the meantime, Thailand imports food.[30]

So far from these countries resolving their unemployment problems and rising to the status of NICs, their more likely course seems to be a gradual slide into stunted growth and a different pattern of unemployment – with more and more small farmers becoming seasonal wage-labourers in commercial agriculture, more and more rural workers being thrown up into the 'informal economy' of the cities and more and more women being mobilised into short-life electronic assembly work and abandoned.[31] But the drive for export-oriented growth and the competition of other UDCs implicates these governments even further in the designs of multinational capital, the strictures of the IMF and the strategies of the World Bank – till their (the governments') interests are no longer the interests of their people but of metropolitan capital, of which they are now the servitors. And what keeps them there is American imperialism.

To come at it from the opposite direction: what keeps Third World labour cheap and captive for industrial conglomerates and enables land to be taken away from the peasants and handed over to agribusiness and the mineral resources to mining companies and brings whole countries within the economic jurisdiction of the agents of multinational capital, the IMF and World Bank, is the installation and maintenance of authoritarian Third World regimes by western powers.

Setting up the new order

Trade no longer follows the flag; the flag follows trade. Capital has broken its national bounds, technology allows it, and governments must follow in capital's wake to set up the political and social orders within which it can safely and profitably operate – if needs be with force, but with culture first.

Via culture

Today that culture is transmitted not through education or through a genteel propaganda of superiority (British Council style) but subliminally, subcutaneously: in the food you eat, the clothes you wear, the music you hear, the television you watch, the newspapers you read. You do not eat a hamburger, the universal 'food', without taking in the American way of life with it:* you do not watch television (and it is mostly American in the Third World) without accepting the American world view; you do not listen to pop music – your pop, their pop, it's all pap – without losing your ability to hear other voices, your ability to reflect, weigh, meditate; you do not read the newspapers without losing your sense of truth.

Fast food for the culture of cooking, ready-made clichés for the act of thinking, style for content, sound in place of music, noise in place of sound, reading shorn of reflection, an easy superficiality for uneasy depth, sentimentality passed off as love, individual greed in place of collective good – corporate American culture is a surrogate for culture. It dwarfs the mind, limits horizons, warps the imagination, impoverishes passion – consider the impact of Murdoch-culture (his nationality is irrelevant) on a country like Sri Lanka, which is still to recover from the cultural imperialism of another occupation – and smoothes the way for American hegemony.

And tourism is not just a vehicle of that culture, but its vanguard: a defoliant that destroys the native culture as it advances, clears the ground for corporate industry to replace it with theirs.

Tourism is not travel: search, curiosity, attachment. Tourism is reified leisure designed to relieve you (for a time) of your reified life. So, what it carries with it is the desperate excesses of its own culture and what it adopts and fetishises is the creative aspects of the native culture. Sri Lanka's beaches, a few years ago, were recommended by a paedophilia group in Britain as a good tourist venue for procuring children. And India which once had *sanyasis*† galore now has Swamis Inc.

Tourism transforms personal relationships into commercial relationships, use value into exchange value, breaks down the

---

* 'Fast foods are becoming a way of life', acclaimed *Business Week*, as McDonalds' 'Americanisation of the Japanese... reached a new peak', and *Advertising Age* confirmed that fast food 'is the food of the jeans generation, the new people who are looking to a common culture. South East Asians a generation ago thrived on Coca-Colanisation. Now their children are in the middle of a hamburger happening.'[32]

† People who have given up worldly things and chosen poverty as a way of life.

last vestiges of communalism and replaces it not with bourgeois culture but with post-bourgeois nihilism.

Via war

But if culture fails to win subject peoples to their own subjugation under regimes ordained by imperialism, there is always force, war – not necessarily direct, though that too, as in the invasion of Grenada, but indirect, through low intensity warfare or conflict (LIC) aimed at subverting resistance and preventing revolutionary movements from coming into being. LIC, according to the US Joint Chiefs of Staff's declaration in 1985, is protracted war involving 'diplomatic, economic, and psycho-social pressures through terrorism and insurgency'[33] – which, spelt out, means 'insurgency and counter-insurgency operations, terrorism and counter-terrorism, surgical direct action military operations, psychological warfare, and even operations by conventional or general purpose forces'.[34] At one end of the spectrum, LIC is soft war, concealed war at the grassroots level, a war of paralysis of the will to resist, but at the other it is hard war, using terrorism and counter-insurgency and armed force. PSYOP (psychological operations), for instance, was the 'primary component' of LIC in El Salvador for a while and combined propaganda based on Coca-Cola selling techniques with precise disinformation put out by an Institute for Popular Education set up by the CIA in the Ministry of Communications and Culture. 'Descending upon remote villages', reported Dan Siegel and Joy Hackel, 'with *mariachi* bands, multicolored leaflets, clowns and candies for children, and taped advertisements targeting their parents, the military engaged in a major public relations blitz across the country.' At the same time TV, radio and newspapers carried on a sustained campaign to 'undermine the image of the guerillas while enhancing that of the government'. And on the international front carefully doctored material was 'leaked' by the National Security Council to selected reporters 'to change the country's image abroad and persuade the US Congress to continue to supply aid'.[35]

In Nicaragua the CIA PSYOP manual urged '"political proselytism" and civic-action operations working side-by-side with peasants... building, fishing, repairing etc'. But this was to be coupled with 'the selective use of violence', whereby 'contra provocateurs "armed with clubs, iron rods, placards, and if possible small fire arms" would instigate mob riots in the cities'.[36]

Besides fomenting 'preventive counter-revolution' (the phrase is Marcuse's), LIC also aims at de-stabilising 'unfriendly' Third World regimes such as Mozambique, Angola, Nicaragua by providing 'diplomatic, military and economic support... for an insurgent force seeking freedom from an adversary government'[37] – insurgent forces such as MNR, UNITA and the Contras. In the case of Nicaragua, however, LIC has also involved the sowing of mines in the country's harbours 'to disrupt the flow of shipping essential to Nicaraguan trade during the peak export period' (Oliver North in a 'top secret' memorandum)[38] and the destruction of its oil facilities – both operations conducted by a specially trained force of 'unilaterally controlled Latino assets' (UCLAs). But in 1983 the LIC merchants combined with the World Bank to stop Nicaragua getting a loan to build a fleet of fishing boats on the grounds that the oil that was necessary to operate the boats (a condition imposed by this non-political Bank specially for Nicaragua) had run out in the meantime – thanks to the setting fire of its oil tanks by 'unknown' raiders from a mother-ship off-shore.[39]

The fomentation of insurgencies and local wars also helps western powers to sell even more arms to Third World countries – to fuel the wars that fuel the arms sales – and get them deeper and deeper into debt and dependency. 'Without these sales', commented Tom Gervasi, Director of the Center of Military Research, in a TV programme recently, 'the developing nations cannot maintain the industry, and unemployment and bankruptcy will follow.' Besides, 'in order to arm ourselves properly, we have got to arm the world; to get the price down to what we can afford, we must sell more'.[40]

Of course, the whole point of LIC, in the final analysis, is to provide multinationals with a climate hospitable to trade and

investment – all sorts of trade and investment – or, as Colonel
Motley put it in the *Military Review*, 'to influence politico-military
outcomes in the resource-rich and strategically located Third
World areas'.[41] In Latin America the desired 'politico-military
outcomes' have led to a variety of military juntas, from the savage
in Chile (where the monetarist theories of Friedman's 'Chicago
boys' were first practised) to the confused in Bolivia. In South East
Asia they have resulted in all sorts of authoritarian regimes, from
the dictatorships of South Korea and (till recently) the Philippines
to the parliamentary oligarchies of Singapore and Sri Lanka.
The NICs, both of Latin America and South East Asia, seem, by
and large, to have the outright dictatorships (mutants perhaps
of their own socio-political history), while the UDCs appear to
sport varieties of parliamentary authoritarianism. Which would
point to the theorem that the greater and/or faster the growth of
Third World countries, the quicker their graduation into fully-
fledged dictatorships. Or even that totalitarian regimes are as
much the form of government 'tolerable' to silicon age imperialism
as mock-Westminster was to industrial colonialism. Except that
in recent years the United States has shown a certain flexibility
in changing dictatorships around to 'friendly democracies', as in
the Philippines, or recycling them through democratic processes
such as elections and referenda, as in Chile and Haiti – so as to
keep US interests in place.

Casualties of imperialism

The economic depredations of multinational capital, the political
repression of the regimes that host it and the LIC waged by
western powers to keep these regimes in situ all combine to effect
the brutal dislocation and displacement of people all over the
Third World and force them to flee their countries. Whether as
economic refugees or as political asylum-seekers is no matter
– for, however their arrival at the centre may be categorised, their
ejection from their countries is, as I have shown, both economic
and political at once. To distinguish between them is not just to
wilfully misunderstand the machinations of imperialism today, but

to pretend that the struggle against imperialism is not also here, at the centre, or has nothing to do with workers' struggles here.

For, apart from everything else, these – the refugees, migrants and asylum seekers, the flotsam and jetsam of latter-day imperialism – are the new underclass of silicon age capitalism. It is they who perform the arduous, unskilled, dirty jobs in the ever-expanding service sector, who constitute the casual, ad hoc, temporary workers in computerised manufacture, who provide agribusiness with manual farm labour. They are the invisible workers in the service industries, serving in the up-front kitchens at McDonald's, as porters and cleaners in hospitals and shops, as waiters and petrol pump attendants, security guards and night watchmen, servants and slaves. They are the peripheral workers in manufacture, peripheral in the manufacturing sense too, because modern production processes do not require a permanent workforce but a functionally flexible 'core group' which can adjust to changes in technology and a numerically flexible 'peripheral group' which can be adjusted to changes in the market. They are the sweat-shop workers in the primitive putting-out system of the garment industry. They are tomato-pickers for agribusiness.[42] They are, in a word, the cheap and captive labour force – rightless, rootless, peripatetic and temporary, illegal even – without which post-industrial society cannot run.

Their condition has been graphically described in *Ganz Unten* (published recently in English as *Lowest of the Low*[43]) by a German investigative journalist, Günter Wallraff, who in the guise of a Turkish labourer, Ali, lived through a year of a migrant worker's life. And, like any migrant worker, Wallraff/Ali is hired and fired at will, sat upon and spat upon, used and abused, vilified, reified and thrown upon a heap (in Turkey for preference) when he is done with. At first he hires himself out – to all sorts of menial jobs in restaurants and building sites and construction works – but soon discovers that he can continue to work only if he comes under the aegis, the protection, of a sub-contractor who hires him out to a contractor who contracts to do the dirty work for reputable firms who do not want to know that they are doing it. And that work ranges from clearing frozen sludge from massive pipes on high buildings in 17 degrees of frost and shovelling hot, grimy coke dust hour after hour below ground level to being hired out as a human guinea-pig to a pharmaceutical firm and cleaning out a nuclear power station, the carcinogenic effects of which would show only after Ali has returned to Turkey (the condition on which he got the job in the first place).

And the firms that get his work have no responsibility for him. For Ali is hired out to them by labour contractors who have obtained him as part of a labour gang from sub-contractors and sub-sub-contractors and so on down the line. And all that Ali gets is what is left of his wages when everybody above him has taken his cut. He has no national insurance, no pension rights, no right to health care and social security, no right to a fair wage – and if he baulks at it, he is handed over to the police and deported home to a worse fate. He is the apotheosis of captive labour, dispensable, disposable, yielding absolute surplus value – right here in the centre.

You do not have to go to Germany to find the Alis of this world, though. They are here in Britain too, among the refugees from Colombia, Chile, Sri Lanka, Sudan, Eritrea, Iran, the Philippines, Ghana – from every part of the world where imperialism has set foot.

The moment of socialism

But if these are the new circuits of imperialism made possible by the revolution in the productive forces, it is that same revolution that allows us to break the circuit and move towards socialism. The liberation of the productive forces must mean the liberation of man and woman kind – all men and women in the Third World, the First, wherever – not the greater liberation of a few at a greater cost to the many. But to do that we have got to seize the technology, put ourselves in command of it, not let it run away with itself into capital's terrain.

It is inconceivable that when we can produce more food that we should throw it away, that when we can run factories without debasing workers that we should debase them, that when we have found the leisure to be more creative in we should turn ourselves into mindless junkies, that when we have invented the ultimate weapon of destruction we should not live in peace, that when we have learnt to master nature we should not let nature put out its thousand blooms, that when we have reached the summit of individual freedom we should not be working for the collective good.

Socialism is a moral creed, a secular faith – tolerant, loving, creative, increasing all to increase the one. It is that morality above all that the movement of workers has garnered and fostered and kept alive all these generations to in-form and fashion our societies when Prometheus had been unbound again. What we have learnt from the labour movement, what we must hold on to, are not the old ways of organisation, the old modes of thought, the old concepts of battle against capital, but the values and traditions that were hammered out on the smithy of those battles: loyalty, solidarity, camaraderie, unity, all the great and simple things that make us human.

That is the morality of socialism that the working-class movement, the peasants' movement, the women's, black and gay movements, the green and anti-nuclear movement – all the movements of liberation have sung out. Technology can now make it flesh, and we cannot let capital take it away from us.

We can now ordain our societies so that there is greater productivity with less labour, improved consumption for all and more time to be human in. When our problem is no longer the production of goods as such, we should be looking to their more equitable distribution; when large numbers of workers are no longer necessary for such production, we should be looking to the more equitable distribution of work. If the same number of goods can be produced by half the workforce, it follows that the whole workforce need work only half the time rather than leave the other half unemployed. Not because work itself is sacrosanct, but because the culture of self-esteem and worth erected on the notions of working and earning will be a long time a-dying. We can set the process in motion, however, by providing everybody with a minimum wage irrespective of whether he or she works or not – so assuring effective demand, on the one hand, and replacing the work ethic with the leisure ethic, on the other. But such leisure will be active, creative leisure – not reified or nuclearising of us, but growing, organic, connecting us to people again: old people, children, the sick and disabled, the oppressed and the exploited. And education will be geared not just to jobs but to using leisure intelligently and creatively, to working things out for ourselves – for the technology that does all the thinking for us in the machines we produce is also the technology that requires us to return to the basic principles that produce such thinking: it requires that we not only know that 2 and 2 make 4, but why. It enables us to return to fundamentals, to holistic thinking, to an authority over our own experience and so removes us from our captive submission to the media, politicians, the video civilisation.

We have cultures of resistance to create, communities of resistance to build, a world to win. Now is the moment of socialism. And capital shall have no dominion.

10

A BLACK PERSPECTIVE ON THE GULF WAR*

This is not our war, this is not the war of black and Third World peoples. This is not a war for us, this is a war against us wherever we are – whether in Europe, the United States or any part of the Third World. That is my first point.

Secondly, the terms of debate on which this war is being conducted are not our terms of debate. They are not our questions, they are not our principal concerns. We are not concerned with whether or not Saddam Hussein is a dictator so much as with who put him there. We cannot be concerned with Iraqi small power designs on Kuwait to the exclusion of American big power designs on the Third World that the 'liberation' of Kuwait is going to entail. It is not our question whether the incursion into Kuwait and the occupation of Palestine are linked. It is not our question whether Israel has the right to exist or not.

Of course Israel has the right to exist. Israel does exist. It is the one existence that none of us can deny. It exists in our everyday lives. It exists in every consciousness of our being. It exists in the maiming of our children, the dispossession of our old peoples, the brutalisation of our young. It exists in the decanting of the Palestinian population from Palestine through justifiable homicide, through judicious and judicial imprisonment, through political exile – as once the Caribbean was 'decanted' of the Arawaks, the Americas of the Indians and Australia of its Aboriginal population. Israel exists.

---

* Text of a speech given at the inaugural meeting of Black People Against War in the Gulf, Camden town hall, London, 5 February 1991.

Israel exists, above all, in the collective unconscious of the oppressed and the exploited as once that consciousness existed in them. Israel exists, above all, as an object lesson to us that we do not ourselves become oppressors in the name of our oppression.

Of course Israel has the right to exist. That is not a problem for us, for black and Third World people. We do not deny Israel's right to exist. What we do deny is Israel's denial of the Palestinians' right to exist – in Palestine.

That for us is the crux of the matter. The rights of the Palestinian people to their land and to their existence – that is central to the concern of black and Third World peoples in this war and after this war.

As for the question of linking the Iraqi invasion of Kuwait with the Israeli occupation of the West Bank and Gaza Strip, that is not really a question for us. Because everything in our lives is linked. The invasion of Kuwait is linked with the occupation of Palestine, the invasion of Lebanon is linked with the occupation of Grenada, the invasion of Panama is linked with the occupation of East Timor. Hunger and famine are linked to exploitation; race and power and poverty are linked. The presence of Third World peoples over here and the presence of multinational corporations in the Third World are linked. They are all links in the chain of imperialism.

And racism and imperialism are linked. We see the links in our everyday lives, we know the links viscerally, in our guts. We have no problem with linkages. Our problem is to stop the white powers-that-be from de-linking us from ourselves, detaching us from our histories. That is our problem.

Nor is the question of whether Saddam Hussein is a dictator or not of so much import to us as who put him there. For if he is a dictator, he is a dictator created by, and kept in situ by, American capitalism – like all the dictators of the Third World, like all the authoritarian regimes, pseudo-parliamentary or openly totalitarian, in the Third World – in Chile, Haiti, Sri Lanka, South Korea, El Salvador, Guatemala. The names are legion. In every single Third World country almost without exception the powers that rule us are the powers that have been installed by American imperialism and the satraps of American imperialism. Getting rid of our dictators does not get rid of the system that put them there. Black dictatorship and white imperialism are two sides of the same coin. Our problem is to get rid of both.

Our problem is to decide our own governments, to make our own choices, our own mistakes – and put them right as and when we think fit – to make our own histories. We need to have the political freedom to decide our governments, the economic freedom to make our choices, the cultural freedom to make, and remake, our histories. That is what democracy means to us – not the 'democracy' that is foisted on us, for our own good, by those who know what is best for us. Not the democracy that pretends to fight a war for democratic values while denying those values in the very act of prosecuting the war. For not only is this war a war of sanitised warfare, bereft of real people, but a war also of sanitised values, bereft of real morality. Not only is this a war being fought on the basis of technology, but our consent to the war is being bought on the basis of technology. The technology that fights the war on our behalf is also the technology that disinforms us as to why we are fighting it. The controllers of the technology of communication condition not only what we see and hear but how we think and feel – or, rather, by conditioning what we see and hear, they make sure that we do not think or feel any differently from them. We are in a time of technological authoritarianism.

Men and women are going off to die in a war that they were led to believe could not be avoided for a lie they were led to believe in. They are as much unwitting cannon fodder as those who died on the fields of Flanders. And foremost among them are the blacks, the Hispanics and the poor whites, those victims of Reaganite policies who have no employment, no prospects, no way out of the ghetto. Is it any wonder that they should swell the ranks of the so-called volunteer army of the US of A? Or that African-Americans should represent 25 per cent of the fighting force (when they are only 12 per cent of the population) or that they should be the majority in the front line? What choice do they have? What democracy for them?

What, then, if these are not our terms? What are our terms, what are our concerns? How should we look at what is happening today? How should we look at this war from the black and Third World perspective – from the experience of our own history and our own consciousnesses?

What concerns black and Third World people is not just the war but the new order, the new imperium, which is emerging from the ending of the cold war. I see this war as an interlude – or, rather, a rite of passage from the old American imperialism to the new. The ending of the cold war has left the United States the sole super-power in the world. The contestation between the West and the East is over, and the West is free to range over the South, marauding it at will. This war, the war with Iraq, is a flexing-of-the-muscles exercise, a casing-the-joint exercise, a testing of the opposition, a sounding of the hangers-on. It is an exercise in establishing the unipolar, monolithic super-power hegemony of the USA. It is a dry run for the second American century, but this time under the pretended aegis of the United Nations.

Remember, once before, when Britain ruled over us, how, by inveigling us into its way of life, its language, its beliefs, it made us, the subject peoples, a party to our own subjugation – the black skin, white masks syndrome? Today, it is not the peoples of the Third World who are being won over but the states of the Third World, and not so much through a cultural imperialism that denotes a way of life as through a cultural imperialism that denotes a way of governing. It is a sort of political cultural imperialism – the imperialism, that is, of a political culture which, on the one hand, defines as non-democratic, and therefore untenable, any regime that does not serve western interests and is prepared, on the other, to overlook, and indeed sustain, the most brazen dictatorships so long as they serve western interests. And it is that same political culture which, at another level, holds that all nations are equal in the United Nations but that those who serve western interests are more equal than others. Once more we are being set against each other and made accomplices in our own despoliation.

At the very moment that western powers have acknowledged that the United Nations has something to say in the settling of international disputes, the United Nations has ceased to say anything to us. From being ineffectual and irrelevant, the UN has now become a pliant tool of American imperialism. And the new uncontested American imperium is going to land the Third World with the rulers that it does not want, a standard of living which is barely above starvation level, and with ecological devastation to keep western petticoats clean.

Only a few weeks ago, at the GATT talks in Geneva, the industrialised countries warned that if Indonesia continued to ban the felling and export of raw logs so as to protect its own environment, the corporations in the USA which needed timber for raw material would be hit; Indonesia would have to remove its export ban on logging or face trade sanctions. Another aspect of the new imperium was also evidenced at the same talks when William Brock, a senior GATT negotiator, pointed out that 'We must get away from the anachronism that developing countries need to feed themselves, given the ready availability of US cereals.' He therefore called for the removal of government subsidies on food production in Third World countries. Let them eat wheat, was his curt message, American wheat!

If the war in the Gulf is a passage to a new political and military order, the GATT talks are the passage to a new economic and commercial order.

But that is not to say that the war in the Gulf is not also an economic and commercial war over the price and availability of petroleum and, therefore, a war about the standard of living of the American peoples and the peoples of the West – and not just because America needs oil for energy, but because western life-style is petroleum-based. Your shirts, your furnishings, your nylons, your curtains, your fabrics, your insecticides, your fungicides, your fertilisers, your washing-up liquids, your detergents are all petroleum-based. The West's economy is founded on petroleum-based industry, petroleum-based agriculture, petroleum-based life-styles. And the US consumes 25 per cent of the world's oil while producing only 4 per cent.

It is this political, economic and military penetration of Third World countries by western governments that has begun once again to dispossess and displace our people and lead to the vast and rapid-fire shift of whole populations in our part of the world – from countryside to town to oil-rich country and to Europe and America. And it is these migrants from the more impoverished parts of the Third World – Palestinians, Egyptians, Filipinos, Indians, Sri Lankans, Pakistanis, Vietnamese – who have built the infrastructure of the sheikhdoms and serve in their homes as servants and slaves. In Kuwait alone there are over 1.5 million (72 per cent) non-nationals, over half of whom are from the Middle East and over a third from Asia. Given that the population of Kuwait is just over 2 million, the number of Kuwaitis who actually work must be even less than the number of Kuwaitis who actually vote. And yet no western commentator on this war has bothered to remark on these Third World workers left stranded and close to starvation in huts and tents, or on the consequences of that to their dependants back home. This is not their war either.

Nor is it the war of the migrants and refugees and asylum seekers who have been thrown up on the shores of Europe and serve as the flexible and disposable workforce of post-industrial capitalism. And yet it is these people, designated as 'Pakis' or Arabs or Muslims (anybody dark would do to qualify), who are being subjected to an increasingly undifferentiated racism in the media and on the streets. Mosques from Marseilles to Batley have been fire-bombed, women have had their head-scarves torn off in the middle of our city centres, individuals are stopped at random and beaten if they do not denounce Saddam Hussein, Arab community centres are daily receiving death threats.

The arbitrary rounding-up, detention and deportation of Middle East nationals by the government has further sanctioned the idea that we have here in Britain a fifth column, an enemy within. But then, anti-Arabism and anti-Islamic sentiments have never been far from the surface of British life – as was shown in the Rushdie affair, when everyone from street thugs to politicians and 'intellectual socialists', with varying degrees of brazenness and coyness, gave vent to their racist sentiments against Muslims and Arabs. We are once more in the midst of a Crusade against 'the barbarians' (the phrase belongs to the Belgian Minister of the Interior).

As a consequence, all the bits and pieces of racist belief have become telescoped into each other, and every stereotype reinforces another. The Arab gets telescoped into the Muslim, Iranians become Arabs, Khomeini and Islamic fundamentalism gets mixed up with oil sheikhs holding the West to ransom, the Turks who clean the streets of Western Europe and provide domestic help to its middle classes are suddenly become part of an invading army. All Asians are 'Pakis', and 'Paki' passes as a synonym for mad Muslim. And all Muslims are Iraqis.

This new racism makes no distinction between one black and another, between refugee and settler, between Muslim and Hindu. Our fight, then, is not only against the new imperium, but against the new racism, the anti-Arab racism, the anti-Muslim racism.

We are all Muslims now!

11

POVERTY IS THE NEW BLACK*

Racism has always been an instrument of discrimination. And discrimination has always been a tool of exploitation. Racism, in that sense, has always been rooted in the economic compulsions of the capitalist system. But it manifests itself, first and foremost, as a cultural phenomenon, susceptible to cultural solutions such as multicultural education and the promotion of ethnic identities. Redressing the problem of cultural inequality, however, does not by itself redress the problem of economic inequality. Racism needs to be tackled at both levels – the cultural and the economic – at once, remembering that the one provides the rationale for the other. Racism, in sum, is conditioned by economic imperatives, but negotiated through cultural agency: religion, literature, art, science, the media and so on.

Which of these agencies, though, holds sway in a particular epoch is itself dependent on the economic system of that epoch. Thus, in the period of primitive accumulation, when the pillage and plunder of the new world by Spanish conquistadors was laying the foundations of capitalism, it was religion in the form of the Catholic Church that gave validity to the concept that the native Indians were *sub-homines*, the children of Ham, born to be slaves, and could therefore be enslaved and/or exterminated at will. In the period of merchant capital, when the monarch was no longer subordinate to the Church and the bourgeoisie was in its ascendancy, the racialist ideas of the earlier period became secularised in popular literature, political discourse and education and served to rationalise and justify the trade in black slaves.

---

* This essay was written in August 2001.

With the development of industrial capitalism and its corollary, colonialism, the racialist ideas of the previous epochs congealed into a systemic racist ideology to condemn all 'coloured' peoples to racial and cultural inferiority. By the end of the nineteenth century, at the height of the imperial adventure, the ideology of racial superiority began to take on a pseudo-scientific validity in the Social Darwinism of Gobineau and Chamberlain – which in turn further popularised the view of racial hierarchies.

Today, under global capitalism which, in its ruthless pursuit of markets and its sanctification of wealth, has served to unleash ethnic wars, balkanise countries and displace their peoples, the racist tradition of demonisation and exclusion has become a tool in the hands of the state to keep out the refugees and asylum seekers so displaced – even if they are white – on the grounds that they are scroungers and aliens come to prey on the wealth of the West and confound its national identities. The rhetoric of demonisation, in other words, is racist, but the politics of exclusion is economic. Demonisation is a prelude to exclusion, social and therefore economic exclusion, to creating a peripatetic underclass, international *Untermenschen*.

Once, 'they' demonised the blacks to justify slavery. Then they demonised the 'coloureds' to justify colonialism. Today, they demonise asylum seekers to justify the ways of globalism. And, in the age of the media, of discourse, of spin, demonisation sets out the parameters of popular culture within which such exclusion finds its own rationale – usually under the guise of xenophobia, the (natural) fear of strangers. Such a term, it is thought, would include white refugees and asylum seekers streaming in from Eastern Europe, whereas the term racism strictly refers to people of a different race and colour. Xenophobia, besides, is innocent, racism culpable.

But the other side of the coin of 'the fear or hatred of strangers' is the defence and preservation of 'our people', our way of life, our standard of living, our 'race'. If it is xenophobia, it is – in the way it denigrates and reifies people before segregating and/or expelling them – a xenophobia that bears all the marks of the old racism, except that it is not colour-coded. It is a racism that is not just directed at those with darker skins, from the former colonial countries, but at the newer categories of the displaced and dispossessed whites, who are beating at Western Europe's doors, the Europe that displaced them in the first place. It is racism in substance but xeno in form – a racism that is meted out to impoverished strangers even if they are white. It is xeno-racism.

Xeno-racism is a feature of the Manichaean world of global capitalism, where there are only the rich and the poor – and poverty is the new black. Where the national state works primarily in the interests of multinational corporations, where the national bourgeoisie collaborates with international capital, where the middle class is effete and self-serving and the working class, disaggregated and dispersed by technology, has lost its political clout.

That is the context within which we have got to adjudge the changing nature of racism and from that, conversely, adjudge the nature of the society we live in.

In Britain, with its long tradition of racism over five centuries and three continents, racial prejudice has become an intrinsic part of popular culture, racial discrimination has come to inhere in the institutions of society and racist laws and policies have characterised state intervention at the point of economic need. But today, the state is much more regulatory and interventionist – in the interests, ironically, of an unregulated market – though wanting to appear open and democratic. Thus, in its avowedly liberal mode, it is prepared to go along with the Macpherson recommendations and dismantle institutional racism, especially in the public sector, but in its self-justifying regulatory mode, it brings institutional discrimination back into the system through the Immigration and Asylum Act, with its dispersal schemes, its voucher system and detention camps. And it is this demonisation of refugees and asylum seekers rather than the move to dismantle institutional racism that has caught the public's attention, resonating as it does with its misgivings about the 'alien invasion' – and so stoked the fires of popular racism. In the course of which, the fight against institutional racism itself has taken a beating.

There are other changes in the law, too, which, though affecting the population in general, impact more harshly on black communities and further institutionalise racism in the criminal justice system. Thus the proposal to abolish the right of defendants to elect to be tried by a jury for offences such as minor theft, assault and criminal damage, will affect black people more adversely because they are over-represented in those areas – not least because they are stopped and searched, arrested and charged more often than white people. To remove their right to request trial by jury, therefore, and put them up for summary trial before magistrates, who are perceived to be on the side of the police, is to deny them one of the few remaining legal safeguards against unfair treatment.

So too the Terrorism Act 2000, which gives the Home Secretary powers to proscribe any organisation which, according to him, threatens violence to advance 'a political, religious, or ideological cause' criminalises the liberation struggles of those who have fled the tyrannies of their own countries and, in the process, stigmatises them as terrorists.

In sum, the laws, the administration, the criminal justice system – the whole state apparatus in Britain – is rife with racism and gives the lie to the government's pretensions to counter institutional racism and the culture which gives it a habitation and a name. At first glance, British racism would appear to have three faces – state, institutional, popular – but, in effect, it has one face with three expressions, the face of the state. To put it another way, institutional racism and popular racism are woven into state racism and it is only in unravelling that that you begin to unravel the fabric of racism.

Except that now there is another problem compounding racial conflict: poverty – the systemic poverty of a society which, at the dictates of a free market economy, is becoming increasingly polarised between the haves and the have-nothings. This has often been characterised as the north/south divide, with the north belonging to dead industries and the south to the modern economy. But there are pockets of poverty both in the north and the south, where mills and mines, docks and shipyards, steel and textiles have disappeared or been relocated by technology and the global factory. What is more to the point, however, is not so much the geography of decay as the composition of the working class in these industries and its subsequent disaggregation and segregation.

Some of these industries, such as mining, dock-work and ship-building, had a workforce that was almost wholly white, whereas the steel and textile mills of Yorkshire and Lancashire, and textiles in particular, had also recruited labour from the Indian subcontinent. And it was these mill towns that the government, either by default or design, failed to bring into the modern economy, through investment or retraining, when the old industries had died. The white workers were able to move out to other jobs elsewhere, but racism and family ties (which was the only 'network' available to them) pointed Bangladeshis and Pakistanis towards restaurant work and mini-cabbing – and the sense of solidarity and comradeship between white and Asian workers that had been engendered on the factory floor was lost. Segregation in housing, resulting from local government policies, separated the communities further and led to the segregation in schooling of the next generation. Multiculturalism in its updated Scarman model, ethnicism, deepened the fissures between ethnic groups. And ethnic funding, instead of improving the local economy as a whole, helped only to improve the personal economy of a few – some of whom made it into the town halls and Tammany Hall style politics, where the currency of corruption was not money so much as communalism and religion.

All of which served to brand the Bangladeshis and Pakistanis as self-segregating and better served by local authorities than the local whites. That the former were mostly Muslim Asians, as distinct from other Asians, served to focus white hate on Islam. And it was that potent combination of racial and religious hatred that provided the breeding ground for the electoral politics of the British National Party, on the one hand, and the *goonda* politics of the National Front, on the other – and provoked the uprisings of young Asians in Oldham, Bradford, Burnley, Leeds, Stoke.

What were the youth to do? They had been born here, schooled here, grown up here, had been media-maddened by all the good things in life that could be, should be, available to them – and yet all around them were 'the rocks, moss, stonecrop, merds' of the industrial wastelands of derelict Britain. Whatever leadership there was had either retreated into the safety of religion or defected to the service of local and central government, from where they condemned the youth while feathering their own nests.

No economic infrastructures or hope of socialisation through work. No political parties, no ideology, no political culture – to unite the fragmented communities, to develop an alternative politics, to emerge as a political force – all that had died with New Labour. Locked into their degradation and defeat by a racist police force, vilified by a racist press and violated, finally, by the true fascists. What were the youth to do but break out in violence, self-destructive, reactive violence, the violence of choicelessness, the violence of the violated?

NOTES

1 The Liberation of the Black Intellectual

1. Aimé Césaire, in his address to the Congress of Black Writers and Artists, Paris, 1956, reported in 'Princes and powers', in James Baldwin, *Nobody Knows My Name* (London, 1961).
2. T.S. Eliot, 'The Waste Land', in *Collected Poems*, 1909–1962 (London, 1963).
3. The British media uses the 'coloured intellectual', whatever his or her field of work, as white Africa uses the Chief: as a spokesman for his tribe.
4. Jean-Paul Sartre, 'Intellectuals and revolution: interview', *Ramparts* (Vol. 9, no. 6, December 1970), pp. 52–5.
5. Ibid.
6. Jean-Paul Sartre, *Black Orpheus* (Paris, n.d.).
7. Black is here used to symbolise the oppressed, as white the oppressor. Colonial oppression was uniform in its exploitation of the races (black, brown and yellow) making a distinction between them only in the interest of further exploitation – by playing one race against the other and, within each race, one class against the other – generally the Indians against the blacks, the Chinese against the browns, and the coolies against the Indian and Chinese middle class. In time these latter came to occupy, in East Africa and Malaysia for example, a position akin to a comprador class. Whether it is this historical fact which today makes for their comprador role in British society is not, however, within the scope of this essay. But it is interesting to note how an intermediate colour came to be associated with an intermediate role.
8. Aimé Césaire, *Return to My Native Land* (Harmondsworth, 1969).
9. 'Black: opposite to white.' *Concise Oxford Dictionary.* 'White: morally or spiritually pure or stainless, spotless, innocent. Free from malignity or evil intent, innocent, harmless esp. as opp. to something characterised as *black.' Shorter Oxford Dictionary.*
10. Frantz Fanon, *Black Skin: White Masks* (London, 1968).
11. Paul Valéry, quoted in Fanon, *Black Skin: White Masks.*
12. Fanon, *Black Skin: White Masks.*

13. Ibid.
14. Thomas Carlyle, 'Occasional discourse on the nigger question', in *Latter Day Pamphlets* (London, n.d.).
15. William Blake, from 'Songs of innocence', in J. Bronowski (ed.), *A Selection of Poems and Letters* (Harmondsworth, 1958).
16. Jean Genet, Introduction to *Soledad Brother: the prison letters of George Jackson* by George Jackson (London, 1970).
17. R.D. Laing, *Politics of Experience and Bird of Paradise* (Harmondsworth, 1970).
18. Fanon, *Black Skin: White Masks*.
19. Césaire, *Return to My Native Land*.
20. T.S. Eliot, 'Tradition and the individual talent', in *The Sacred Wood: Essays on Poetry and Criticism* (London, 1934).
21. Ibid.
22. Dunduzu Chisiza, 'The outlook for contemporary Africa', *Journal of Modern African Studies* (Vol. 1, no. 1, March 1963), pp. 25–38.
23. Julius K. Nyerere, *Uhuru na Ujamaa: Freedom and Socialism: a selection from writings and speeches, 1965–67* (Dar-es-Salaam, 1968).
24. Ibid.
25. Benjamin Rowland, *Art and Architecture of India: Hindu, Buddhist, Jain* (Harmondsworth, 1970).
26. Paul A. Baran and Paul M. Sweezy, *Monopoly Capital: an essay on the American economic and social order* (Harmondsworth, 1968).
27. Frantz Fanon, *The Wretched of the Earth* (London, 1965).
28. He may, of course, become frozen in a narrow cultural nationalism of his own in violent reaction to white culture.
29. Antonio Gramsci, 'The formation of intellectuals', in *The Modern Prince and Other Writings* (New York, 1957).
30. Fanon, *Black Skin: White Masks*.
31. 'Negritude' in the original French.
32. Sartre, *Black Orpheus*.
33. Jacques Roumain, quoted in Fanon, *Black Skin: White Masks*.

2 The Hokum of New Times

1. Stuart Hall, 'Thatcher's lessons', *Marxism Today* (March 1988).
2. Stuart Hall, 'Brave New World', *Marxism Today* (Special issue, October 1988).
3. See A. Sivanandan, 'New circuits of imperialism' [Chapter 9, this volume] and Zygmunt Bauman, 'Fighting the wrong shadow', *New Statesman* (25 September 1987).

4. Martin Jacques, *Marxism Today* (October 1988).
5. Hall, 'Brave New World'.
6. See Sivanandan, 'New circuits of imperialism' [Chapter 9, this volume].
7. Carver Mead quoted in Walter B. Wriston, 'Technology and sovereignty', *Foreign Affairs* (Winter 1988/89).
8. Hall, 'Brave New World'.
9. Hall, 'Thatcher's lessons'.
10. Bharat Patankar, 'Monochromatic green gathering', *Race & Class* (October–December 1989). See also *Race & Class* special issue *Ungreening the Third World* (January–March 1989).
11. T.S. Eliot, 'Burnt Nortun', *Four Quartets* (London, 1970).
12. Rosalind Brunt, 'Bones in the corset', *Marxism Today* (October 1988).
13. Beatrix Campbell in 'Clearing the decks: a roundtable discussion', *Marxism Today* (October 1988).
14. Brunt, 'Bones in the corset'.
15. Hall, 'Brave New World'.
16. Ibid.
17. Campbell in 'Clearing the decks'.
18. Hall, 'Brave New World'.
19. Ibid.
20. Anthony Doran, 'Baa, baa, green sheep!' *Daily Mail* (9 October 1986).
21. Hall, 'Thatcher's lessons'.
22. *After dread and anger* (BBC Radio 4, 21 March 1989).
23. Frank Field, *Losing Out: the emergence of Britain's underclass* (London, 1989).
24. Hall, 'Brave New World'.
25. Frank Field, *Losing Out*.
26. Campbell in 'Clearing the decks'.
27. Hall, 'Brave New World'.
28. Charlie Leadbeater, 'Power to the person', *Marxism Today* (October 1988).
29. Charlie Leadbeater, in 'Clearing the decks'.
30. Hall, 'Brave New World'.
31. Robin Murray, 'Life after Henry (Ford)', *Marxism Today* (October 1988).
32. Stuart Hall and Martin Jacques, 'People Aid – a new politics sweeps the land', *Marxism Today* (July 1986).
33. Ibid.
34. Beatrix Campbell in 'Clearing the decks'.
35. Marshall Berman, *All That Is Solid Melts Into Air: the experience of modernity* (London, 1983).

36. A. Sivanandan, 'The new racism', *New Statesman* (4 November 1988).

4   Race, Class and the State: The Political Economy of Immigration

1. One of those who took part in the Spaghetti House Siege [referred to in Chapter 5 of this volume].
2. See Stephen Castles and Godula Kosack, *Immigrant Workers and the Class Structure in Western Europe* (London, Oxford University Press for IRR, 1973), and E.J.B. Rose et al., *Colour and Citizenship: a report on British race relations* (London, Oxford University Press for IRR, 1969).
3. Ceri Peach, *West Indian Migration to Britain: a social geography* (London, Oxford University Press for IRR, 1969).
4. Ibid.
5. André Gorz, 'The role of immigrant labour', *New Left Review* (No. 61, May–June 1970).
6. Peach, *West Indian Migration to Britain.*
7. See M. Nikolanakos, 'Germany: the economics of discrimination', *Race Today* (Vol. 3, no. 11, November 1971), pp. 372–4.
8. See A. Sivanandan, 'Race, class and power: an outline for study', *Race* (Vol. 14, no. 4, April 1973), pp. 383–91.
9. 'The rate of immigrants into this country', said Gaitskell to the Commons in the debate on the 1962 Act, 'is closely related and, in my view at any rate, will always be closely related to the rate of economic absorption... There has been over the years... an almost precise correlation between the movement in the number of unfilled vacancies, that is to say employers wanting labour, and immigration figures' – House of Commons Official Report, Vol. 649, Col. 793, 16 November 1961.
10. 'Through the 1950s Britain acquired a coloured population in, so to speak, a fit of absence of mind.' Dipak Nandy in the Foreword to *The Multi-Racial School*, by Julia McNeal and Margaret Rogers (Harmondsworth, Penguin, 1971). For the high-minded school, see, for instance, the writings of P. Mason et al.
11. It is significant that at the time the Immigration Bill was being debated Britain was negotiating for entry into the Common Market.
12. The Commonwealth Immigrants Act of 1962 had left no one in doubt as to which part of the Commonwealth (white or black) control was applicable.
13. Already – by 1965 – 40 per cent of all junior hospital medical staff were from the New Commonwealth and nearly 15 per cent

of all student nurses. Without that help some hospitals would have had to close just as without Commonwealth immigrants London Transport would be disrupted (see Lord Stonham, Lords *Hansard* 10 March 1965, Col. 96). And David Ennals told the Commons some days later that in 1963 'immigrant teachers, nurses, professional engineers and chemists numbered only half as many as their British counterparts who left for other parts of the world' (*Hansard* 23 March 1965, Col. 393).

14. *Commonwealth Immigrants Act 1962, Control of Immigration Statistics, 1966*. Cmnd. 3258 (London, HMSO, 1967).
15. See M. Nikolanakos, 'Uber das Nord-Sud Problem in Europa: das Konzept des Europaischen Sudens', *Dritte Welt* (No. 1, 1974), pp. 29–50.
16. Psychologically it might be – but this is of no interest to capital unless there is profit in it. Socially, it is counter-productive.
17. Jamaica and Trinidad and Tobago achieved independence in August 1962, Guyana in May 1966, Barbados in November 1966. Antigua, Dominica, Grenada, St Lucia and other small islands became 'non dependent states' in 1967.
18. Roy Hattersley, quoted in Rose et al., *Colour and Citizenship*.
19. Sheila Patterson, *Immigration and Race Relations in Britain, 1960–67* (London, Oxford University Press for IRR, 1969).
20. 'Address given by the Home Secretary, the Rt. Hon. Roy Jenkins, MP, on 23 May 1966 to a meeting of Voluntary Liaison Committees', London, NCCI, 1966.
21. In a speech supporting immigration control, Roy Hattersley MP (Labour) remarked that it was now 'necessary to impose a test which tries to analyse which immigrants, as well having jobs or special skills are most likely to be assimilated into our national life'. This would, he added, favour the English-speaking West Indians as against the Pakistanis (see Patterson, *Immigration and Race Relations in Britain, 1960–67*).
22. *Times* news team, *The Black Man in Search of Power* (London, Nelson, 1968).
23. See 'The liberation of the black intellectual' [Chapter 1, this volume].
24. In 1974 the median settlement was £23.50. *White Paper on Racial Discrimination* (London, HMSO, September 1975).
25. This refers to the Spaghetti House Siege [see Chapter 5, this volume].
26. 'Gunning for a wage', *Race Today* (Vol. 7, no. 10, October 1975).

27. Antonio Gramsci, *Selections from the Prison Notebooks*, edited by Quintin Hoare and G. Nowell Smith (London, Lawrence and Wishart, 1971).

5 From Resistance to Rebellion: Asian and Afro-Caribbean Struggles in Britain

1. Ruth Glass and Harold Pollins, *Newcomers* (London, Centre for Urban Studies and George Allen & Unwin, 1960).
2. D.R. Manley, 'The social structure of the Liverpool Negro community with special reference to the formations of formal associations', unpublished thesis (1958).
3. *The Keys* (Vol. 3, no. 2, October–December 1925).
4. Edward Scobie, *Black Britannia* (Chicago, Johnson Publishing Co., 1972).
5. From it sprang *Link*, *Carib*, *Anglo-Caribbean News*, *Tropic*, *Flamingo*, *Daylight International*, *West Indies Observer*, *Magnet* and others.
6. 'Without integration, limitation is inexcusable; without limitation, integration is impossible.' Roy Hattersley, 1965.
7. That Fenner Brockway, a ceaseless campaigner for colonial freedom, had introduced a Private Member's anti-discrimination bill year after year after year from 1951 had, of course, made no impact on Labour consciousness.
8. *West Indies Observer* (Vol. 1, no. 19, 4 May 1963).
9. *West Indies Observer* (Vol. 1, no. 22, 15 June 1963).
10. *West Indies Observer* (No. 36, 18 January 1964).
11. Joseph A. Hunte, *Nigger Hunting in England* (London, West Indian Standing Conference, 1965).
12. Commonwealth Immigration Advisory Council, *Second Report* (London, 1964).
13. Department of Education Circular 7/65 (London, 1965).
14. Paul Foot, 'The strike at Courtaulds, Preston', *IRR Newsletter* Supplement, July 1965.
15. Peter Marsh, *The Anatomy of a Strike* (London, IRR, 1967).
16. Raas, a Jamaican swear word, gave a West Indian flavour to Black Power.
17. I remember the time in South London when an old black woman was being jostled and pushed out of a bus queue. Michael went up and stood behind her, an ill-concealed machete in his hand – and the line of lily-white queuers vanished before her – and she entered the bus like royalty.

18. The National Federation of Pakistani Associations was formed in 1963.

19. *Times* news team, *The Black Man in Search of Power* (London, Nelson, 1968).

20. A. Sivanandan, *Race and Resistance: the IRR story* (London, IRR, 1974). See also Jenny Bourne and A. Sivanandan, 'Cheerleaders and ombudsmen: the sociology of race relations in Britain', *Race & Class* (Vol. 21, no. 4, 1980).

21. In real life and real struggle, the economic, the political and the ideological move in concert, with sometimes one and sometimes the other striking the dominant note – but orchestrated, always, by the mode of production. It is only the marxist textualists who are preoccupied with 'determinisms', economic and otherwise.

22. Dilip Hiro, *Black British, White British* (Harmondsworth, Penguin, 1971).

23. *The Times* (24 October 1967) quoted in *IRR Newsletter*, December 1967.

24. *IRR Newsletter*, December 1967.

25. Ibid.

26. Such as the Naxalites, Adivasis, Dalit Panthers in India, and the Pakhtun, Sindhi and Baluchi oppressed people's movements in Pakistan. In 1974 organisations of untouchables in Britain came together at the (new) IRR to organise an International Conference on Untouchability (which for financial reasons never got off the ground).

27. Quoted in E.J.B. Rose et al., *Colour and Citizenship* (London, Oxford University Press for IRR, 1969).

28. There were in fact about 66,000 at this time who were entitled to settle in Britain.

29. Jagmohan Joshi, quoted in C. Karadia, 'The BPA', *IRR Newsletter*, June 1968.

30. A reference to Powell's Birmingham speech (April 1968) in which he said: 'As I look ahead, I am filled with foreboding. Like the Roman, I seem to see "the River Tiber foaming with much blood".'

31. The Bill proposed to give immigrants who were refused entry the right of appeal to a tribunal.

32. A. Sivanandan, 'Imperialism and disorganic development in the silicon age' [see Chapter 8, this volume].

33. JCWI was set up in 1967 as a one-man welfare service for incoming dependants at Heathrow Airport, but later burgeoned into a case-work and campaigning organisation.

34. According to a letter in the *Guardian* of 10 September 1981 from members of Jawaharlal Nehru University (Delhi), there are still

'20,000 people of Indian origin from East Africa... waiting in India for their entry vouchers to the UK'.

35. See, for example, Robert Moore and Tina Wallace, *Slamming the Door* (London, Martin Robertson, 1975).

36. See 'Notes and documents' in *Race & Class*, special issue, 'Rebellion and repression: Britain '81' (Vol. 23, nos 2/3, 1981/2).

37. John La Rose had been Executive of the Federated Workers' Trade Union in Trinidad and Tobago.

38. It was one of the founders of this school, Tony Munro, who was later to be involved in the Knightsbridge Spaghetti House siege.

39. The BWM (Black Workers' Movement) was the new name the Black Panthers took in the early 1970s.

40. Louis Kushnick, 'Black Power and the media', *Race Today* (November 1970).

41. See Institute of Race Relations, *Police Against Black People* (London, 1979), and various issues of *Race Today* for the important trials of this period.

42. Stuart Hall et al., *Policing the Crisis* (London, Macmillan, 1978).

43. IRR, *Police Against Black People*.

44. These included representatives from Indian, Pakistani and West Indian associations and from black political organisations such as the BPFM, BUFP, BCC and the Black Workers' Coordinating Committee, etc.

45. For all the above strikes, see various issues of the *BPFM Weekly*, (later *Uhuru*), the *BWAC Weekly Review*, *Black Voice* and *Race Today*.

46. See Colin Prescod, 'The people's cause in the Caribbean', *Race & Class* (Vol. 17, no. 1, 1975); Horace Campbell, 'Rastafari: culture of resistance', *Race & Class* (Vol. 22, no. 1, 1980) and Paul Gilroy, 'You can't fool the youths', *Race & Class* (Vol. 23, nos 2/3, 1981/2).

47. The Community Relations Commission (CRC) emerged as the successor to the NCCI in the Race Relations Act of 1968.

48. A. Sivanandan, 'Race, class and the state: the political economy of immigration' [see Chapter 4, this volume].

49. Sir Robert Mark, *In the Office of Constable* (London, Collins, 1978).

50. See Tony Bunyan, *The Political Police in Britain* (London, Julian Friedmann, 1976), and S. Chibnall, *Law and Order News* (London, Tavistock, 1977).

51. 'Race and the press', *Race & Class* (Vol. 17, no. 1, Summer 1976).

52. IRR, *Police Against Black People*.

53. Campaign Against Racism and Fascism/Southall Rights, *Southall: the birth of a black community* (London, IRR, 1981).

54. See 'Grunwick', *Race & Class* (Vol. 19, no. 1, 1977), and 'UK commentary', *Race & Class* (Vol. 19, no. 3, 1978).
55. A. Sivanandan, 'From immigration control to "induced repatriation"', see *Race & Class* (Vol. 20, no. 1, 1978).
56. Campaign Against Racism and Fascism/Southall Rights, *Southall*.
57. 3 July 1981 – the day on which Asian youths burnt down a public house at which a racist pop group and its skinhead fans had gathered. This event was part of the 1981 uprisings.
58. Tax relief in respect of dependent children was replaced by child benefit paid to wives – but those with children abroad were not entitled to it, even if they were supporting them.
59. See 'Notes and documents', *Race & Class* (Vol. 23, nos 2/3, 1981/2).
60. Symbolically, the man who had initiated so many of the black working-class and community movements of the early years and clarified for us all the lines of race/class struggle, Jagmohan Joshi, died on the march, of a heart attack.
61. Campbell was arrested on 1 March 1980 on charges he claimed were false. From 10 March he refused food and drink. On the 26th he was force-fed. On the 31st he was found dead in his cell. Steve Thompson, who was also a Rasta, had a year earlier been forcibly shorn of his locks and following his protest sent to Rampton Mental Hospital. A Home Office circular denying recognition of Rastafarianism as a religion in prisons had been issued in 1976 (60/76). In 1977, a white sociologist showed in a Cranfield Police Study how the Rastas were terrorising the police of Handsworth (Birmingham). In April 1981, the Home Office confirmed its circular. In June, 'Tubby' Jeffers collapsed in prison from refusing food that violated his Rasta beliefs.
62. The Race Today Collective emerged from the radicalisation of the Institute of Race Relations (1969–72) as an independent black journal and had grown, under Darcus Howe and John La Rose, into an activist collective.
63. For example, Greater Manchester Chief Constable James Anderton referred to police critics 'as creepy and dangerous minorities… who are obviously using the protection imparted by our very constitution in order first to undermine it and then eventually to displace it' (September 1980).
64. Juries, opined Sir Robert Mark, 'perform the duty rarely, know little of the law, are occasionally stupid, prejudiced, barely literate and often incapable of applying the law as public opinion is led to suppose they do' (*Observer*, 16 March 1975).

65. Declaring that 'prejudice is a state of mind brought about by experience', Detective Superintendent Holland identified long-haired, unshaven youths as the ones likely to have cannabis and West Indians hanging around in jeans and T-shirts as likely 'muggers' (*Guardian*, 14 September 1981).

6 RAT and the Degradation of Black Struggle

1. J.L. Watson, 'Introduction: immigration, ethnicity and class in Britain', in J.L. Watson (ed.), *Between Two Cultures: migrants and minorities in Britain* (Oxford, Blackwell, 1977).
2. P. Weinreich, 'Ethnicity and adolescent identity conflicts: a comparative study', in Verity Saifullah Khan (ed.), *Minority Families in Britain: support and stress* (London, Macmillan, 1979).
3. Roger Ballard and Catherine Ballard, 'The Sikhs: the development of South Asian settlements in Britain', in Watson (ed.), *Between Two Cultures*.
4. Sandra Wallman, 'The scope for ethnicity', in Sandra Wallman (ed.), *Ethnicity at Work* (London, Macmillan, 1979).
5. 'The Brixton disorders, 10–12 April 1981: report of an inquiry by… Lord Scarman' (London, HMSO, 1981).
6. US Department of Labor, *The Negro Family: the case for national action*, compiled by D.P. Moynihan (Washington, USGPO, 1965).
7. See also Martin Barker and Anne Beezer, 'The language of racism – an examination of Lord Scarman's report on the Brixton riots', *International Socialism* (Winter 1982–3), pp. 108–25.
8. *Report of the National Advisory Commission on Civil Disorders*, Chairman Otto Kerner (New York, Bantam Books, 1968).
9. US Commission on Civil Rights, 'Racism in America and how to combat it' (Washington, USCCR, 1970).
10. P.C. Goldin, 'A model for racial awareness training of teachers in integrated schools', *Integrated Education* (No. 43, January–February 1970), pp. 62–4.
11. P. Bidol and R.C. Weber, *Developing New Perspectives on Race: an innovative multimedia social studies curriculum in race relations for secondary level* (Detroit, Detroit New Speakers Bureau, 1970), and P. Bidol, 'A rap on race – a mini lecture on racism awareness', *International Books for Children* (Vol. 3, no. 6, 1974), pp. 9–10.
12. R.W. Terry, *For Whites Only* (Detroit, William B. Eerdmans, 1970).
13. See Judy H. Katz, *White Awareness Handbook for Anti-Racism Training* (Norman, University of Oklahoma Press, 1978).
14. Quoted in ibid.

15. Quoted in ibid.
16. Quoted in ibid.
17. Ibid.
18. Nadine Peppard, 'Towards effective race relations training', *New Community* (Vol. 8, nos 1/2, Spring–Summer 1980), pp. 99–106.
19. Phil Baker and Elizabeth Hoadley-Maidment, 'The social psychology of prejudice: an introduction' (Southall, National Centre for Industrial Language Training, 1980).
20. See Benedict Anderson, *Imagined Communities: reflections on the origin and spread of nationalism* (London, Verso, 1983).
21. See the CRE report, *Local Government and Racial Equality* (London, CRE, 1982); Joint Government/Local Authority Association Working Group, *Local Authorities and Racial Disadvantage* (Department of the Environment, 1983); and the conference which followed, 'Local authorities and racial disadvantage', London, 21 March 1984 (Bichard Report); 'Race equality – strategies for London boroughs', report of the LBA/CRE/LACRC conference for councillors, Sussex, 1–3 July 1983.
22. Home Office Press Release, 21 March 1984.
23. *Evening Standard* (16 October 1984).
24. Colin Brown, *Black and White in Britain: the third PSI survey* (London, Heinemann, 1984).
25. Committee of Inquiry into the Education of children from ethnic minority groups, 'West Indian children in our schools', Chairman Anthony Rampton (London, HMSO, June 1981).
26. NAS/UWT, 'Multi-ethnic education', Birmingham, NAS UWT [1984].
27. D. Ruddell and M. Simpson, 'Recognising racism: a filmstrip, slide and cassette presentation for racism awareness training' (Birmingham, Education Department, 1982).
28. 'Towards anti-racist strategies: a course for teachers' (ILEA Centre for Anti-Racist Education, 1984).
29. Nadine Peppard, 'Race relations training: the state of the art', *New Community* (Vol. 2, nos 1/2, Autumn/Winter 1983), pp. 150–9.
30. Quoted in T. Holden, *People, Churches and Multi-Racial Projects* (London, Methodist Church, 1984).
31. Ecumenical Unit for Racism Awareness Programmes, Annual Report, 1983–4.
32. National Convention of Black Teachers, 'Police racism and union collusion – the John Fernandes case' (London, NCBT, 1983).
33. P. Southgate, 'Racism awareness training for the police: report of a pilot study by the Home Office (London, Home Office, 1984).

34. See 'Scabbing against Fernandes', *Asian Times* (28 October 1983), and 'Racism Awareness Programme Unit', *Asian Times* (25 November 1983).
35. For a description of a RAT course, and a critique, see the CARF articles in *Searchlight* (January and February 1985, nos 115 and 116).
36. Lewisham Racism Awareness Training Unit, Black awareness programme, 9–10 August 1984.
37. Denise Winn, 'Would you pass the colour test?' *Cosmopolitan* (January 1985).
38. See Jenny Bourne, 'Towards an anti-racist feminism' (London, IRR, 1984), *Race & Class* pamphlet no. 9.
39. See Ruddell and Simpson, 'Recognising racism'; Ashok Ohri, Basil Manning and Paul Curnow (eds), *Community Work and Racism* (London, Routledge and Kegan Paul, 1982).
40. Martin Webster, in *Spearhead* (May–June 1979).

8 Imperialism and Disorganic Development in the Silicon Age

1. GATT was set up to regulate trade between nations, the IMF to help nations adjust to free trade by providing balance-of-payments financial assistance, the World Bank to facilitate the movement of capital to war-torn Europe and aid to developing countries.
2. See *Ampo*, special issue, 'Free trade zones and industrialisation of Asia' (Vol. 8, no. 4 and Vol. 9 nos 1–2, 1977).
3. Even in the period of import-substitution – more succinctly described by the Japanese as 'export-substitution investment' – the multinational corporations were able to move in 'behind tariff barriers to produce locally what they had hitherto imported'. (*Ampo*, op. cit.)
4. The first Free Trade Zone was established at Shannon airport in Ireland in 1958 and was followed by Taiwan in 1965. In 1967 the United Nations Industrial Development Organisation was set up to promote industrialisation in developing countries and soon embarked on the internationalisation of Free Trade Zones into a global system. South Korea established a Free Trade Zone in 1970, the Philippines in 1972 and Malaysia in the same year. By 1974, Egypt, Gambia, Ivory Coast, Kenya, Senegal, Sri Lanka, Jamaica, Liberia, Syria, Trinidad and Tobago and Sudan were asking UNIDO to draw up plans for Free Trade Zones. (*Ampo*, op. cit.) Sri Lanka set up its Free Trade Zone last year soon after a right-wing government had taken power, albeit through the ballot box.

5. Jeff Frieden, 'The Trilateral Commission: economics and politics in the 1970s', *Monthly Review* (Vol. 29, no. 7, December 1977).

6. Richard Falk, 'A new paradigm for international legal studies', *The Yale Law Journal* (Vol. 84, no. 5, April 1975).

7. Selangor Graduates Society, *Plight of the Malaysian Workers in Singapore* (Kuala Lumpur, 1978).

8. Walter Easey, 'Notes on child labour in Hong Kong', *Race & Class* (Vol. 18, no. 4, Spring 1977).

9. Jon Stewart and John Markoff, 'The microprocessor revolution', *Pacific News Service*, Global Factory, Part II of VI.

10. Association of Scientific Technical and Managerial Staffs (ASTMS), *Technological Change and Collective Bargaining* (London, 1978).

11. D. Butler, abstract, *The Convergence of Technologies*, Report Series no. 5, Butler Cox Foundation, quoted in ASTMS, *Technological Change and Collective Bargaining*.

12. Ieuan Maddock, 'Beyond the Protestant ethic', *New Scientist* (23 November 1978).

13. Ibid.

14. Harry Braverman, *Labor and Monopoly Capital* (New York, 1974).

15. Counter Information Services, *The New Technology*, Anti-Report no. 23 (London, 1979).

16. Philip Virgo, *Cashing in on the Chips* (London, 1979).

17. Cited in Rachael Grossman, 'Women's place in the integrated circuit', *Southeast Asia Chronicle* (No. 66, Jan–Feb 1979).

18. Ibid.

19. 'Workers who must dip components in acids and rub them with solvents frequently experience serious burns, dizziness, nausea, sometimes even losing their fingers in accidents... It will be 10 or 15 years before the possible carcinogenic effects begin to show up in women who work with them now.' *Southeast Asia Chronicle* (No. 66, Jan–Feb 1979).

20. Cited in ibid.

21. See A. Lin Neumann, '"Hospitality girls" in the Philippines', *Southeast Asia Chronicle* (No. 66, Jan–Feb 1979).

22. See 'The Day After tomorrow', by Peter Large, *Guardian*, 17 February 1979.

23. For the purposes of the general analysis presented here, I make no distinction between periphery and developing periphery.

24. Amilcar Cabral, *Return to the Source* (New York, 1973).

9   New Circuits of Imperialism

1. Sir Ieuan Maddock, 'Beyond the Protestant ethic', *New Scientist* (23 November 1978).

2. Robin Murray, 'Ownership, control and the market', *New Left Review* (No. 164, July/August 1987).

3. Paul Handley, 'Long road to success', *Far Eastern Economic Review* (28 January 1988).

4. Peter Large, 'Pirelli slips into total automation on its Welsh industrial Kibbutz', *Guardian* (4 August 1988).

5. Nick Garnett, 'The culture shock of automation', *Financial Times* (7 October 1988).

6. Wladimir Andreff, 'The international centralisation of capital and the re-ordering of world capitalism', *Capital and Class* (No. 22, Spring 1984).

7. Charles Leadbeater, 'Dagenham's decline is Genk's gain', *Financial Times* (30 January 1989).

8. 'South Korea embarks on a mass memory test', *Far Eastern Economic Review* (18 August 1988).

9. John McBeth and Mark Clifford, 'Ambitious flight plans filed: South Korea wants to buy an aerospace industry', *Far Eastern Economic Review* (9 June 1988).

10. Bob Johnstone, 'Taiwan has designs on booming niche markets', *Far Eastern Economic Review* (18 August 1988).

11. *Latin American Monitor* (Vol. 6, no. 1, February 1989).

12. *Multinational Monitor* (Vol. 8, no. 2, February 1987).

13. *Latin American Monitor* (Vol. 6, no. 1, February 1989).

14. Nigel Harris, *The End of the Third World: newly industrialising countries and the decline of an ideology* (London, 1987).

15. Ibid.

16. Clive Hamilton, 'Can the rest of Asia emulate the NICs?', *Third World Quarterly* (Vol. 9, no. 4, October 1987).

17. Peter Evans, *Dependent Development: the alliance of multinational, state and local capital in Brazil* (Princeton, New Jersey, 1979).

18. Walter Schwarz, *Guardian* (13 February and 27 February 1989); Louise Byrne, *Observer* (26 February 1989), and 'The world this week', Channel Four TV (26 February 1989).

19. Harris, *The End of the Third World*.

20. Susan George, *A Fate Worse Than Debt* (London, 1988).

21. 'South Korea embarks on a mass memory test', op. cit.

22. Bob Johnstone, 'Diverting the brain drain: Taiwan science park woos hi-tech entrepreneurs', *Far Eastern Economic Review* (28 January 1988).

23. Carl Goldstein, 'Government pushes Singapore into wafer fabrication', *Far Eastern Economic Review* (18 August 1988).

24. See A. Sivanandan, 'Imperialism and disorganic development in the silicon age' [Chapter 8, this volume], and Swasti Mitter, *Common*

Fate, Common Bond: women in the global economy (London, 1986).

25. Global and Conceptual Studies Branch Division for Industrial Studies, *Restructuring World Industry in a Period of Crisis – the role of innovation* (Vienna, UNIDO, 1981).
26. Nick Seaward, 'A rethink on rationalisation', *Far Eastern Economic Review* (24 March 1988).
27. Carl Goldstein, 'Malaysia's back-end boom', *Far Eastern Economic Review* (25 August 1988).
28. Nick Seaward, 'The race to stay ahead', *Far Eastern Economic Review* (8 October 1987), and Nick Seaward, 'A new pragmatism', *Far Eastern Economic Review* (21 January 1988).
29. Paul Handley, 'Long road to success', *Far Eastern Economic Review* (28 January 1988), and Michael Vatikiotis, 'The energy to change', *Far Eastern Economic Review* (21 January 1988).
30. Carl Goldstein, 'Asia's supermarket', *Far Eastern Economic Review* (29 December 1988), and Paisai Sricharatchanya, 'Not just chicken feed', *Far Eastern Economic Review* (3 March 1988).
31. Saskia Sassen, *The Mobility of Labor and Capital* (Cambridge, 1988).
32. Quoted in Armand Mattelart, *Transnationals and the Third World* (Massachusetts, 1983).
33. Michael T. Klare, 'The interventionist impulse', in Michael T. Klare and Peter Kornbluh, *Low Intensity Warfare* (New York, 1988).
34. Lieutenant Colonel John M. Oseth, quoted in Klare, 'The interventionist impulse'.
35. Daniel Siegel and Joy Hackel, 'El Salvador: counterinsurgency revisited', in Klare and Kornbluh, *Low Intensity Warfare*.
36. Peter Kornbluh, 'Nicaragua: US proinsurgency warfare', in Klare and Kornbluh, *Low Intensity Warfare*.
37. *Joint Low-Intensity Conflict Project Final Report*, quoted in Michael T. Klare and Peter Kornbluh, 'The new interventionism', in Klare and Kornbluh, *Low Intensity Warfare*.
38. Quoted in Kornbluh, 'Nicaragua: US proinsurgency warfare'.
39. 'The masters of war', *The Four Horsemen*, Central TV (9 April 1986).
40. Ibid.
41. Quoted in Klare and Kornbluh, 'The new interventionism'.
42. A. Sivanandan, 'Racism 1992', *New Statesman & Society* (4 November 1988).
43. Günter Wallraff, *Lowest of the Low* (London, 1988).

BIBLIOGRAPHY OF WRITINGS BY A. SIVANANDAN

Books and pamphlets

Race and Resistance: the IRR story (London, Race Today Publications, March 1975)

A Different Hunger: writings on black resistance (London, Pluto Press, 1982)

Communities of Resistance: writings on black struggles for socialism (London, Verso, 1990)

When Memory Dies (a novel) (London, Arcadia, 1997)

Where the Dance Is (short stories) (London, Arcadia, 2000)

Articles and papers

'The Ceylon scene', *IRR Newsletter* (March 1966)

'Fanon: the violence of the violated', *IRR Newsletter* (N.S. Vol. 1, no. 8, August 1967)

'White racism and black', *Encounter* (Vol. 31, no. 1, July 1968)

'A farewell to liberalism', *IRR Newsletter* (N.S. Vol. 3, no. 4, April 1969)

'The politics of language 3: Ceylon, an essay in interpretation', *Race Today* (Vol. 2, no. 6, June 1970)

'Culture and identity', *Liberator* (Vol. 10, no. 6, June 1970)

'Revolt of the Natives', *Liberator* (Vol. 11, nos 1–2, January/February 1971).
  Also in *Twentieth Century* (Vol. 177, no. 1038, 1968), original title, 'Black's move'

'Black power: the politics of existence', *Politics and Society* (Vol. 1, no. 2, February 1971)

'The passing of the king', *Race Today* (Vol. 3, no. 4, April 1971)

'Thoughts on prison', *Race Today* (Vol. 3, no. 10, October 1971)

'The anatomy of racism', paper presented at *Race Relations Research Conference*, London, IRR, 18 February 1972

Skin: a one-act play, *Race Today* (Vol. 4, no. 5, May 1972)

'Angelus', *Race Today* (Vol. 4, no. 7, July 1972)

'Anatomy of racism: the British variant', *Race Today* (Vol. 4, no. 7, July 1972)

'Race, class and power: an outline for study', *Race* (Vol. 14, no. 4, July/April 1973)

'Opinion on academic violence', *Race Today* (Vol. 5, no. 6, June 1973)

'The Institute story: the unacceptable face', *Race Today* (Vol. 6, no. 3, March 1974)

'Alien Gods', in B. Parekh (ed.), *Colour, Culture and Consciousness: immigrant intellectuals in Britain* (London, George Allen and Unwin, 1974)

Also in *Race & Class* (Vol. 18, no. 4, Spring 1977) as 'The liberation of the black intellectual'

Also in *Economic Review* (February 1976)

'Race, class and the state: the black experience in Britain', *Race & Class* (Vol. 17, no. 4, Spring 1976)

'Race and resistance: Asian youth in the vanguard', *Sandesh International Supplement* (4 July 1976)

'Race, class and the state 2: Grunwick: report on the West Indian community', *Race & Class* (Vol. 19, no. 1, Summer 1977)

'Report from Sri Lanka, August 1977', *Race & Class* (Vol. 19, no. 2, Autumn 1977)

'Sri Lanka: uses of racism', *Economic and Political Weekly* (Vol. 12, no. 41, 8 October 1977)

'Grunwick 2', *Race & Class* (Vol. 19, no. 3, Winter 1978)

'From immigration control to induced repatriation', *Race & Class* (Vol. 20, no. 1, Summer 1978)

'The case for self-defence', *Rights* (Vol. 3, no.3, January/February 1979) (with Jenny Bourne)

'From immigration to repatriation: "the imperial imperative": research perspectives in the field of immigrant labour', paper, Berlin, Berliner Institut für Vergleichende Sozialforschung, June 1979

'Imperialism and disorganic development in the silicon age', *Race & Class* (Vol. 21, no. 2, Autumn 1979)

Also in *Monthly Review* (Vol. 32, no. 3, July/August 1980)

Also as '*Von der Einwanderung sur Rückwanderung: die Imperative des Imperialismus*', Berlin, Berliner Institut für Vergleichende Sozialforschung, June 1979

Also (excerpts) in *The Witness* (Vol. 64, no. 11, November 1981)

'*Die Neue Industrielle Revolution*', in J. Blaschke and K. Greussing (eds), '*Dritte Welt' in Europa: Probleme der Arbeitsimmigration* (Frankfurt, Syndikat, 1980)

'Race, class and caste in South Africa: an open letter to No Sizwe', *Race & Class* (Vol. 22, no. 3, Winter 1981)

'White man, listen', *Encounter* (July 1981)

'From resistance to rebellion: Asian and Afro-Caribbean struggles in Britain', *Race & Class* (Vol. 23, nos 2/3, Autumn 1981/Winter 1982)

'The black struggle in Britain', *Heritage* (No. 1, 1984)

'London's black workers', *Jobs for a Change* (No. 8, May 1984)

'Sri Lanka: racism and the politics of underdevelopment', *Race & Class* (Vol. 21, no. 1, Summer 1984)

'RAT and the degradation of black struggle', *Race & Class* (Vol. 26, no. 4, Spring 1985)
   Also in London Strategic Policy Unit, *Racism Awareness Training: a critique* (London, LSPU, 1987)

'In the castle of their skin', *New Statesman* (7 June 1985) (extracts from 'RAT...')

'The sentence of racism', *New Statesman* (14 June 1985) (extracts from 'RAT...')

'Britain's Gulags', *New Socialist* (November 1985)
   Also in *Race & Class* (Vol. 27, no. 3, Winter 1986)

'Britain and the anatomy of racism', *Racial Justice* (No. 3, Spring 1986)

'Race, class and Brent', *Race & Class* (Vol. 29, no. 1, Summer 1987)

'Left, Right and Burnage: no such thing as anti-racist ideology', *New Statesman* (27 May 1988)
   Also in *Race & Class* (Vol. 30, no. 1, July/September 1988)

'The new racism', *New Statesman and Society* (4 November 1988)
   Also in *Race & Class* (Vol. 30, no. 3, January/March 1989)

'Rules of engagement', *International* (February 1989)

'New circuits of imperialism', *Race & Class* (Vol. 30, no. 4, April/June 1989)
   Also in *Etudes Marxistes* (No. 4, August/September 1989)

'Racisme', *La Breche* (No. 445, 16 February 1990)

'All that melts into air is solid: the hokum of New Times', *Race & Class* (Vol. 31, no. 3, January/March 1990)

'The enigma of the colonised: reflections on Naipaul's arrival', *Race & Class* (Vol. 32, no. 1, July/September 1990)

'Whatever happened to imperialism?' *New Statesman and Society* (11 October 1991)

'Black struggles against racism', in CCETSW, *Setting the Context for Change* (London, CCETSW, 1991)

'Letter to God', *New Statesman and Society* (Christmas supplement, 1991)

'From resistance to rebellion', in *Texte zur Rassissmus Diskussion* (Berlin, Schwarze-Risse, 1992)

'Into the waste lands', *New Statesman and Society* (19 June 1992)

'Race against time', *New Statesman and Society* (15 October 1993)
Also in *Race & Class* (Vol. 35, no. 3, January/March 1994) as 'Millwall and after'

'Capitalism, globalization and epochal shifts: an exchange', *Monthly Review* (Vol. 48, no. 9, February 1997)

'The making of home to the beat of a different drum', *Race & Class* (Vol. 39, no. 3, January/March 1998)

'Globalism and the Left', *Race & Class* (Vol. 40, nos 2/3, October 1998/ March 1999)

'Seize the time', *CARF* (No. 48, February/March 1999)
Also in *Black Housing* (No. 105, April/May 1999)

'The rise and fall of institutional racism', *CARF* (No. 54, December/ January 2000)

'How Labour failed the Lawrence test', *Guardian* (21 February 2000)
Also in *Multicultural Teaching* (Vol. 18, no. 2, Spring 2000)

'Refugees from globalism', *CARF* (No. 56, August/September 2000)
Also in *Race & Class* (Vol. 42 no. 3, January/March 2001)

'Reclaiming the struggle', *Race & Class* (Vol. 42, no. 2, October/ December 2000)

'Poverty is the new Black', *Guardian* (17 August 2001)
Also in *Race & Class* (Vol. 43, no. 2, October/December 2001) and excerpt in *CARF* (No. 64, October/November 2001)

'Jan Carew, renaissance man', *Race & Class* (Vol. 43, no. 3, January/ March 2002)

'Globalism's imperial war', *CARF* (No. 70, Spring 2003)

'We the (only) people', *CARF* (No. 71, Summer 2003)

'*Race & Class* – the next thirty years', *Race & Class* (Vol. 46, no. 3, January/March 2005)

'It's anti-racism that was failed, not multiculturalism that failed', *IRR News* (12 October, 2005, www.irr.org/2005/october/ak000021. html)

'How Britain lets down minorities', *Observer* (16 October 2005)

'Racisme, globalisering og krigen mot terror', *Samora* (No. 4/5, 2006)

'Race, terror and civil society', *Race & Class* (Vol. 47, no. 3, January/ March 2006)

'The rules of the game', in Tony Bunyan (ed.), *The War on Freedom and Democracy: essays on civil liberties in Europe* (Nottingham, Spokesman, 2006)

'Britain's shame', *Catalyst* (July/August 2006)

'Attacks on multicultural Britain pave the way for enforced assimilation', *Guardian* (13 September 2006)

'Liberal elitists who ignore the context of power and privilege', *Guardian* (30 November 2006)

Texts of speeches

'Race: the revolutionary experience', given at World Council of Churches Consultation on Racism, 19–24 May 1969, in *Race Today* (Vol. 1, no. 4, August 1969)

'Challenging racism: strategies for the '80s', given at GLC's Consultation on Racism, 12 March 1983, in *Race & Class* (Vol. 25, no. 2, Autumn 1983)

'Our struggles are one', given at Friends' House, 21 March 1984, in *Asian Times* (13 April 1984)

'The struggle for Black Arts in Britain', given at Africa Centre, 8 May 1986, in *Race & Class* (Vol. 28, no. 1, Summer 1986)

'Britain as it is: socio-economic-political perspective', *Report of the Western Europe Urban Rural Mission Consultation, 18–22 April 1988* (Geneva, World Council of Churches, 1988)

'Reclaiming the fight against racism', *Southall Review* (Spring 1989)

'The international perspective', excerpts from a speech given at Communities of Resistance Conference, Hackney, 11 November 1989, in *Communities of Resistance 1992* (London, Communities of Resistance Network, 1991)

'A Black perspective on the war', given at Black People Against War in the Gulf, 5 February 1991, in *Race & Class* (Vol. 32, no. 4, April/June 1991)

'Address to the 10th National Congress of the Azanian People's Organisation (AZAPO)', *Race & Class* (Vol. 33, no. 2, October/December 1991)

'Our passports on our faces', excerpts from a speech given to the Refugee Council's Annual Conference, November 1991, in *CARF* (No. 6, January/February 1992)

Address to FBHO Ninth Annual Conference, *Black Housing* (October/November 1992)

'Racism: the road from Germany', expansion of talk given at PDS Europaischer Kongress gegen Rassissmus, 13–15 November 1992, in *Race & Class* (Vol. 34, no. 3, January/March 1993)

'Proposals for an anti-racist policy in Europe', given at the Anti-Racist Congress of the Party of Democratic Socialism (PDS), Berlin, 13 November 1992 Also (abridged) in *New Statesman and Society* (4 December 1992)

'Why teach? The role of the educator in social work', given at CCETSW workshop, 27–28 January 1993, in *Issues for Black Tutors*, CCETSW, January 1993

'Beyond statewatching', talk given at the Statewatching the New Europe Conference, 27 March 1993, in T. Bunyan (ed.), *Statewatching the*

New Europe: a handbook on the European state (London, Statewatch, 1993)

'The Black politics of health', address to the King's Fund Consultation for Black Health Workers, in *Race & Class* (Vol. 34, no. 4, April/June 1993)

'Hilary Arnott 1944–1994', given at the memorial meeting, 31 January 1995, in *Race & Class* (Vol. 36, no. 4, April/June 1995)

'*La trahison des clercs*', given at the ICA, 18 May 1995, in *Race & Class* (Vol. 37, no. 3, January/March 1996)

Also in *New Statesman and Society* (14 July 1995)

Also in *Polyglot* (Vol. 1, 1996)

'Communications of resistance', given at 2nd AMARC Pan-European Conference of Community Radio Broadcasters, 16–19 October 1996, in *Voices Without Frontiers Conference Report* (Sheffield, AMARC, 1996)

'The contours of global racism', given at the Crossing Borders Conference, London Metropolitan University 15/16 November 2002, in *IRR News* (www.irr.org.uk/2002/november/ak000006.html)

'Racism in the age of globalisation', given at 3rd Claudia Jones Memorial Lecture, 28 October 2004, in *IRR News* (www.irr.org.uk/2004/october/ha000024.html)

'The development of the Institute and its library', given at the opening of the Sivanandan Collection at the University of Warwick Library, 27 April 2006, in *IRR News* (www.irr.org.uk/2006/may/ha000007.html)

'The global context', keynote speech at IRR's 'Racism, Liberty and the War on Terror' conference, September 2006, in *Race & Class* (Vol. 48, no. 4, April/June, 2007)

Interviews

'The bobby is back on the beat(ing)', interview conducted by Paul Gilroy, *Afdrule*, undated

Untitled interview, *Sunday Times* (Sri Lanka), September 1977

'If they come for us in the morning, they will come for you in the night', *Big Flame* (March 1978)

'Fighting Tory racism', interview by CARF, *Race & Class* (Vol. 21, no. 3, Winter 1980)

Also in *Searchlight* (No. 54, December 1979)

'The Institute is a servicing-station for black people on their way to liberation', *Shakti* (November 1983)

'Race and class', *London Labour Briefing* (No. 43, October 1984)

'Blacks and the Black Sections', interview by CARF, *Race & Class* (Vol. 27, no. 2, Autumn 1985)
  Also as 'Black sections and the Labour Party', *Searchlight* (No. 124, October 1985)
  Also in *Brighton Labour Campaigner* (No. 5, December 1985)
Untitled interview, *Sri Lanka Human Rights Bulletin* (No. 7, October 1987)
Untitled interview, *The Journal* (No. 6, Spring 1988)
'Racism, education and the black child', *Links* (No. 34, 1989)
'Signs of the times', interview by Paul Grant, *Race & Class* (Vol. 33, no. 4, April/June 1992)
  Also in P. Grant and R. Patel (eds), *A Time to Act: Kairos 1992* (Birmingham, Evangelical Christians for Racial Justice, 1992)
  Also in *Silsila – Zeitschrift gegen Rassissmus und Imperialismus* (January 1993)
'Black is a political colour...', *Labour Briefing* (February 1993)
'Communities of Resistance', *New Times* (No. 54, 19 March 1994)
'Fighting our fundamentalisms', interview by CARF, *Race & Class* (Vol. 36, no. 3, January/March 1995)
  Also in *CARF* (No. 24, February/March 1995)
'Heresies and prophecies: the social and political fall-out of the technological revolution', *Race & Class* (Vol. 37, no. 4, April/June 1996)
  Also in J. Davis, T. Hirschl and M. Stack (eds), *Cutting Edge: technology, information capitalism and social revolution* (London, Verso, 1997)
  Also in *cy-rev* (No. 5, 1998)
'The colour line is the poverty line', in S. Greenberg (ed.), *Hate Thy Neighbour: the dividing lines of race and culture* (London, Camden Press, 1998) (Mindfield series)
'The struggle for a radical black culture', in Kwesi Owusu (ed.), *Black British Culture* (London, Routledge, 1999)
'The challenge of September 11', *CARF* (No. 65, December/January 2002)
'Racism and the market-state', *CARF* (No. 69, Winter 2002/3)
  Also in *Race & Class* (Vol. 44, no. 4, April–June 2003)
'Bombesikker oppskrift', *Klassenkampen* (14 February 2006)
'Freedom of speech is not an absolute', *Race & Class* (Vol. 48, no. 1, July–September 2006)
'The neoliberal attack on cultural diversity', *Socialist Worker* (21 October 2006)

Obituaries

'Orlando Letelier', *Race & Class* (Vol. 18, no. 2, Autumn 1976)

'Malcolm Caldwell', *Race & Class* (Vol. 20, no. 4, Spring 1979)

'Walter Rodney 1942–80', *Race & Class* (Vol. 22, no. 1, Summer 1980)

'Thomas Hodgkin 1910–1982', *Race & Class* (Vol. 24, no. 1, Summer 1982)

'Ken Jordaan 1924–1988', *Race & Class* (Vol. 30, no. 3, January/March 1989)

'N. Shanmugathasan: an appreciation', *Tamil Times* (15 March 1993) Also in *Race & Class* (Vol. 34, no. 4, April/June 1993)

'James Boggs 1919–1993', *Race & Class* (Vol. 35, no. 2, October/ December 1995)

'Keith Buchanan 1919–1997', *Race & Class* (Vol. 39, no. 2, October/ December 1997)

'The Rt Hon Enoch Powell MP 1912–1998: a racist for all seasons', *Race & Class* (Vol. 39, no. 4, April/June 1998)

'Philip Mason 1906–1999', *Race & Class* (Vol. 40, no. 4, April/June 1999)

'Eqbal Ahmad 1932–1999', *Race & Class* (Vol. 41, no. 3, January/March 2000)

'Hugh Tinker 1921–2000', *Race & Class* (Vol. 42. no. 1, July/September 2000)

'Paul Sweezy 1910–2004', *Race & Class* (Vol. 46, no. 1, July–September 2004)

'Basker Vashee 1944–2005', *IRR News* (www.irr.org.uk/2005/august/ ak00002.html)

Editorials

'Put politics in command', *Race Today* (August 1973)

Untitled, *Race* (Vol. 15, no. 4, April 1974)

'The corporate face of capital', *Race & Class* (Vol. 17, no. 1, Summer 1975)

Untitled, *Race & Class* (Vol. 20, no. 2, Autumn 1978)

Untitled, *Race & Class* (Vol. 25, no. 2, Autumn 1983)

Untitled, *Race & Class* (Vol. 25, no. 3, Winter 1983)

Untitled, *Race & Class* (Vol. 26, no. 1, Summer 1984)

Untitled, *Race & Class* (Vol. 30, no. 3, January/March 1989)

Untitled, *Race & Class* (Vol. 32, no. 3, January/March 1991)

Untitled, *Race & Class* (Vol. 35, no. 4, April/June 1994)

Untitled, *Race & Class* (Vol. 36, no. 2, October/December 1994)

Untitled, *Race & Class* (Vol. 39, no. 1, July/September 1997)
'We the (only) people', *Race & Class* (Vol. 45, no. 1, July–September 2003)

Book reviews

'Moral atonement', review of *Black Suicide* by Herbert Hendin, in *New Society* (23 April 1970)

Review of *Soledad Brother* by George Jackson, in *New Society* (1 April 1971)

'Bucking the burden', review of *A Rap on Race* by Margaret Mead and James Baldwin, in *New Society* (22 July 1971)

'Fake's progress', review of *Rampal and His Family: the story of an immigrant* by Ursula Sharma, in *New Society* (19 August 1971)

'Let them come', review of *If they Come in the Morning: voices of resistance* by Angela Davis and others, in *New Society* (7 November 1971)

Review of *Racial Tensions and National Identity* edited by E.Q. Campbell, in *Caribbean Studies* (Vol. 13, no. 3)
    Also in *Race* (Vol. 15, no. 4, April 1974)

'Another wound', review of *No Name in the Street* by James Baldwin, in *New Society* (No. 498, April 1972)

'Sower and seed', review of *Blood in My Eye* by George Jackson, in *New Society* (4 May 1972)

'From sir', review of *Reluctant Neighbours* by E.R. Braithwaite, in *New Society* (No. 35, October 1972)

Review of *The Politics of Sri Lanka 1947–1973* by A. Jayaratnam Wilson, in *Race & Class* (Vol. 16, no. 2, October 1974)

Review of *The Private Life of Islam* by Ian Young, in *Race & Class* (Vol. 16, no. 3, January 1975)

Review of *The World and China 1922–1972* by John Gittings, in *Race & Class* (Vol. 16, no. 4, April 1975)

Review of *James Baldwin* edited by K. Kinnaman, in *Race & Class* (Vol. 17, no. 1, Summer 1975)

Review of *The Import of Labour* by Adriana Marshall, in *Race & Class* (Vol. 17, no. 1, Summer 1975)

Review of *A Seventh Man* by John Berger and Jean Mohr, in *Race & Class* (Vol. 17, no. 1, Summer 1975)

Review of *The Facts of Racial Discrimination: a national survey* by David J. Smith, in *Race & Class* (Vol. 17, no. 4, Spring 1976)

Review of *A Bibliography of Ceylon: volume 3* by H.A.I. Goonetileke, in *Race & Class* (Vol. 18, no. 4, Spring 1977)

Review of *Roots*, in *Race & Class* (Vol. 19, no. 1, Summer 1977)

Review of *Black Testimony: the voices of Britain's West Indians* by Thomas Cottle, in *Race & Class* (Vol. 20, no. 4, Spring 1979)

Review of *Paul Robeson Speaks: writings, speeches, interviews 1918–1974*, edited by Philip S. Foner, in *Race & Class* (Vol. 21, no. 3, Winter 1980)

Review of *Imperialism: pioneer of capitalism* by Bill Warren, in *Race & Class* (Vol. 24, no. 2, Autumn 1982)

Review of *Hand on the Sun* by Tariq Mehmood, in *Race & Class* (Vol. 25, no. 2, Autumn 1983)

Review of *Staying Power: the history of Black people in Britain* by Peter Fryer, in *Race & Class* (Vol. 26, no. 2, Autumn 1984)

Review of *The Making of the Black Working Class in Britain* by Ron Ramdin, in *Race & Class* (Vol. 28, no. 4, Spring 1987)

Review of *Those Long Afternoons: childhood in colonial Ceylon* by E.F.C. Ludowyk, in *Race & Class* (Vol. 31, no. 4, April/June 1990)

Miscellaneous

Compiler, *Coloured Immigrants in Britain: a select bibliography* (London, IRR, 1965); also 2nd edition 1967 and 3rd edition 1969

Compiler, *Commonwealth Immigrants in Britain: a preliminary check-list of research* (London, IRR, May 1966)

Editor, *Register of Research on Commonwealth Immigrants in Britain* (London, IRR 1967); also 3rd edition with S. Bagley, May 1968; 4th edition with J.M. Evans, September 1969; with H. Waters December 1970; with C. Kelly, 1972

Introduction to *Police Against Black People* (London, IRR, 1979)

'Black Sections: radical demand... or distraction', round table discussion with others, in *Marxism Today* (September 1985)

In the Eye of the Needle, report of the Enquiry into Greater London Arts, chair A. Sivanandan (London, GLA, 1986)

Introduction to *Policing Against Black People* (London, IRR, 1987)

Introduction to Günter Wallraff, *The Lowest of the Low: the Turkish worker in West Germany* (London, Methuen, 1988)
Also in *Race & Class* (Vol. 28, no. 2, Autumn 1986)

Introduction to *Deadly Silence: black deaths in custody* (London, IRR, 1991)
Also in *Race & Class* (Vol. 33, no. 1, July/September 1991)

Foreword to *Community Care: the Newham black experience* (London, December 1992)

Introduction to J. Bourne, L. Bridges and C. Searle, *Outcast England: how schools exclude black children* (London, IRR, 1994)

Introduction to Chris Searle, *Living Community, Living School* (London, Tufnell Press, 1997)

Introduction, with Hazel Waters, to 'Cedric Robinson and the philosophy of Black resistance', *Race & Class* (Vol. 47, no. 2, October/December 2005)

Foreword to Liz Fekete, *They Are Children Too: a study of Europe's deportation policies* (London, IRR, 2007)

Foreword to Arun Kundnani, *The End of Tolerance: racism in 21st century Britain* (London, Pluto Press, 2007)

Preface to Liz Fekete, *Integration, Islamophobia and Civil Rights in Europe* (London, IRR, 2008)

INDEX

7/7 168, 170, 171
9/11 168

Ali, Altab 129
Ali Baig, Akhtar 129, 136
Ali, Ishaque 129
Ali, Quddus 60
anti-colonial struggle 96
anti-deportation campaigns 51
anti-Muslim racism 168
anti-terror legislation
   anti-terror bill 2005 171, 173
   Anti-Terrorism Crime and
      Security Act 2001 171
   Prevention of Terrorism Act
      2005 172
   Terrorism Act 2000 171, 226
assimilation xvi
asylum seekers xiv, 51, 168, 210

Baraka, Amiri (formerly LeRoi
   Jones) 109, 113
Bean, John 96
Berman, Marshall 47
Birmingham 99
Black Day of Action 137
Black Eagles 113
Black House 109
black identity 6–7, 10, 14, 16–17,
   96
black intellectual 3–18, 37,
   55–62
Black Liberation Front 118
Black Panther Movement 114,
   119
black papers 119, 129
Black Parents' Movement 118

Black People the Way Forward
   conference 85
Black People's Alliance (BPA)
   113
Black People's Freedom
   Movement 123
black petit-bourgeoisie 146
Black Power 103, 105, 108, 117,
   119–22, 152
Black Sections (in the Labour
   Party) 146–7
black self-organisation 94, 96,
   107, 118–21
Black Socialist Alliance 129
Black Trade Union Solidarity
   Movement 146–7
Black Unity and Freedom Party
   (BUFP) 118, 119
Black Women's Centre 135
black workers (and workers'
   organisations) 92, 93, 117,
   122–6
black youth 87–9, 126–30,
   137–9, 143, 227
Blacks Against State Harassment
   (BASH) 129
Blair, Tony 167, 168, 170, 174
Blake, William 9
bourgeois freedoms 55
Boyle, Sir Edward 101–2
Bradford
   Bradford 12 case 50
   Manningham 50, 128
   'riots' 170
   youth movement 129
Brazil 197, 198, 200–2
Bristol bus boycott 100, 102

British National Party (BNP) 60, 97, 107, 226
British Union of Fascists 96
British values xv, xvii, 174
British West Indian Association 100
Brixton Black Women's Group 135
Brixton 'riots', 137–9, 143
Broadwater Farm 49
Brockwell Park 122, 126
Brunt, Rosalind 33
Bush, George W., 167
bussing 102

Cabral, Amilcar 192
Callaghan, James 114
Campaign Against Racial Discrimination (CARD) 81, 103, 104, 106
Campbell, Beatrix 33, 34, 41, 52
capital 25, 27, 47, 55–6, 181, 206
Carib Club 122
Caribbean Artists' Movement 113
Caribbean Workers' Movement 120
Carmichael, Stokely 81, 108
carnival 98
'Cartoon' Campbell 136
Césaire, Aimé 3, 7, 19
Chapeltown (Leeds) 122, 126
children 13
Church 158–9, 222
Coard, Bernard 118
Cochrane, Kelso 97–8
colonial independence 95, 103
colonial labour 70–1
colour bar 91
Coloured People's Progressive Association 98

Committee of African Organisations 97
Commonwealth 70–2
Commonwealth Immigrants Act 1962 72, 75, 96, 99–100 1968 74, 82, 111
Commonwealth Immigrants' Advisory Council (CIAC) 101
Communities of Resistance campaign 52
Community Relations Commission (CRC; later Commission for Racial Equality, CRE) 83–5, 89, 126
community relations councils 84
Co-ordinating Committee Against Racial Discrimination (CCARD) 99
Conference of Afro-Asian-Caribbean Organisation 99
control orders 172
Council for Interracial Books 153–4
Courtauld's Red Scar Mill strike 86, 102, 104, 108
Crepe Sizes dispute 123
cultural politics 59
cultural imperialism 3–18, 206–8
culturalism 169

Dashiki 119
De Menezes, Jean Charles 168
dependency 200–2
disorganic development 180, 190–2
Dragons Teeth 153
DuBois, W.E.B. 90, 151

Educationally Sub-Normal (ESN) schools 81, 118
Edwards, Brother Herman 119

Egbuna, Obi 108, 113
employment vouchers 72–3
Enlightenment, the 174
Equal Rights 112
ethnicism (and ethnic funding) 58, 141–2, 144, 155, 169, 226
Eurocommunism 20, 22, 37
Export Processing Zones (EPZs) 194
Ezzrecco, Frances 98

Fanon, Frantz 7
Fernandes, John 159
Ferreira, Michael 129
Fordism 23–6, 35
Free Trade Zones (FTZs) 181–2, 184
fundamentalism 175

Garvey, Marcus and Amy 98
Gastarbeiter 75, 183
General Agreement on Tariffs and Trade (GATT) 56, 179, 219
Ghose, Ajoy 109, 118
Gibson, Ashton 119
Glass, Ruth 91
globalisation xiii, 55, 167, 174
GNP 190–1
Gorz, André 68
Gramsci, Antonio 16, 87, 140
Grassroots 121
Greater London Council (GLC) 40
Griffiths, Peter 104
Grunwick strike 130–1
gurdwaras 125

Hall, Stuart 24, 26, 34, 36, 39, 43–4
Harambee 119
health 135, 136

Home Affairs Committee on Racial Disadvantage 141–2, 144
housing
  black organisation around 93
  discrimination in 67, 91, 101
  shortage 68
Human Rights Act 173
Huntington, Samuel 167
Hussein, Saddam *see* Saddam Hussein

identity politics 32, 36, 41
immigrant labour 66–9, 98
Immigration Act 1971 75, 115–16
Immigration Appeals Act 1969 114
immigration control 66, 69, 75–6, 132
  (*see also* Commonwealth Immigrants Acts)
Imperial Typewriters strike 86, 125
imperialism xv, 45, 193–214, 216
incitement to racial hatred (prosecution of blacks) 104, 109
India 12, 197
Indian Workers' Associations (IWAs) 90, 93, 95, 98, 99, 110, 113
individualism 42–3
industrial capitalism 27, 55, 194
Industrial Relations Act 1971 116, 125
information society 38, 60
Institute of Race Relations (IRR) 63, 106, 169
integration 78–83, 84, 170–1
  commission on 168
  definition xvii, 80

intellectual 37–8, 55–62
International African Service
    Bureau 95
international division of labour
    180
International Monetary Fund
    (IMF) xiv, 56, 179, 200,
    206
Iraq xvi, 215, 218
Islamophobia 177, 220
Israel xviii, 173, 215–16

Jacques, Martin 23
Jallianwala Bagh massacre 90,
    133
Jamal, Abdullah (formerly
    Jermaine Lindsay) 170
James, C.L.R. 90, 95
Jenkins, Roy xvii, 71
Joint Council for the Welfare of
    Immigrants (JCWI) xiv, 117
Jones, Claudia 98–9, 104
Jordan, Colin 96
Joshi Jagmohan 99, 112
jury trial 225

Kahn, Mohammad Sidique 171
Katz, Judy 150–3
Kenyan Asians 71, 74, 111–12
Kenyatta, Jomo 74, 90, 95
Kerner Commission 148
Keskidee 119
Keys, The 94
King, Martin Luther 81, 103,
    112
    People's March on Washington
    99
Kurdish refugees 52

La Rose, John 118
labour 23, 27, 181, 204
Labour Party 19–20, 23, 29
    New Labour 227

language 8–9, 81
Leadbeater, Charlie 42–3
League of Coloured Peoples 94
League of Empire Loyalists 96,
    107
Live Aid 45–6
London Transport 66, 96
low intensity conflict 208–10
Lowest of the Low 211
Ludmer, Maurice 99
Lumumba, Patrice 99
Lyotard, Jean-François 61

McDonald, Trevor 83
McGoldrick affair 36
McKinnon, Judge Neil 131
McNee, Sir David (Metropolitan
    Police Commissioner) 133
Macpherson, Sir William's report
    169, 224
Maddock, Sir Ieuan 187, 193
Magna Carta xvi
Makonnen, Ras 90, 95
Malawi Asians 128
Malcolm X 103, 107
Manchanda, Abimanyu 104
Mangrove trial 120–1
Manley, Norman 98
Mansfield Hosiery strike 86,
    123–4
Mark, Sir Robert (Metropolitan
    Police Commissioner) 127
market system xvii, 174–5, 225
marxism 21, 37, 140
Marxism Today 19–23, 33
Marxists
    new 28, 38, 41, 45, 47
    old 23
    white 15
Memoranda of Understanding
    172–3
Merseyside West Indian
    Association 93

Michael X (formerly Abdul Malik and Michael de Freitas) 103–13
microelectronics 186
migrant workers 48, 52, 70
millenarian movements 175
Moody, Dr Harold 94
morality 54, 213
Mosley, Sir Oswald 96–7
Movement for Colonial Freedom 99
Moynihan, Daniel 144
mugging 121–2
Mukti 129
multiculturalism xvi, 141, 168, 170, 175–6
multinational corporations 46, 184, 189
Murdoch, Rupert 61
Murray, Robin 35, 44, 195
Muslims 168, 220–1

National Committee for Commonwealth Immigrants (NICCI) 73, 79, 80, 104–5
National Federation of Pakistani Associations 105
National Front (NF) 107, 131–2, 196, 226
National Labour Party 97
nationality laws 71–2, 91, 128, 134
nativism 168
Nehru, Jawaharlal 98
New Cross fire 136–7
new social movements 30–2, 34, 39
Newham, London Borough of 50–1
newly industrialising countries (NICs) 196–206
Nicaragua 209
'nigger-hunting' 101

Nkrumah, Kwame 90, 95
North London West Indian Association 118
Notting Hill 97–8, 99, 106, 120, 126
Nottingham 122, 123
Nyerere, Julius 11

O'Dwyer, Sir Michael (Lieutenant Governor of the Punjab) 90
oil xiv
oppression 6, 14
Organisation of Women of Asian and African Descent (OWAAD) 135–6

Padmore, George 90, 95
'Paki-bashing' 120
Pakistani Welfare Associations 110
Pakistani Workers' Associations 98
Pakistani Workers' Union 120
Palestine xvi, 51, 173, 215–16
Pan-African Congress 90, 95
Pan-African Federation 95
'pardner' system 93
patrials 115
Peach, Blair 49–50, 133
Peach, Ceri 68
Peppard Nadine 15
periphery 181
Perivale Gütermann strike 125
Pitt, Lord 83
pluralism 86
police
    racism and struggles against 100, 120–2, 137–9, 145
    Racism Awareness Training 159
Political and Economic Planning (PEP) 80
positive action 144

postmodernism 59, 61–2
poverty 225–7
Powell, Enoch 79, 83, 111–12,
    128, 132
power, personalising of 35
Prevention of Terrorism Act 2005
    172
production
    changes in 195
    control of the means of 28
    hierarchies of 196
    level of 27, 188
    method of 38
    relations of 27

Race Relations Act 176
    1965 79, 80, 104
    1968 82–3
    1976 85, 86–9, 126, 128
Race Relations Board 80, 82–5,
    89, 104, 118
race 'riots' (including urban
    rebellions)
    1919 94
    1958 69, 97
    1981 137–9, 155
    2001 170
Race Today 137
Racial Action Adjustment Society
    (RAAS) 103–4, 107–9, 113,
    119
racial disadvantage 143–4
racial discrimination 70–1, 77,
    82, 88, 91–3
Racial Preservation Society 107
racial segregation 168, 170, 226
racial violence (race hatred,
    attacks and racial murders)
    50, 60, 96–7, 106–7, 112,
    127, 129, 132, 136
racialism 91–2, 96, 162
racism 16, 58, 69, 77, 89, 222–7
    against Muslims xv, 168, 220

definition of 161–3
fight against 36, 59, 92–138,
    176
in the police 100
in trade unions 122, 124
institutionalised 73, 78, 106,
    145, 157, 169
psychology of 150–2, 154
state 100, 116
xeno- 168, 224
Racism Awareness Programme
    Unit (RAPU) 153, 159
racism awareness training (RAT)
    36, 141–66
Rampton Committee 156
Read, Kingsley 131
recruitment of workers 66
refugees 57, 52
Rockware Glass strike 103
Rodney, Walter 113
Runnymede Trust 84

Saddam Hussein 215–16, 220
Salmon, Lord Justice 97
Samaj in'a Babylon 129
Sartre, Jean-Paul 5–6, 12, 17
Sawh, Roy 103, 108, 109, 119
Scarman report 141–69, 176
schooling 101–2, 118
Searchlight 99
second generation 86–9
Second World War 95
secularism 174
separation of powers 172
silicon age 185
Singapore 183–4
Singh Chaggar, Gurdip 127–8,
    131
Singh, Udham 90, 93
Smethwick 104
Social Contract 131
socialism 212–14
'sou-sou' system 93

South East Asia 183, 189, 194,
196–9, 204–5
Southall 49, 127, 130, 133–4,
137
Southall Black Sisters 136
Southall Youth Movement 128
Soyinke, Wole 113
Spaghetti House siege 90, 127
Special Patrol Group (SPG) 122,
131, 133
Sri Lanka 51, 182, 207
state terrorism 173
strikes 86, 102, 103, 109, 110,
122–6, 130, 136, (*see also*
Courtauld's, Woolf's,
Mansfield Hosiery, Imperial
Typewriters, Grunwick)
Structural Adjustment
Programmes (SAPs) xiv, 56
Subject People's Conference 95
suicide bombers 170
supplementary schools 118
'Sus' (section 4 of the 1824
Vagrancy Act) 115, 120

Tanweer, Shehzad 171
technological revolution 55, 177,
184, 185, 203
information technology 27,
185–8
Terrorism Act 2000 171, 226
Terry, Robert 149
Thatcher, Margaret 132, 134
Thatcherism 19–20, 28–9, 40, 46
Third World 57–8
Times, The 105
tourism 207
trade union racism 122, 124
Trades Union Congress (TUC)
124, 131
Transport and General Workers
Union (TGWU) 123, 125,
130

Trilateral Commission 179, 181

Ugandan Asians 117, 125
underclass 87, 138, 223
under-developed countries
(UDCs) 196–206
Union of Post Office Workers 130
Union Movement 96
United Nations 218–19
United States xv, 208, 217
Commission on Civil Rights
148
Defense Department 147
Embassy (march on) 99
in Nicaragua 209
Universal Coloured People's
Association (UCPA) 108–9,
113, 119–20

Valéry, Paul 7
Vietnam protest 104, 108
virginity test 117

Wallace-Johnson, I.T.A. 90, 95
Wallraff, Günter 211–12
war 208
in Iraq 169
Gulf war 215–22
low intensity 208–10
Second World War 95, 181
Warren, Bill 47
welfare state 174
West African students 94
West Indian Federation 97, 101
West Indian Gazette 98, 104
West Indian Standing Conference
(WISC formerly Standing
Conference of West Indian
Organisations in the UK) 98,
101, 104, 109, 113
West Indian Workers' Association
98–9
White Defence League 96–7

white guilt 152, 162–6
White Paper 1965 73, 75, 78,
    104–5
White Paper 1975 65, 126
Wilson, Harold 83, 104, 111
Women in Black 51
women's struggles 119, 130, 134,
    135–6

Woolf Rubber Company strike
    86, 95
World Bank 56, 179, 200, 206

youth 137–9

xenophobia 223
xeno-racism 168, 224